OLYMPIC AND WORLD RECORDS

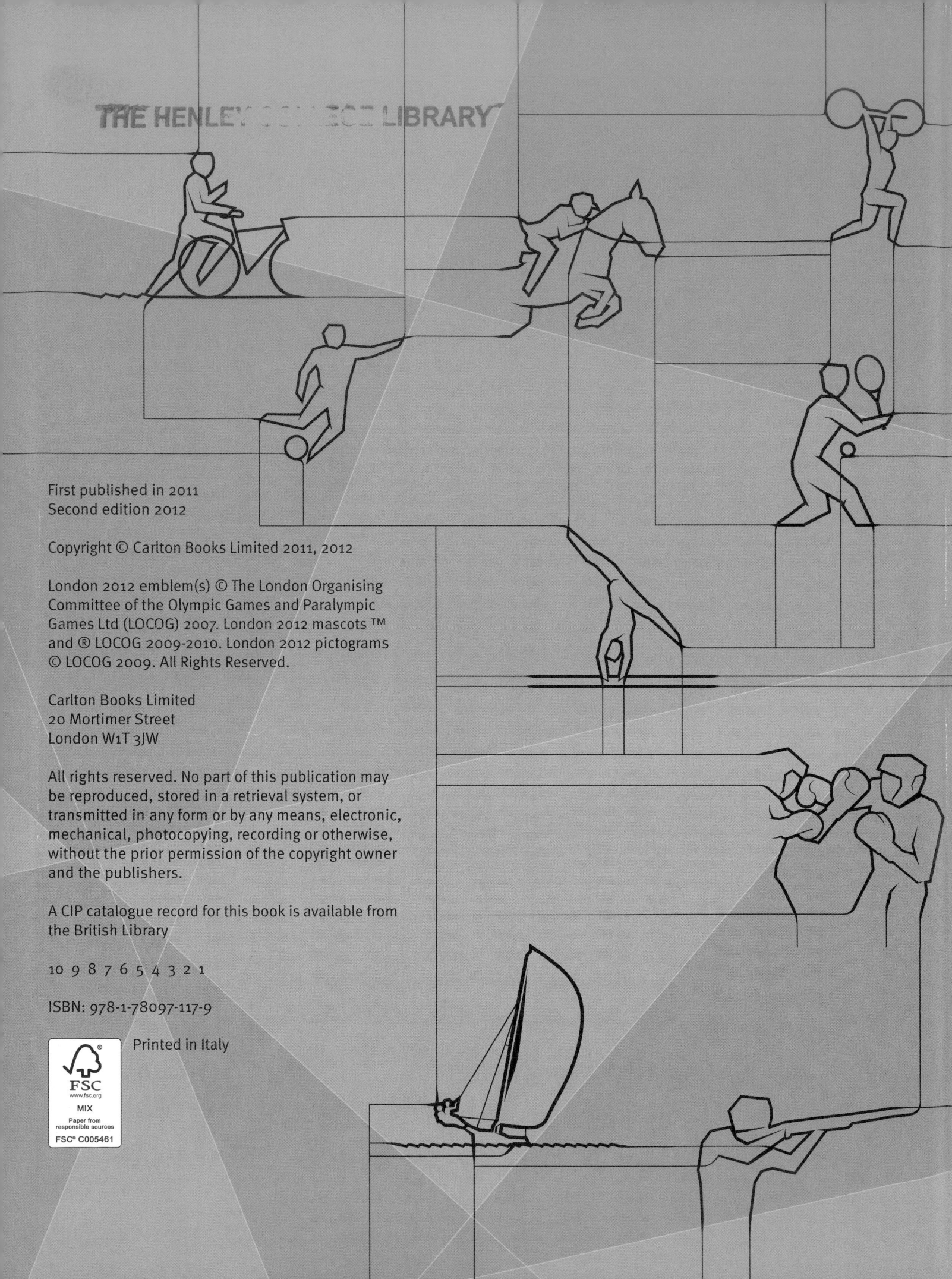

First published in 2011
Second edition 2012

Copyright © Carlton Books Limited 2011, 2012

London 2012 emblem(s) © The London Organising
Committee of the Olympic Games and Paralympic
Games Ltd (LOCOG) 2007. London 2012 mascots ™
and ® LOCOG 2009-2010. London 2012 pictograms
© LOCOG 2009. All Rights Reserved.

Carlton Books Limited
20 Mortimer Street
London W1T 3JW

A CIP catalogue record for this book is available from
the British Library

10 9 8 7 6 5 4 3 2 1

ISBN: 978-1-78097-117-9

Printed in Italy

FSC
www.fsc.org
MIX
Paper from
responsible sources
FSC® C005461

OLYMPIC AND WORLD RECORDS

An official London 2012 Olympic Games publication

KEIR RADNEDGE

CARLTON

Contents

↗ *Mo Farah won gold in the 5000m and 10,000m at London 2012.*

➔ *Michael Phelps took his tally of Olympic Games Swimming medals to 22.*

⬅ *Jessica Ennis missed the Beijing 2008 Games Heptathlon but made it up by winning the event at London 2012.*

➔ *Victoria Pendleton rode her way to gold and silver medals at London 2012.*

Introduction

The date 6 July 2005 is etched in the annals of British sport. That was the day when Jacques Rogge, President of the International Olympic Committee, revealed to the world that the Host City for the 2012 Olympic Games would be ... 'London!'

A little more than seven years later Rogge, in closing the Games of the XXX Olympiad and along with most of Britain and billions around the world, was hailing the 'happy and glorious Games' which had sparkled and dazzled in terms of sporting achievement in a social and organisational context deemed to have set new standards for the Olympic Movement.

Nine cities initially bid for the 2012 Summer Games. One year before the final decision Havana, Istanbul, Leipzig and Rio de Janeiro were eliminated from the process. That left London, Madrid, Moscow, New York and Paris.

Four rounds of voting were needed at the 117th IOC Session in Singapore. The city receiving fewest votes was eliminated each time. Moscow fell first, then New York City, then Madrid, then Paris. London topped the votes tally in only one round ... the last, the one which mattered, by a margin of just four votes, 54 to 50.

A vision of legacy for the youth of tomorrow was one of the most persuasive arguments proclaimed by the bid team, led by Seb Coe, and supported by leading politicians and sports stars.

On another historic date – 27 July 2012 – London became the first city to host the Olympic Games on three occasions, having stepped in at short notice in both 1908 and 1948.

The unique status of the Olympic Games lies not only in the drama of high-level, simultaneous competition in so many and varied sports, all in close proximity to each other, but in the link with antiquity which inspired Baron Pierre de Coubertin ... and in the ideals which the Olympic Movement seeks to spread worldwide through sport's inspirational, unifying medium.

The London 2012 Olympic Games was a stunning showcase of sporting performance which promised, as LOCOG Chair Seb Coe had proffered, to 'Inspire a generation' of future athletes, regenerate the East End of the city and deliver the organisational triumph for the Host Nation. London confidently put on a Games that will live long in the memory across the world.

As Coe said, in his closing address: 'When our time came, Britain, we did it right.'

The first modern Olympic Games were held in 1896 in Athens. This book recounts the achievements of heroes and heroines from that day to this. But, in the context of the Olympic Games, it is merely the story so far ...

← Jamaican sprinter Usain Bolt wrote his name in the history books at London 2012 when he retained his 100m, 200m and 4 x 100m Relay Olympic titles.

Chapter One
Olympic Games heritage

The history of the Olympic Games dates back to 776 BC. That was when the Ancient Greeks held sporting contests on a plain above a village in the Peloponnese called Olympia. These Olympic Games grew from a single event to widespread popularity across the city states of Greece. They lasted until AD 393, when they were discontinued by decree of the Roman Emperor Theodosius, who considered them a pagan festival.

In the years after the Franco-Prussian war of 1871, a young Frenchman called Pierre de Coubertin travelled to England and the United States. There he saw the growth of competitive sport in schools, colleges and clubs and decided that sporting competition would be beneficial not only for his country and its youth in particular but for others throughout the world.

In 1894, still only 31, he gathered like-minded men from across the world at the University of the Sorbonne in Paris, founded the International Olympic Committee and persuaded them to revive the Olympic Games. The first games of the modern era were scheduled for Athens in 1896.

These were modest beginnings. Fewer than 250 athletes took part from a dozen nations and all were men. Since then the Games have overcome many obstacles to become the greatest sporting show on earth. De Coubertin, who died in 1937, would have been amazed to see just how much his brainchild has grown.

When the Olympic Flame burned at London 2012, nearly 11,000 competitors from 204 countries were present. Almost half the competitors were women, and in all there were a staggering 302 gold medal events in 26 sports.

The London 2012 Olympic Games Opening Ceremony delivered a magnificent spectacle involving history, humour, music, dance and an incredible Olympic Cauldron lighting.

Olympic Games stadiums

The word 'stadium' takes its name from the ancient length of the same name in Latin. This was the length of the track or the equivalent of 180 metres. At the Olympic Games of antiquity held in Olympia, sporting contests took place in conjunction with a religious festival. The stadium was next door to the temple.

⬆ *The White City Stadium in west London was the all-purpose venue for the 1908 Olympic Games.*

Athens 1896 and 2004

The centrepiece of the 1896 Games was the Panathenaic Stadium, a marble structure built in the fourth century BC. Greek benefactor Georgios Averof paid for the renovation. Shaped almost like a horseshoe, with spectators seated on three sides, the running track featured tight turns at either end. To the delight of the crowd, Spiridon Louis of Greece came home to win the first Olympic Marathon. At the 2004 Games, the stadium again staged the finish of the Marathon, as well as Archery.

⬇ *Crowds gather for the Opening Ceremony at the Panathenaic Stadium in Athens ahead of the 1896 Games, the first of the modern era.*

London 1908 and 1948

The stadium used for the London 1908 Games was originally called the Great Stadium, but it soon became known as White City. It featured cycling and running tracks and even a swimming pool on the infield and offered a legacy ahead of its time, staging athletics, rugby league, football, speedway and greyhound racing before it closed in the mid-1980s. London joined Paris – 1900 and 1924 – in hosting a second Summer games in 1948, when Wembley Stadium was the main venue. King George VI declared the Games open, 26 years after he had laid the stadium's first foundation stone. Dutch housewife Fanny Blankers-Koen dominated the headlines, winning four gold medals on a cinder track.

Los Angeles 1932 and 1984

The Los Angeles Memorial Coliseum was built in the early 1920s to honour the fallen in the First World War. It staged the Games first in 1932 and again in 1984, when a jet-powered rocket man began the proceedings. Some 84 pianists played Gershwin's Rhapsody in Blue before Ronald Reagan became the first incumbent American president to open the Games. Carl Lewis made the stage his own during the following days with four gold medals. The Games ended with a spectacular light show finale featuring a spaceman who bade farewell.

Berlin 1936

A giant bell tolled above Berlin's Olympic Stadium to welcome the world to the 1936 Olympic Games. Designed by Werner March, the stadium was monumental in design and held more than 100,000 in its heyday. The first Olympic Flame brought by relay from Olympia burned here. Adolf Hitler declared the Games open, but the star was Jesse Owens, who won four gold medals on the track. The stadium formed part of an overall sports complex. The Olympic swimming pool was next door and vast gymnastic displays were held on the Maifeld, an arena behind the stadium.

Atlanta 1996

The stadium used for the 1996 Centennial Games in Atlanta held 85,000 fans and incorporated a series of underground passages to allow for dramatic set pieces during the Opening Ceremony. Boxing champion Evander Holyfield brought the flame through one of these tunnels to reach the stage, and later Muhammad Ali lit the Olympic Flame on a free-standing tower outside the stadium itself! After the Games the entire arena was rebuilt for the Atlanta Braves baseball team, and the running track was given to a local university.

Barcelona 1992

The Estadi Montjuic in Barcelona was built on a hill overlooking the city with the 1936 Olympic Games in mind. However, Barcelona lost out to Berlin in the IOC vote in 1931. When the city was finally chosen to host the 1992 Olympic Games, the interior was completely renovated, while the impressive facade was maintained.

Munich 1972

Munich's Olympiastadion, built for the 1972 Games, has a futuristic roof made of self-cleaning acrylic glass plates. With a surface area of 75,000 square metres, it offers a unique and dramatic tented effect. Two years after the Games the stadium was used for the 1974 World Cup final.

Melbourne 1956

Melbourne Cricket Ground was the main centre for the 1956 Olympic Games and hosted Athletics, the Football final and a demonstration event, Australian Rules Football. Built in 1853 as a base for the Melbourne Cricket Club, it staged the first cricket Test match in 1877 and is also home to Australian Rules Football, Rugby Union and Rugby League.

Helsinki 1952

The stadium used for the Helsinki 1952 Games pays homage to Finland's athletics heritage. Visitors are greeted by a giant statue of long-distance runner Paavo Nurmi, the 'Flying Finn', who lit the Olympic Flame in the stadium at the start of the Games.

Beijing 2008

Dubbed the 'Bird's Nest' by locals and visitors alike, Beijing's Olympic Stadium was constructed using 45,000 tonnes of steel. During the Games, it held 91,000 and hosted Athletics and the men's Football final. A complex system of steel wires above the stadium made possible some spectacular displays, none more than when gymnast Ning Li soared through the air to light the Olympic Flame on the stadium roof.

⬇ *Built at a cost of US$423 million, the Bird's Nest Stadium was the magnificent focal point of the Beijing 2008 Games.*

London 2012

↑ *The Olympic Stadium was the centrepiece of the London 2012 Games.*

The beating heart of the Games

London's Olympic Stadium was designed and built with an 80,000 capacity but with a potential to be trimmed down to 50,000 and/or 25,000 for economic and legacy use going forward. This was a crucial factor in Britain/London later winning the right to host the 2017 World Athletics Championships.

Sustainability was an important issue in the design and the 14 lighting towers were not merely a design feature but played a key broadcasting role to provide the high-powered lighting essential to high-definition TV coverage. Altogether the stadium was lit by 532 individual floodlights.

More than 30 buildings were demolished on the site and around 800,000 tonnes of soil was removed before construction could begin, enough to fill the Royal Albert Hall nine times over. The stadium was built on an 'island', with waterways on three sides, providing spectator access via five bridges.

Chair of the Organising Committee Seb Coe described the stadium as 'the beating heart of the Olympic Park'. Facilities included not only the 400m running track but also state-of-the-art support facilities in terms of changing rooms, medical support and an 80m warm-up track. One of the key employees was a hawk named Willow whose role was to circle in and around the stadium and prevent pigeons from nesting.

The surrounding Olympic Park featured seven other permanent sports venues including the high speed Velodrome and the remarkable Aquatic Centre whose wave-shaped roof measured 12,000 square metres, one and a half times the size of the Wembley football pitch.

Host Cities

The battle to host an Olympic Games is a long and, for the victors, a rewarding one. London, which in 2012 was the first city to have the honour of hosting the Games three times, promised regeneration of the local area and a legacy for young and aspiring sports people. Host Cities always leave their own individual stamp on the Games and create sporting memories which last a lifetime.

Longest games

The London 1908 Olympic Games were the longest in history. They began on 27 April at Queen's Club, in West Kensington, when Evan Baillie Noel won the first gold medal in Racquets. They came to an end on the last day of October, when England won the Hockey final. They included a strange mixture of events including Ice Skating, Motor Boating, Lacrosse, Rugby Union and even Tug of War.

Political change

Berlin was awarded the 1936 Games five years earlier, before the Nazis came to power. A bitter critic of the Olympic Movement, Adolf Hitler later tried to hijack the Games for political gain. His theories of racial superiority were confounded by the exploits of American Jesse Owens, who won four gold medals and forged a life-long friendship with his German rival in the Long Jump, 'Luz' Long. For the first time full results from every event were set down.

Heading down south

Melbourne in 1956 was the first southern hemisphere city to stage the Olympic Games. Never before had an Olympic Games begun in November. They became known as 'The Friendly Games' despite a tense Cold War political backdrop as a result of the Suez crisis and the Hungarian uprising. The sporting competition launched the career of Australian swimmer Dawn Fraser, who dominated the women's 100m Freestyle over the next three Olympic Games.

Doubling up

Paris was the first city to host the Olympic Games twice. In 1900 they were run in conjunction with the Paris Exhibition and were, to a certain extent, overshadowed by the fun of the fair. They lasted five months but were surrounded by confusion over what were official events. The Games returned in 1924 and are associated with the story of British athletes Eric Liddell and Harold Abrahams, later celebrated in the Oscar-winning film *Chariots of Fire*.

Stockholm stand-in

Stockholm was thrust into the Olympic spotlight for the second time in 1956. Australian quarantine laws prevented the transit of horses to Melbourne, the designated Host City, so the equestrian events were held earlier in the year in the Swedish capital. They took place in the stadium that had been used for the 1912 Games. Gymnast Karin Lindberg was chosen to light the Olympic Flame, becoming the first woman to do so.

⬆ *Colonel Frank Wheldon receives the gold medal on behalf of the victorious British Eventing team at Stockholm in 1956.*

Hiroshima remembered

The 1964 Games in Tokyo were the first held in Asia. Tokyo had been designated as Host City for 1940 before the war intervened. The Olympic Flame was lit by Yoshinori Sakai, born in Hiroshima the day the atom bomb was dropped. These were the first Games to be televised by satellite. The traditional Japanese sport of Judo was included on the programme for the first time, but to the dismay of the host nation the blue riband open category was won by the giant Dutchman, the late Anton Geesink.

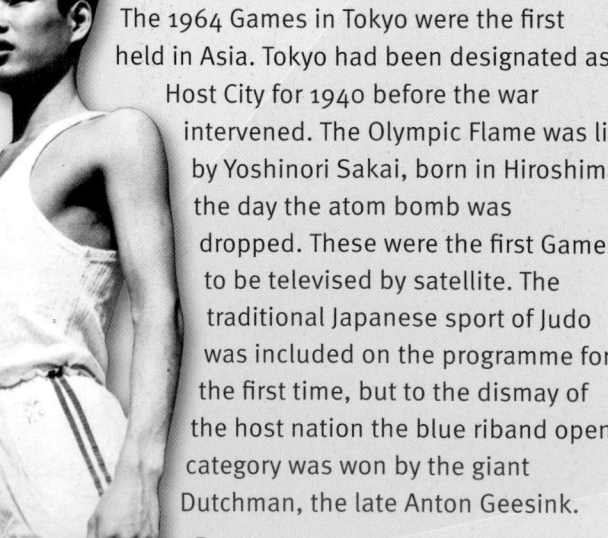

⬅ *Hiroshima survivor Yoshinori Sakai about to light the Olympic Flame in Tokyo in 1964.*

Beating the boycott

In the build-up to the 1980 Games in Moscow, the International Olympic Committee struggled to prevent a western boycott. The United States chose to stay away as a protest against the Soviet invasion of Afghanistan, along with Canada, Japan and the Federal Republic of Germany. Great Britain did compete, but British chef de mission Dick Palmer marched alone in the Opening Ceremony carrying the Olympic Flag. Other nations also competed under the IOC flag or that of their National Olympic Committee.

Harmony breakthrough

Seoul unexpectedly beat the Japanese city of Nagoya to win the 1988 nomination. At the time Korea had only hosted one World Championship event (in shooting), but the Games proved a great success. Some 149 nations marched in the Opening Ceremony, the last at a Summer Games to be held in daylight. The 'Games of Harmony' were the first in 12 years to be attended by both the Soviet Union and the United States. Soviet gymnast Vladimir Artemov won four gold medals, in Horizontal Bars, Parallel Bars, All-Around Individual and Team Combined exercises.

Altitude advantage

In 1968, Mexico City became the first Central American city to stage the Games. Athletes from altitude prospered in the distance events. Kenyans Kip Keino (men's 1500m) and Naftali Temu (men's 10,000m) and Ethiopian Mamo Wolde in the men's Marathon all took gold. The Track events also produced a world record harvest: Jim Hines (men's 100m) Tommie Smith (men's 200m), Lee Evans (men's 400m) and, most famously, Bob Beamon in the men's Long Jump.

More than a games

Barcelona finally won the right to stage the Olympic Games in 1992, some 60 years after having bid first. These proved spectacular Games from the moment Paralympic archer Antonio Rebollo lit the Olympic Flame with a burning arrow. The home crowds were delighted by the men's 1500m success of Fermin Cacho on the track, and across town Spain won Football gold at the iconic Nou Camp Stadium with a team including Barcelona's own Pep Guardiola.

London 2012

Winning the bid and beyond

London was awarded the 2012 Olympic Games – formally the XXX Olympiad – at the 117th Session (congress) of the International Olympic Committee in Singapore on 6 July 2005. The bid committee was led by Seb Coe. It projected a vision of legacy for both the East End of London and British youth sports participation combined with an international outreach project. Four rounds of voting were needed in Singapore. Moscow was eliminated first then New York followed by Madrid. This left London and favourite Paris but London won with 54 votes to 50. That ensured it would be the first city to host the modern Games on three occasions after 1908 and 1948. The London 2012 Games were a huge success in every way, with millions of fans cheering home athletes to levels of success not seen in more than 100 years and sustained brilliance from Olympic legends Michael Phelps and Usain Bolt.

Organising the Games

The London Organising Committee of the Olympic Games, subsequently known by the acronym LOCOG, began work formally in October 2005. Coe was chairman with Paul Deighton as chief executive. Its primary role was the staging of the Games while the construction was entrusted to the newly created Olympic Delivery Authority. Central involvement at Government level came from the Government Olympic Executive, set up within the Department of Culture, Media and Sport. A change of Government in 2010, from Labour to a Conservative/Liberal Democrat Coalition, made no difference to the project because of the cross-party support, which had been evident ever since the launch of the bid process.

➔ *The amazing Orbit in the Olympic Park attracted thousands of visitors during the London 2012 Games.*

Famous firsts

Twenty-seven Olympic Games held in the modern era (since 1896) and the numerous editions of the Ancient Games – held in Greece, normally on a four-yearly basis, between 776BC and 393AD (when they were suppressed by Theodosius I in an attempt to impose Christianity on the region) – have produced numerous landmarks. Here is a selection of the most significant of them.

Out in front

The first recorded Olympic champion was a man called Coroebus. He lived close to Olympia in the province of Elis and won the stadion race over a distance of approximately 180 metres in 776 BC. A baker by profession, he received an olive branch for his trouble and could be described as the first celebrity chef.

How it began

A heat of the men's 100m was the first event to be held at the first Olympic Games of the modern era in 1896. American Frank Lane was the first to cross the line. The first gold medal to be decided came in the men's Triple Jump. Harvard student James Connolly had made the trip to Athens against the advice of the dean at his university but returned home with the first-ever gold medal awarded at the Games. He later ran for Congress, but without success.

← *American athlete James Connolly holds the distinction of winning the first-ever Olympic Games gold medal, in the men's Triple Jump at Athens 1896.*

Oath of respect

The Olympic Oath was taken first at the Antwerp 1920 Games by the Belgian fencer Victor Boin. A journalist and member of the organising committee, Boin had previously represented his country in Water Polo and Swimming. He grasped the Belgian national flag as he swore the Oath, promising to respect the rules. Since 1984 the Olympic Flag has been used in the Opening Ceremony instead of a national flag, and an anti-doping clause has been added. An Oath for judges was introduced in 1972.

↑ *Belgian fencer Victor Boin (centre) becomes the first athlete in history to swear the Olympic Oath, introduced for the first time at the 1920 Games.*

All-round winner

American Eddie Eagan was the first man to win Summer and Winter gold medals. In 1920 he boxed his way to Light Heavy Weight gold at the Summer Games in Antwerp. A law student, he attended both Harvard and Yale universities and later Oxford, but returned to the Olympic arena to make history as part of the US Four-man Bobsleigh team that won gold at the 1932 Winter Games at Lake Placid.

Women's breakthrough

Great Britain's Charlotte Cooper was the first woman to win an Olympic gold medal. She beat the local favourite Hélène Prévost to win the women's Tennis Singles at the Paris 1900 Olympic Games. She added a second gold with Reggie Doherty in the Mixed Doubles. Cooper won the women's singles title at Wimbledon on five occasions and lived to the grand old age of 96.

All in the swim

The long-distance Swimming events held in Beijing were not the firstto be held in open water. In 1896 all events were in the bay of Piraeus and, in 1900, the River Seine was used. Swimming was not held in an indoor pool until the 1948 Games in London.

Ice in summer

The first gold medals for Ice Skating were awarded at the London 1908 Olympic Games. Florence 'Madge' Syers won the women's competition and skated to a bronze in the Pairs with her husband Edgar. Sweden's Ulrich Salchow was the winner of the men's competition. Figure Skating was also held at the Antwerp 1920 Olympic Games, but from 1924 it was included in the Winter Olympic Games.

Comaneci perfection

Nadia Comaneci was only 14 when she flew off the Parallel Bars to execute a perfect landing on the first day of competition in Gymnastics in 1976 in Montreal. The judges awarded her a perfect ten. Her routine during the Team Competition established her as the star of the Games. She received a further ten on Balance Beam and achieved the same score five times more en route to three individual gold medals.

↑ *Nadia Comaneci's perfection earned not only top marks but also headlines around the world.*

Cultural competition

Competitions for artists were introduced for the first time at the Stockholm 1912 Olympic Games, making it possible to win a gold medal for painting, sculpture, music, literature and even architectural design. Olympic founding father Baron Pierre de Coubertin won a prize for his 'Ode to Sport'. He submitted his entry under the pseudonyms George Hohrod and M. Eschbach. The artistic contests were discontinued following the London 1948 Games, but art and music are now included in the Cultural Olympiad, which runs in conjunction with the Games.

Benoit's Marathon

Joan Benoit of the USA became the first woman to win an Olympic gold medal in the Marathon. The event was only introduced at the 1984 Olympic Games in Los Angeles. There was an 800m race for women at the 1928 Games in Amsterdam, but it was considered unsuccessful and there were no women's events at any distance longer than 200m until the 800m was revived for the 1960 Games in Rome. The first 400m was at Tokyo in 1964, 1500m at Munich in 1972 and 3000m also in 1984.

London 2012

Gender equality

London 2012 saw all nations represented, for the first time, by both male and female competitors. Steady pressure from the IOC had been rewarded by Brunei Darussalam and Qatar then, finally, Saudi Arabia agreeing to send women to the Games. Wojdan Shahrkhani became the first Saudi woman to compete at the Olympic Games when she took part in the over 78kg category in Judo; Sarah Attar, in the 800m heats, was the first Saudi woman to compete in the Athletics. The 80,000 crowd cheered Attar as she finished 43 seconds behind heat winner Janeth Jepkosgei Busienei of Kenya.

The 'Blade Runner'

South African Oscar Pistorius – known as the 'Blade Runner' – became the first double amputee to compete in the Olympic Games. He ran in the 400m and 4 x 400m Relay, heading for a unique double with appearances scheduled, a month later, at the London 2012 Paralympic Games. Pistorius had won a silver medal in the team relay at the 2011 World Athletics Championships in Daegu.

↗ *Oscar Pistorius made the semi-final of the men's 800m at London 2012.*

London firsts

- China's Siling Yi won the first gold medal at London 2012 in the women's 10m Air Rifle on 28 July at the Royal Artillery Barracks.
- Dong Hyun Im, the Republic of Korea's visually impaired archer, set the first world record at London 2012 in breaking his own 72-arrow mark of 696 by three points.
- Usain Bolt became, at London 2012, the first man to retain both 100m and 200m sprint titles.
- Jamaica's men's 4 x 100m Relay team broke the 37-second barrier for the first time when shattering their own world record to win gold in 36.84 seconds.
- Kenya's David Rudisha became the first man to run the 800m inside one minute 41 seconds when he set a winning world record of 1:40.91.
- Nicola Adams of Great Britain won the first gold medal in women's Boxing when she outpointed China's Cancan Ren to win the Fly Weight (51kg) title.
- Jade Jones won Great Britain's first gold medal in women's Taekwondo in the Under 57kg category.
- London was the first city to host the modern Olympic Games three times, after 1908 and 1948.

Famous gold medal hauls

Thousands of athletes have achieved their dream of competing at the Olympic Games over the years, some of them have entered Games folklore by winning a gold medal and a select few have achieved legendary status by striking gold on at least three occasions. The following can be considered to be among the greatest Olympians of all time.

↑ *Emile Zatopek won men's 5000m, 10,000m and the Marathon gold at Helsinki 1952.*

↑ *Larissa Latynina won nine gold medals at three Olympic Games.*

Ewry's standing start

In the early Games, jump events from a standing start were included on the roster and Ray Ewry was a master at it, winning the Standing High Jump, Standing Long Jump and Standing Triple Jump at the 1900 and 1904 Games and the Standing High Jump and Long Jump in 1908. His eight gold medals are a record for a field event athlete.

The unique Zatopek

Czechoslovak Emil Zatopek had already served notice of his ability as a long-distance runner by winning men's 10,000m gold in 1948 in London, but it was in Helsinki in 1952 that he carved his name in the history books. Zatopek retained his 10,000 title and completed the long-distance track double with victory over 5000m. Only three days later, he took part in his first Marathon and won it. In one single week he had raced four times over a total distance of some 62 kilometres. He remains the only athlete in history to win all three long-distance events at a single Olympic Games.

Lucky nine for Larissa

Over three Olympiads, from 1956 to 1964, Ukrainian-born Larissa Latynina dominated women's Gymnastics. A member of the all-conquering Soviet team, individually she won four golds in Melbourne in 1956, including the blue riband All-Around title which she retained four years later. Her ninth and final gold came with the USSR team in 1964. She also won a further five bronze and four silver medals, and her 18 Olympic medals remain a record. In her entire Olympic career she finished outside the medals in only one event.

Captain Canada

Canadian showjumper Ian Millar began his Olympic career in Munich in 1972 but had to wait until his ninth Olympic Games before he won a medal. Still going strong in 2008, aged 61, he was a member of the Canadian silver medal winners in the Team Jumping event held in Hong Kong.

History man Phelps

No man has enjoyed more success at the Olympic Games than Michael Phelps. He had already written his name in the annals of world swimming before he competed at Beijing in 2008. He surpassed compatriot Mark Spitz with eight golds at a single Olympiad, all but one set in world record times and all in morning sessions. The magical eight was completed in the men's 4 x 100m Medley Relay. In Athens he had already stormed to victory in six events to bring his career tally to 14. He has also won two bronze medals.

Four for Lewis

Carl Lewis emulated his countryman Jesse Owens by winning four gold medals at a single Games. At Los Angeles 1984, he took gold in the men's 100m, 200m, the 4 x 100m Relay and the Long Jump. Although his dominance in the sprints faded, his power in the Long Jump never waned and his victory at Atlanta 1996 gave him four consecutive titles, equalling the feat of discus thrower Al Oerter.

Family fortunes

Italian brothers Piero and Raimondo D'Inzeo were the first men to compete together at eight consecutive Games. In 1948, older brother Piero competed in Showjumping and Raimondo in Eventing. They competed as team-mates in 1956, with Raimondo winning silver and Piero bronze plus a team silver. Raimondo went on to win Individual Jumping gold in 1960. The brothers' final appearance came at the 1976 Games. Between them they won 12 Olympic medals.

Redgrave's record

Sir Steve Redgrave's five gold medals in Olympic Rowing have given him legendary status. In 1984, he was a member of the Coxed Four that won Great Britain's first Rowing gold in 36 years. In 1988, he won gold in the Coxless Pairs partnered by Andy Holmes and then formed a powerful alliance with Matthew Pinsent, eight years his junior. Together they won gold in the Coxed Pairs in 1992 and 1996. Both men were chosen for the Coxless Four in Sydney where, amid feverish speculation, Redgrave played his part to win a fifth consecutive gold at 38, a staggering feat in an endurance event. Redgrave was later knighted, as was Pinsent after he won his fourth gold medal, again in the Coxless Four, at Sydney 2000.

Hat-trick in the ring

Hungarian Lazlo Papp was the first boxer to win three consecutive gold medals at the Olympic Games. He beat home favourite John Wright to win the Middle Weight title at the London 1948 Games, then claimed further gold medals at Light Middle Weight in 1952 and 1956. Afterwards he was allowed to turn professional, a rarity in the communist era.

➜ *Lazlo Papp was Hungary's hat-trick hero.*

London 2012

Fabulous Phelps

United States swimmer Michael Phelps retired after the London 2012 Olympic Games as the most decorated Olympian ever, with a total of 22 medals. He won six gold and two bronze at Athens 2004, a record eight gold at Beijing 2008 and four gold and two silver at London 2012. Former Soviet gymnast Larisa Latynina, who held the record for nearly 50 years, was at London 2012 to cheer on Phelps. She won 18 medals (nine gold), at Melbourne 1956, Rome 1960 and Tokyo 1964. Phelps's total is double that of any other male swimmer at the Games. Eleven medals each had been won by fellow Americans Mark Spitz (nine gold), Matt Biondi (eight gold) and London 2012 Swimming rival Ryan Lochte (five gold).

➜ *Michael Phelps's total of 22 Olympic Games medals may never be beaten.*

Hoy's record haul

Sir Chris Hoy's victories in Cycling's Team Sprint and Keirin at London 2012 took his total of Olympic gold medal tally to a Great Britain record of six, one more than rower Sir Steve Redgrave. Hoy also extended his overall medals total to a British joint-record seven. Fellow cyclist Bradley Wiggins also has seven medals, but with four gold, one silver and two bronze. Great Britain's total of 65 medals in all with 29 golds made London 2012 the most successful Games since the first time London had hosted them, in 1908. In a very different era, Great Britain won 139 medals including 55 gold.

London 2012 medals top 10

Rank	Country	G	S	B	Total
1	United States of America	46	29	29	104
2	People's Republic of China	38	27	23	88
3	Great Britain	29	17	19	65
4	Russian Federation	24	26	32	82
5	Republic of Korea	13	8	7	28
6	Germany	11	19	14	44
7	France	11	11	12	34
8	Italy	8	9	11	28
9	Hungary	8	4	5	17
10	Australia	7	16	12	35

Opening Ceremonies

The ceremonial aspects of the Olympic Games set them apart from other international sports events, with the splendour of the Opening Ceremony helping to heighten the anticipation of the coming days of sporting action.

⬆*Queen Elizabeth II opens the 1976 Olympic Games.*

Speech-making

IOC rules not only expect there to be certain ceremonial speeches made at the Opening Ceremony; they even provide the precise wording that officials are supposed to use. This meant that on the evening of 27 July 2012, in her Golden Jubilee year, Her Majesty Queen Elizabeth II uttered the words: 'I declare open the Games of London celebrating the 30th Olympiad of the modern era.' It was not the first time that The Queen has made the speech at an Opening Ceremony. At Montreal, in 1976, Her Majesty declared the Games open and, mindful that she was in the French-speaking province of Quebec, the first language that she used was French.

The right flag

Olympic rules were re-written ahead of the Moscow 1980 Olympic Games to allow teams to march behind 'a' flag, rather than their national flag. The United States had called for a boycott of Moscow following the Soviet Union's invasion of Afghanistan – but the British Olympic Association defied its government's orders and let its athletes follow their own conscience about whether they should compete. As a result, the British team in Moscow marched behind the Olympic Flag, and the likes of Duncan Goodhew, Steve Ovett and Allan Wells never heard 'God Save the Queen' when they received their gold medals. Indeed, Seb Coe had to come back and win the men's 1500m for a second time in 1984 to have that experience.

Growth of the Games

When the first modern Olympic Games were staged in Athens in 1896, the Opening Ceremony featured competitors from 22 national Olympic committees. At London in 2012, for the first time ever, all 204 IOC member nations sent competitors to the Games.

Parade of nations

The Olympic Charter demands that 'each delegation dressed in its official uniform must be preceded by a name-board bearing its name and must be accompanied by its flag'. The Charter's rules also determine the marching order for all Opening Ceremonies, with Greece, as the first home of the Games, given the honour of leading the parade. To bring a show to a suitable climax, the Charter stipulates that the country hosting the Games should always be the last to enter the Stadium.

⬆*As is the custom, Greece – considered the mother nation of the Olympic Games – was handed the honour of leading the Parade of Nations at the Opening Ceremony at the Beijing 2008 Olympic Games.*

Flag games

The Olympic Flag has been used at the Opening Ceremony in 1992 by the 'Unified Team' – comprising competitors from the states of the former Soviet Union – and by Timor-Leste in 2000. On other occasions, a special flag has been used by delegations, such as when the two Koreas marched together in Sydney in 2000 and again in Athens in 2004.

Flaming climax

The ceremonial all leads to the biggest set-piece of the Opening Ceremony, the lighting of the Olympic Flame, which burns brightly over the stadium, and the Host City, signifying a two-week truce. The lighting of the Flame has seen some spectacular moments at recent Games: Muhammad Ali, winner of a Boxing gold medal in 1960, performed the task at Atlanta 1996; Cathy Freeman, seemingly standing in a shower of fire, was handed the honour of lighting the Flame at Sydney 2000; and, most spectacular of all, Spanish archer Antonio Rebollo sending his flaming arrow arcing into the Barcelona night sky in 1992.

⬆ *Australian athlete Cathy Freeman finds herself centre stage as she lights the Olympic Flame at the climax of the Opening Ceremony at the 2000 Olympic Games in Sydney.*

London 2012

Wonder of London

Fears that the Opening Ceremony for the London 2012 Olympic Games could not match the scale of the Beijing 2008 event were dispelled by the craft and creativity of the 'Isles of Wonder' spectacle produced on 27 July 2012 by Oscar-winning director Danny Boyle and music directors Rick Smith and Karl Hyde of the electronic music duo Underworld.

The opening stadium scene presented the British country idyll: country cottages, hills, valleys, even 40 live sheep, 12 horses, nine geese, 10 ducks, three cows, two goats and three sheepdogs, plus clouds, a water wheel and a maypole. A countdown clock flashed across the spectators in the stands before the Red Arrows roared overhead with perfect timing – at 20.12 – burning red, white and blue smoke trails.

A show of relentless pace began with a rapid-fire film following the Thames from its source live into the stadium where the 2012 Tour de France winner Bradley Wiggins rang the Olympic Countdown Bell to launch a pageant of Britain's greatest music and words.

The artistic legacy of Sir Edward Elgar, William Blake and William Shakespeare was transformed into the might of the industrial revolution, before actor Daniel Craig's James Bond brought – apparently – Her Majesty Queen Elizabeth II parachuting in from Buckingham Palace.

Other stars cascaded, with appropriate invention: such as Rowan Atkinson in a dream scene from *Chariots of Fire*, leading into a run through the decades to catch up with the world of social media, courtesy of worldwide web creator Sir Tim Berners-Lee. The country-by-country parade of athletes was followed by the formal opening of the Games by The Queen.

The Olympic Torch was brought into the stadium by British rowing legend Sir Steve Redgrave and the lighting of the Olympic Flame was performed by seven young athletes, all of whom had been nominated by British gold medallists. Sir Paul McCartney performed 'Hey Jude' ... and the Games of the XXX Olympiad could, at long last, begin.

⬆ *The London 2012 Games Opening Ceremony was a roaring success.*

⬅ *IOC President Jacques Rogge (left) and Her Majesty Queen Elizabeth II (right) watch the Opening Ceremony before they declared the Games open.*

Closing Ceremonies

Steeped in protocol, the Closing Ceremony has become an integral, memorable and spectacular part of the Olympic Games. It climaxes with extinguishing the Olympic Flame, singing the Olympic Hymn and, finally, to the sound of a farewell song, the symbolic lowering of the Olympic Flag before it is carried out of the arena.

Eight for luck

At the 2008 Olympic Games in Beijing, London's Boris Johnson, in common with the receiving mayors of previous Host Cities all the way back to the Antwerp Games in 1920, waved the newly received Olympic Flag from side to side eight times, as required by tradition. Once the Olympic Flag was symbolically in London's hands, a short performance was staged within the vast Bird's Nest Stadium to offer the 100,000 spectators, and the world watching on TV, a taster of what London would have to offer. The show featured a bold red double-decker bus as the stage for a spectacular display by scores of dancers, many carrying umbrellas, plus Jimmy Page, from the rock group Led Zeppelin, playing guitar to accompany singer Leona Lewis, together with various sound clips from BBC radio and the folk tune 'Greensleeves', all rounded off by David Beckham kicking a football.

Closing rules

Many of the elements of the Closing Ceremonies are governed more by tradition than by International Olympic Committee rules. Usually Flagbearers from each participating country enter the stadium in single file, and behind them march all of the athletes who have competed in the Games, not in strict team order – as the protocol of the Opening Ceremony demands – but mixed together informally. Certain key sports always used to be staged on the final day of the Games: the Individual Showjumping Grand Prix was often the centrepiece of the final day's action, the event sometimes being staged in the main stadium. The final Athletics event to be run, with exhausted runners drifting into the stadium before the Closing Ceremony began, was the men's Marathon, though this was not the case at London 2012, as the race did not finish in the Olympic Stadium. Perhaps because of the Marathon's close connections with the Olympic Games' Greek roots, the medal ceremony for the race is usually integrated into the Closing Ceremony.

Flag days

Flags play a massively significant part in the formalities of the Closing Ceremonies. One key part is the symbolic transfer, from the host city to the next hosts, of the Olympic Flag. For nearly 70 years, the flag used was the 'Antwerp Flag', so called because it had been presented to the IOC by the Belgian hosts at the 1920 Summer Games, where this part of the ceremony was introduced. This flag was used until the 1988 Games in Seoul, when the Korean organisers gave the IOC a near-identical replacement, known at the 'Seoul Flag'. The Winter Olympic Games have a similar ceremony at the end of the Games, where the 'Oslo Flag', presented to the IOC at the 1952 Winter Games, is used.

⬇ *The essential flags at the 2008 Games Closing Ceremony: Greece, the Olympic Flag, China (the host nation) and Great Britain (the next hosts).*

Ceremonial and oaths

Once all the athletes have entered the stadium, three national flags are hoisted on flagpoles, while the corresponding national anthems are played: the flag of Greece on the middle pole to honour the birthplace of the Olympic Games, the flag of the host country on the left-hand pole, and the flag of the country hosting the next Games on the right-hand pole. In 2012, this third flag was that of Brazil, as Rio de Janeiro will host the 2016 Olympic Games.

Medal surge

At the early stagings of the modern Games at the beginning of the 20th century, all the medal presentations were staged at the Closing Ceremony. However, if this had been done in London in 2012, with gold, silver and bronze medals handed out in more than 300 events across 26 sports, the 2½-minute medal presentation ceremonies alone would have lasted for more than 12 hours.

Handover Ceremony

The formality of handing over 'possession' of the Games from one Host City to the next was incorporated into the Closing Ceremony at the Montreal 1976 Games. A formal protocol governs the procedure, with the mayor of the Host City joining the President of the IOC on the rostrum and returning to him the Olympic Flag. The IOC President then places it in the hands and the trust of the mayor of the next Host City.

Appointments and accolades at the Closing Ceremony

The Closing Ceremony is now used by the International Olympic Committee (IOC) to conclude some of the business it has conducted outside the sporting arenas. During the Games, all competitors are invited to elect new members of the IOC Athletes' Commission, the body that represents the competitors' views, and which comprises active or recently retired Olympians. On behalf of the athletes, one of these new members then presents a bouquet of flowers to a Games volunteer as a mark of tribute and gratitude for their work during the duration of the event.

The dying flame

After all the speeches, the time has finally come to end the Games, and as the IOC itself says, 'The last protocol element is undoubtedly the most moving.' The Olympic Flame, which will have been burning above the city for the previous 17 days, will slowly be extinguished while the Olympic Hymn plays and the Olympic Flag is lowered from its flagpole and carried from the stadium.

Last words

The flag-raising at the Closing Ceremony is followed by an address from the chairman of the host organising committee. In London, the IOC President formally closed the Olympic Games by saying: 'I declare the Games of the XXX Olympiad closed and, in accordance with tradition, I call upon the youth of the world to assemble four years from now in Rio de Janeiro to celebrate the Games of the XXXI Olympiad.'

London 2012

Partying off to Rio

The Closing Ceremony of the London 2012 Olympic Games was described as the 'best after-show party there has ever been' by director Kim Gavin.

The culmination of 16 days of competition was titled 'A Symphony of British Music' and began with British actor Timothy Spall appearing as Winston Churchill atop Big Ben in the Olympic Stadium set.

After welcoming HRH Prince Harry and IOC President Jacques Rogge, the next hour was an unbroken segue of popular British music featuring appearances from acts such as Ray Davies, The Pet Shop Boys, Madness and Annie Lennox amongst others. David Bowie's 'Fashion' played while supermodels such as Lily Cole, Kate Moss and Naomi Campbell appeared in the centre of the Olympic Stadium to celebrate the British fashion industry.

George Michael performed his 1990 hit 'Freedom' as the 'audience pixels' around the Stadium dazzled with complex patterns and images. The pixel screens were made up of 70,799 small panels mounted between the seats controlled by a single computer. The lights flashed on and around the athletes who were celebrating in the middle of the Stadium.

LOCOG Chair Seb Coe gave a closing speech before Jacques Rogge officially announced the end of the London

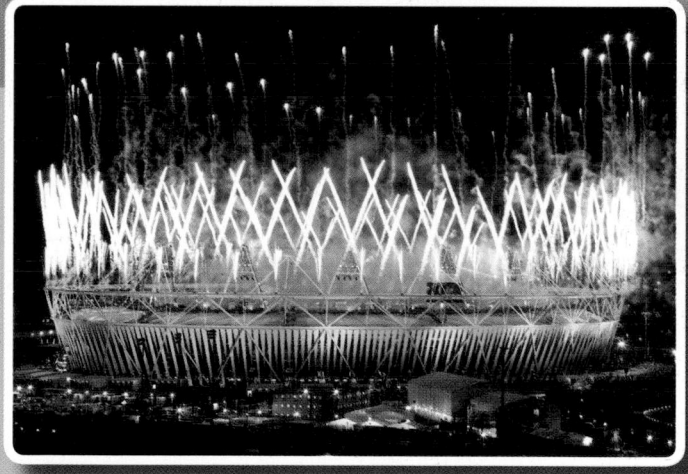

↑ *A pyrotechnic lighting display within the Olympic Stadium came during the London 2012 Closing Ceremony, followed by a stunning fireworks show at its end.*

2012 Games – his final one as IOC President. The Olympic Flame was then extinguished following a ballet performance by Darcey Bussell. The Olympic Flag was passed by the Mayor of London, through the hands of the IOC President, to the Mayor of Rio de Janeiro. Following the official handover, the organisers from the 2016 Olympic Games Host City Rio de Janeiro delivered an eight-minute show with a taste of what the world might expect in 2016: in typical Brazilian fashion it featured two national staples; a carnival atmosphere and Pele.

The evening finished with rock legends The Who playing out the ceremony with their anthem – and, in a way, an unofficial motto for London 2012: 'My Generation'.

Olympic Torch Relays

The modern Olympic Games maintain a link with the Games of Ancient Greece through the ceremonial Olympic Torch Relay, carrying the sacred flame from Olympia, the original site of the Games, to the Host City. There, the lighting of the Olympic Cauldron, usually positioned high above the Athletics Stadium, signifies the precise moment when the Games truly begin.

Flame tradition

The ceremonial surrounding the Torch Relay is strictly controlled by the IOC and the Olympic Charter. Rule 55 of the Charter includes the statement: 'Like the messengers who proclaimed the sacred Olympic truce, the runners who carry the Olympic Flame carry a message of peace on their journey.'

Greek actress Maria Nafpliotou (right) assumes the role of high priestess during the lighting ceremony at Ancient Olympia for the 2008 Games in Beijing.

IOC fire

The International Olympic Committee says: 'In the context of the modern Games, the Olympic Flame represents the positive values that man has always associated with fire. The purity of the flame is guaranteed by the way it is lit using the sun's rays. The choice of Olympia as a starting point emphasises the link between the Ancient and Modern Games and underlines the profound connection between these two events.'

The ancient relay

When the Games were staged in Rome, Italy, in 1960, the Torch Relay was used to shine a spotlight on the two poles of classical civilisation: Athens and Rome. Lesser-known ancient sites in Greece and Italy were brought to the public's attention. For the first time, the relay was televised and the event was closely followed by the media.

The divine Flame

The Ancient Greeks considered fire a divine element and they maintained perpetual fires in front of their temples, including the one at Olympia, where they would stage sporting Games during a period of truce. Before each modern Games, the Flame is lit in a solemn ceremony at Olympia by 11 women representing vestal virgins. The Flame was originally lit using the rays of the sun, to ensure its purity, and a skaphia, the ancestor of the parabolic mirror used today for lighting the Olympic Flame.

The relay to the new world

In 1968, when Mexico City hosted the Games, the Torch Relay's journey retraced the steps of Christopher Columbus to the New World. The last runner on Spanish soil was Cristóbal Colón de Carbajal, a direct descendant of the great navigator. The Olympic Flame made a stop at the Great Pyramid of the Moon in Teotihuacan, where a 'New Fire' ceremony was held. In the Aztec tradition, this marked the end of a 52-year cycle, and the reappearance of the sun at dawn symbolised the renewal of the world.

Relight the fire

The fire ceremony was reintroduced at the modern Games for the first time in Amsterdam in 1928. The Torch Relay was first staged at the suggestion of Carl Diem, the head of the local organising committee for the 1936 Games staged in Berlin. Inspired by torch races that were held in Ancient Greek times, Diem suggested that a flame be lit in Olympia and transported to Berlin for what would be the first Olympic Torch Relay.

➡ *The final leg of a relay involving more than 3,000 runners comes to a close as the last Olympic Torch-bearer reaches Lustgarten in Berlin prior to the 1936 Games.*

British athlete John Mark lights the Olympic Flame at Wembley Stadium in 1948.

The relay of peace

The 1948 Games saw a war-ravaged London take on the first Games for 12 years with a sense of peace and reconciliation, and a strong symbol of this was the Torch Relay. More than 1,400 Torchbearers were used, all on foot, carrying the Flame 3,365 kilometres from Olympia to London's Wembley Stadium, via Italy, Switzerland, France, Luxembourg and Belgium. In homage to the restorer of the Games, the relay passed through Lausanne, in Switzerland, and a ceremony was organised at Pierre de Coubertin's tomb in Bois-de-Vaux.

Relay's hard slog

The last time the Torch Relay was conducted entirely on foot, without any flights or sea crossings, was for the 1980 Games in Moscow. Originally, the Torch Relay runners were mainly selected from local athletics clubs, but gradually celebrities and the general public have begun to participate. Each Games now designs its own, distinctive version of the Torch, and Torchbearers can opt to buy the Torch after they have carried the Flame their set distance and transferred it to the next relay runner.

London's new Relay

The 2012 Olympic Torch Relay started on 19 May and lasted more than two months before the Flame was brought up the Thames to the Olympic Stadium right on cue for the lighting of the Cauldron at the climax of the Opening Ceremony. Around 3,000 runners each carried the Torch 300 metres in the relay. The 2012 Torch Relay toured the United Kingdom, visiting national heritage sites, venues with sporting significance, cultural festivals and many schools. The concept of an international relay was abandoned after problems during the 2008 run.

Novel conveyance

Traditionally, the Torch Relay was conducted entirely on foot. More recent Games have seen the Torch Relay use the pony express through the United States and a camel caravan across the Australian outback. As well as travelling by boat, some Torch Relays have even taken the Flame underwater. It has travelled faster than the speed of sound on Concorde, and the Torch has even been taken in to space by astronauts – twice. Before the 2008 Games in Beijing, the Torch Relay visited the summit of Mount Everest, the world's highest mountain.

London 2012

David Beckham (left) lights the Olympic Torch at RNAS Culdrose, Cornwall.

Lighting up London

London Olympic Games organisers had always forecast that the Torch Relay would fire the public's enthusiasm and excitement in the run-up to the Games but even they may have under-estimated the wave of excitement which the Torch lit throughout the nation. The Flame was brought from Athens on British Airways Flight BA2012 to begin its journey at Land's End on 19 May, with gold medal sailor Ben Ainslie as the first Torchbearer. It completed its mission 70 days later with David Beckham bringing it up the Thames and Sir Steve Redgrave running into the Olympic Stadium for the Cauldron-lighting climax to its journey. Some 3,000 Torchbearers ran the Flame around the country, its visits including a host of sporting, historical and cultural sites. It also undertook a one-off trip out of the United Kingdom into the Republic of Ireland and on to Dublin on 6 June. Organisers estimated that the Flame travelled within 10 miles of 95 per cent of the population.

HM The Queen's rowbarge Gloriana carries the Torch along the River Thames.

Games mascots

They may now be an integral part of the build-up to an Olympic Games and an ever-present feature during the event itself, but Games mascots are a relatively new phenomenon, with the first – a German dachshund called Waldi – appearing as recently as 1972. Here is a collection of the most memorable mascots to have appeared over the years.

Waldi the dachshund left his mark at the 1972 Games.

First mascot

The Summer Olympic Games' first mascot – at Munich 1972 – was a cuddly, multi-coloured German dachshund named Waldi. His image appeared on posters, stickers, key-rings and mugs – all in the colours of the Olympic Rings. Four years earlier the 1968 Winter Games in Grenoble had presented a stylised skiing figure, known as Schuss. Although this was sometimes described as the first Games mascot, it was not produced by the French organisers and was therefore not officially recognised.

Sydney went for a three-in-one mascot concept in 2000 with (from left to right) Ollie, Millie and Syd.

Multiple mascots

The trend for multiple mascots, representing different aspects of the Olympic Games and Paralympic Games, was started in 2000, with Sydney's cartoon characters Syd, Millie and Olly – based on native Australian animals.

Memorable Misha

The Games have also produced some memorable 'characters': Misha, the bear adopted by the 1980 Moscow Games, showed the Russians to be engaged with the modernisation of the Games, and four years later Sam, the Los Angeles eagle, was very Disney-like in its styling and demeanour. A statue of Misha still stands inside the entrance to the Luzhniki sports complex in Moscow, which is dominated by the Olympic Stadium.

Missing the point

The least successful mascots of all time are generally thought to be Izzy, the cartoon character produced for the 1996 Centenary Games in Atlanta – the first Games mascot to be designed by computer – and the beaver Amik from Montreal 1976, who also did little to engage public sympathies.

Atlanta's luckless Izzy tried his best in 1996 … but will be remembered as one of the least successful Games mascots.

London 2012

Wenlock and Mandeville

The London 2012 Olympic and Paralympic mascots reflected the multi-media age of the 21st century. Wenlock and Mandeville were everywhere. They featured in a series of animated films and were a presence on social media, both on Twitter and Facebook. The names had Olympic heritage all of their own. Their inspiration was the Shropshire town of Much Wenlock, considered by many as the true birthplace of the modern Olympic Games, and Stoke Mandeville, home of the world-renowned spinal injuries unit where the Paralympic Movement began in 1948 – with the staging of the Stoke Mandeville Games.

⬇ *Wenlock and Mandeville became two of the best-known faces not only in London but also around the world in 2012.*

⬆ *The Shropshire town of Much Wenlock was a visiting point for the Torch.*

The key to success

As with any major modern sporting event, Olympic Games mascots are now an integral part of the overall business plan. A key part of any Olympic budget is revenue from merchandise sales. London's organisers had targeted £1bn from Olympic and Paralympic Games retail sales, with significant sums coming directly from sales of Wenlock and Mandeville branded T-shirts, key rings and other items.

At the movies

The mini-movies of Wenlock and Mandeville's life stories, which were accessible to download from YouTube, were based on scripts created by the children's laureate, Michael Morpurgo, author of *War Horse*. He came up with the concept of the mascots being fashioned from two drops of molten steel spilt in the making of the last steel girder used in the Olympic Stadium. Foundry worker George picks up the drops of steel and fashions them into figures, which he then gives to his grandchildren. Magically brought to life by a rainbow, they turn somersaults for the children before disappearing off on the road to London, and on towards the Games.

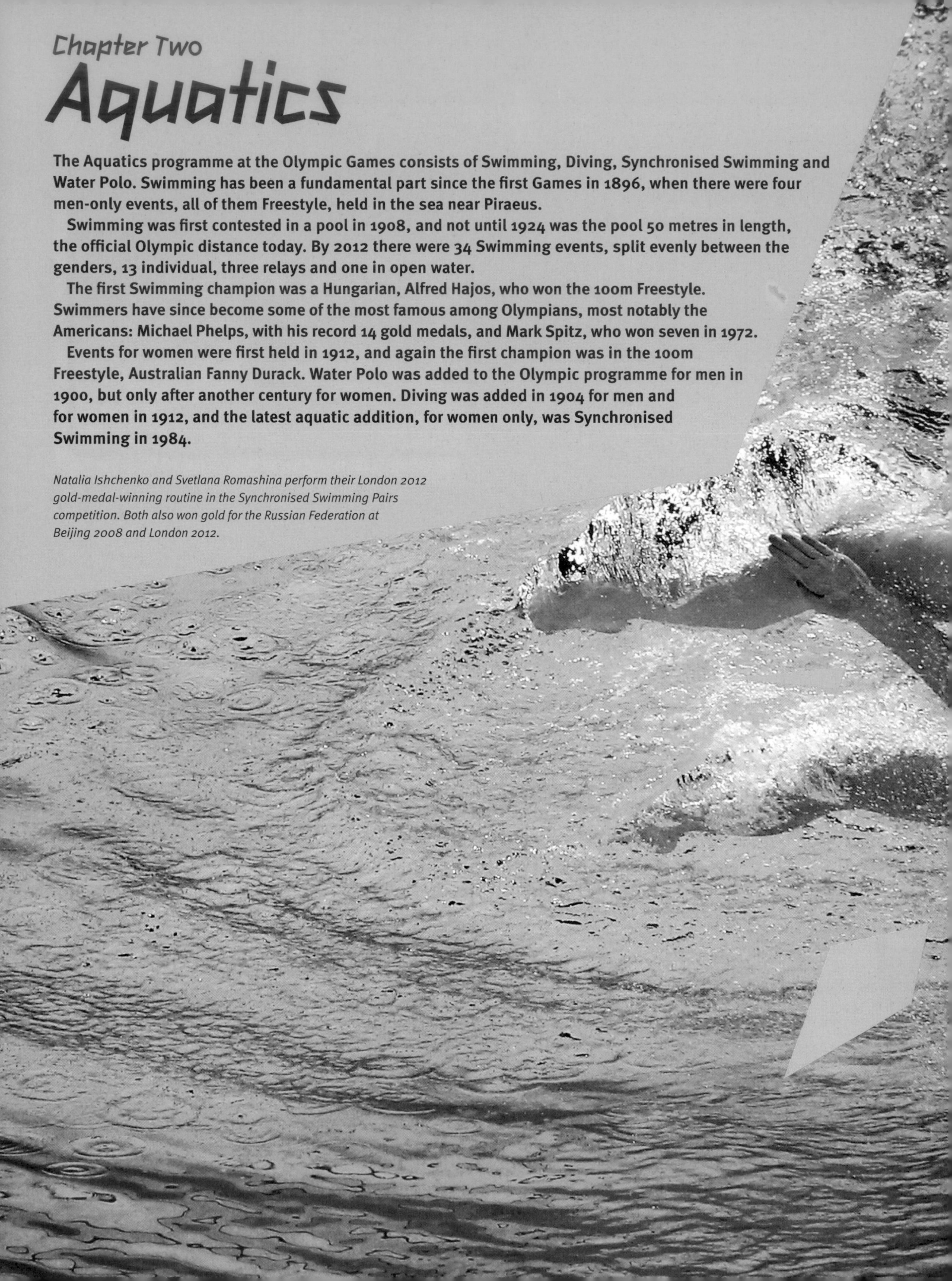

Chapter Two
Aquatics

The Aquatics programme at the Olympic Games consists of Swimming, Diving, Synchronised Swimming and Water Polo. Swimming has been a fundamental part since the first Games in 1896, when there were four men-only events, all of them Freestyle, held in the sea near Piraeus.

Swimming was first contested in a pool in 1908, and not until 1924 was the pool 50 metres in length, the official Olympic distance today. By 2012 there were 34 Swimming events, split evenly between the genders, 13 individual, three relays and one in open water.

The first Swimming champion was a Hungarian, Alfred Hajos, who won the 100m Freestyle. Swimmers have since become some of the most famous among Olympians, most notably the Americans: Michael Phelps, with his record 14 gold medals, and Mark Spitz, who won seven in 1972.

Events for women were first held in 1912, and again the first champion was in the 100m Freestyle, Australian Fanny Durack. Water Polo was added to the Olympic programme for men in 1900, but only after another century for women. Diving was added in 1904 for men and for women in 1912, and the latest aquatic addition, for women only, was Synchronised Swimming in 1984.

Natalia Ishchenko and Svetlana Romashina perform their London 2012 gold-medal-winning routine in the Synchronised Swimming Pairs competition. Both also won gold for the Russian Federation at Beijing 2008 and London 2012.

Men's Diving

The first men's Diving event took place at the 1904 Olympic Games in St Louis, in which athletes contested Platform Diving and a plunge-for-distance event (in which competitors aimed to reach the furthest distance from a standing dive). Today, men compete in 10m Platform and 3m Springboard events – both in individual and, since 2000, synchronised competitions.

Chinese fireworks

China's Jia Hu entered the 10m Platform final at Sydney 2000 in the lead and retained it with a brilliantly executed back 3½ somersault which was awarded a maximum ten by all but one judge. However, with an extremely difficult back 3½ somersault pike, his compatriot Liang Tian scored 101.52 points, then the highest scoring dive in the Games' history. Both men finished with more than 700 points, a record, Tian winning by 11 points with his total of 724.53.

The first perfect ten

The first perfect score of ten was awarded to the only man ever to win the 10m Platform at three straight Olympic Games, the Italian Klaus Dibiasi, and it was awarded for the last dive of a career spanning four Olympic Games. It won him the gold in 1976 by a margin of 23 points and made him the first man ever to score a total of more than 600 in a 10m Platform competition at the Olympic Games.

← *Klaus Dibiasi from Italy set an unbeatable standard over four Olympic Games Diving events between Tokyo 1964 and Montreal 1976.*

Mitcham makes history

Matthew Mitcham, an Australian competing at his first Olympic Games at Beijing 2008, scored 112.10 points in the 10m Platform, the highest total in Olympic history, with his sixth and final dive, a 2½ somersault with 2½ twists in pike position invented by the British Olympic diver Leon Taylor. It earned him four perfect 10s from the seven judges and took him into the gold medal position for the first time in the competition.

Pinkston sets a trend

Clarence 'Bud' Pinkston's gold medal in 10m Platform in 1920 began a run of seven successive victories for the United States that came to an end in 1956, when Mexican Joaquin Capilla Perez took gold. Americans won again in 1960 and 1964, which meant that they had won nine of the ten gold medals in a span of 44 years.

Fading meteor

Shuwei Sun, from Guangdong province in China, had a meteoric rise. He won the 10m platform at the Asian Games aged 14 in 1990, became world champion in 1991, and in 1992 set a world record for the most points earned on a single dive when he was awarded perfect tens on a reverse 3½ somersault tuck for a total of 102 points. The same year, aged 16, he took gold at Barcelona with some ease. That was Sun's peak – he was never to compete at another Games. He missed selection in 1996 and was injured in 2000.

Back to square one...

The first diving championship was organised in Scotland in 1889, featuring a dive from the side and another from a height of 1.8 metres. The first national championship was held in 1895 at Highgate Ponds, in north London, where the country's first permanent diving stage (4.6m high) had been erected in 1893. Another 10m board was built, but was taken down after each staging of the competition, which ended in 1920.

↗ *Sweden's Erik Adlerz, a Platform Diving silver medallist at the 1920 Games, models the discreet swimwear of the era.*

Keeping the men modest

It was not only the women divers who had to cover up when competing. In 1920 the rules decreed men had to wear 'cloth drawers' at least 6 centimetres wide at the hip. The whole trunk and the legs down to the thighs had to be covered, with a hole only 7.5cm from the armpit for the arms.

Lee the master

Sammy Lee was among the greatest authorities on diving technique in the sport's history. The first man to defend the 3m Springboard title at the Games, winning in 1948 and 1952, Lee then coached the two other American men to gain double distinction, Robert Webster (10m Platform, 1960 and 1964) and Greg Louganis (3m Springboard, 1984 and 1988).

⬆ *The moment when Greg Louganis hit the springboard at the 1988 Olympic Games in Seoul.*

Courage worth gold for Louganis

Greg Louganis became the first man to win 3m Springboard and 10m Platform gold medals at two Olympic Games in Seoul in 1988. His victory was not without drama and extreme courage on his part. In a preliminary dive in the Springboard, a reverse 2½ somersault in the pike position, he hit his head on the board and landed clumsily. He was slightly concussed and needed four temporary sutures in the wound, but 35 minutes later he dived again.

London 2012

Boudia beats his demons

American David Boudia, the man who needed advice and support because he was scared of heights, overcame all his demons to carry off gold in the men's 10m Platform at London 2012, Diving's blue riband event, after a gripping final which went to the last dive. The American's score of 568.65 was just enough to beat China's Bo Qiu, who looked distraught to get silver with 566.85. Boudia's gold signalled a welcome renaissance for the United States, who had not won an Olympic Diving medal since Laura Wilkinson won the women's 10m Platform at Sydney 2000. Qiu, the Chinese teenager who came into the event as favourite and world champion, appeared devastated to have failed where Liang Tian had succeeded at Sydney 2000 and Jia Hu at Athens 2004. Australia's defending champion Matt Mitcham was eliminated in the semi-finals.

Daley's delight

Great Britain's Tom Daley was one of the home poster boys of the London 2012 Games and he greeted his bronze medal in the men's 10m Platform with as much glee as if he had won the gold. The 18-year-old who, when he was still just 13 years old, had qualified to compete at the Beijing 2008 Games, as Britain's youngest ever male competitor, made a tentative start to the competition and only scraped into the semi-final in 15th place. But Daley conquered his nerves, and even obtained the right to a re-dive after complaining he had been distracted by a rash of camera-flash bulbs from the 17,500 crowd inside the Aquatics Centre. He even led at the start of the sixth and last round of dives. Afterwards the 18-year-old said his only regret was that his biggest fan, his father Rob, who had died from

⬆ *Great Britain's Tom Daley reacts after winning bronze in the men's 10m Platform competition at the London 2012 Olympic Games.*

cancer the previous year, could not have been there. Daley added: 'This has been the toughest year of my life. It was a shame he wasn't here to see this. The medal means so much to me. I just can't believe it.' It had almost been double success for Daley, as he narrowly missed out on winning a medal in the men's Synchronised 10m Platform competition. He and partner Pete Waterfield had finished fourth, one poor dive costing them the chance of a place on the podium.

Women's Diving

Women's Diving has been part of the Olympic Games programme since Antwerp 1920. As is the case with the men, they compete in 10m Platform and 3m Springboard events, both as individuals and, since Sydney 2000, in synchronised events. Recent competitions have been dominated by Chinese divers.

Too young to dive?

Mingxia Fu was 11 when she won the 1990 Goodwill Games and only 12½ when she won the world title in 10m Platform in 1991. Shocked, FINA, the world body for diving, decreed a minimum age for Olympic competition of 14 years in the Olympic year. Although Fu qualified for the 1992 Games only narrowly, having turned 14 just 20 days before her 10m Platform Final, she won the gold medal by the most decisive margin in 60 years – and won again in 1996.

Like mother like daughter

Patricia McCormick was the first diver, man or woman, to win 3m Springboard and 10m Platform gold medals at two Olympic Games, in 1952 and 1956. Eighteen years later, at the Olympic Games in her home city of Los Angeles, her daughter Kelly missed out on gold in the 3m Springboard by just 3.24 points. Four years later she was to win another medal for the McCormick family, a 3m Springboard bronze.

Young and old

Aileen Riggin, of Newport, Rhode Island, won the first 3m Springboard gold medal, at Antwerp 1920. She was 14 years old and just 1.40 metres tall, the smallest competitor in the entire Games that year. She was diving into an outdoor moat of cold water and there were no hot showers for competitors, as there are today. It obviously did her no harm, because 82 years after her victory (aged 96) she won six age group titles at the World Masters Championships.

American hand-over

The United States dominated women's Diving from 1920 to 1956, but since China's return to the Olympic Games in 1984 in Los Angeles their women have reigned supreme. Jihong Zhou's gold medal in 10m Platform was China's only gold in that comeback Games, but Chinese women have since won the last six 3m Springboard titles, the only three synchronised golds contested and five of the last seven 10m Platform events. Their women won all four gold medals contested when the country hosted the 2008 Games in Beijing.

↖ *Double gold-medal winner Pat McCormick in action at Helsinki 1952.*

Doubling up

Synchronised Diving for pairs was introduced at Sydney 2000, effectively doubling the number of events. Nine judges, instead of seven, officiate, five looking for synchronisation and four for execution, two for each diver. The highest and lowest scores for both phases are discarded, the remainder added and then multiplied by the degree of difficulty. There are no preliminaries or semi-finals. Only eight pairs can qualify for the Olympic Games from major events in the previous year.

↗ *China's Ruolin Chen (front) and Xin Wang (back) put in a collection of gold medal-winning dives at the 2008 Games in Beijing.*

Keeping it in the family

Elizabeth Becker and Clarence 'Bud' Pinkston are the most successful Diving couple in Olympic history. He won gold in the 10m Platform and silver in the 3m Springboard in 1920 and a bronze in 1924. At the latter Games, in Paris, he met Elizabeth Becker, another member of the US Diving team, who won gold in the 3m Springboard and silver in the 10m Platform. They married, had twins, and on their second birthday in 1928 she was back in Europe to win 10m Platform gold and 3m Springboard bronze in Amsterdam, making a family grand total of seven medals (two gold, two silver and three bronze).

No head for heights

Mary Ellen Clark won bronze at Barcelona 1992, diving from the 10-metre board, an exercise which means a body hits the water at 30mph. A year before the 1996 Games, however, she began to feel dizzy every time she dived, even from the 1m board. She was diagnosed with benign paroxysmal position vertigo and for nine months could not dive. After treatment including head swinging, neck collars and acupuncture, she returned to win bronze in 1996, aged 33, to become Diving's oldest medallist.

Lucky break

Three-and-a-half months before the United States Olympic trials in 2000, Laura Wilkinson broke three bones in her right foot in training. The foot was in a cast for ten weeks, but a month after its removal she won selection for the US team. Incredibly, in Sydney six months after the accident, she won the gold medal in 10m Platform after entering the final round in fifth place and going on to beat Chinese diver Na Li by the slenderest of margins – 1.74 points.

⬆ *Minxia Wu enjoyed another 3m Springboard double at London 2012, winning both the women's Individual and Synchronised events.*

Chen's golden double

China's Ruolin Chen was one of the handful of Olympic champions from Beijing 2008 who successfully defended their title at London 2012 when she took gold in the women's 10m Platform. Her score of 422.3 points proved superior only after a high-tension fifth and final round of competition. A string of fine performances meant that the five divers from second to sixth were separated by only 10.3 points. Australia's Brittany Broben took silver on 366.5 and Malaysia's Pandelela Rinong Pamg bronze on 359.2. A major upset was the failure of Yadan Hu, world silver medallist, to press Chen for gold. Hu finished down in ninth place after event nerves appeared to have upset her first two dives. China's Minxia Wu won an unprecedented third consecutive Olympic women's Synchronised 3m Springboard title with partner Zi He.

Switch pays again for Heymans

Emilie Heymans became first female diver to win medals at four consecutive Olympic Games and the first Canadian to win four in a row when she and partner Jennifer Abel took bronze in the women's Synchronized 3m Springboard at London 2012. Yet Heymans had dreamed of Olympic glory, as a child, through Gymnastics. Born in Belgium – for whom her mother competed at Montreal 1976 – that ambition was brought to an end by her doubting coaches when she was 11. That prompted her switch to diving, which was almost instantly rewarded with silver at Sydney 2000. Bronze followed at Athens 2004 then silver in the 10m Platform at Beijing 2008. As she celebrated in London she did not rule out going for medal number five at the Rio 2016 Games.

The diving baby

Californian Marjorie Gestring is the youngest person ever to win an individual gold medal in any sport. Too young to compete under modern rules, she was only 13 years 268 days old when she won the 3m Springboard in 1936. Younger still was another American, Dorothy Poynton, who won silver in the 3m Springboard aged 13 years 23 days in 1928. She later won gold in the 10m Platform in 1932 and 1936.

⬆ *It was lucky 13 for American diver Marjorie Gestring in Berlin in 1936.*

London 2012

Men's Swimming

Swimming was one of the ten sports contested at the inaugural Olympic Games at Athens 1896, with athletes competing in four events: the 50m Freestyle, 100m Freestyle, 500m Freestyle and, surprisingly, the 100m Freestyle for sailors. A part of the programme at every Games since, by 2012 the number of events for men had grown to 17, 16 in the pool and one – the Marathon Swim – in open water.

The dead heat

Australian John Devitt was so certain he had lost the 100m Freestyle final in 1960 that he congratulated 'winner' Lance Larson and left the pool. But then confusion reigned. The two men's times were identical at 55.2 seconds – an Olympic record. Two first-place judges thought Devitt had won, but two second-place judges thought Devitt second, so of six judges three voted for Devitt, three for Larson. A head judge with a casting vote decided it for Devitt.

Ultimate victor

Michael Phelps could have matched Mark Spitz's single Games record of seven gold medals at the Athens 2004 Games. But he gave up his place on the United States 4 x 100m Medley Relay team to Ian Crocker after beating him in the 100m Butterfly by just 0.04sec, so settled for six golds. At Beijing 2008, Phelps broke Spitz's mark with eight gold medals, and his four golds at London 2012 gave him an Olympic Games record 18.

Not like father...

Swimming's first champion was Alfred Hajos, a Hungarian who had become a good swimmer after his father drowned in the River Danube when Alred was 13. The competition in 1896 was held in the sea near Piraeus, with the water temperature only 13° Celsius, an incentive for quick swimming. He later also won the 1,200m Freestyle when rough conditions caused 3.5-metre waves. Some 28 years later he won a prize as an architect in the Olympic Art Contest.

Hungarian Alfred Hajos was a double Olympic Games gold-medal winner: in Swimming at Athens 1896 and in Art at Paris 1924.

Hollywood days

The Olympic swimming pool seemed to lead directly to Hollywood stardom between the two World Wars. First to take his swimming fame to the silver screen was Duke Kahanamoku, who made several silent moves, but more famous was Johnny Weissmuller, a winner of five gold medals in the 1920s who became the most popular of all Tarzans. Eleanor Holm, the 1932 Backstroke champion, later became Jane to another Tarzan, Olympic Decathlon champion Glenn Moore, while Buster Crabbe, the 1932 400m Freestyle champion, became Flash Gordon on screen.

Five-time Olympic Games gold medallist Johnny Weissmuller earned even greater fame as Tarzan in Hollywood's own golden era appearing in 36 films.

The mighty wingspan of Germany's Michael Gross earned him not only his 'Albatross' nickname but also three Olympic Games gold medals and three world records.

Gross the albatross

There was only one feature of the West German swimmer Michael Gross that was greater than his immense height of 2.01m (6ft 7in) – his arm-span. From fingertip to fingertip he measured 2.25 metres. He was nicknamed the 'Albatross', and he used his immense reach to win three gold medals in 1984 and 1988 and set three world records.

Magnificent seven

American Mark Spitz was anticipating a hatful of gold medals in 1968, having won five at the previous year's Pan-American Games. He won just two, both from Relays, and in his final race, the 200m Butterfly in which he held the world record, he finished last. Four years later, it was his first event and he won it in world record time. He went on to win seven gold medals, the first athlete in Olympic Games history to do so.

⬇ *Mark Spitz was the star of the show at Munich 1972, becoming the first Olympian in history to land a haul of seven gold medals at one Games.*

⬆ *There was a golden lining to a school accident for Britain's Duncan Goodhew when he won 100m Breaststroke gold at the 1980 Olympic Games in Moscow.*

Goodhew proves his point

Swimmers invariably wore tight-fitted rubber caps to reduce water drag from their hair. Some even shaved their heads. Duncan Goodhew, a dyslexic Briton, did not need anything artificial. He lost his hair permanently from the trauma of falling from a tree at his Sussex school when he was ten, thereafter suffering years of adolescent abuse. His determination to overcome his problems was channelled into swimming and he won 100m Breaststroke gold at the 1980 Games.

Golden reward for iceman ross

Richard Ross should not have taken part in the 400m Individual Medley at the Tokyo 1964 Olympic Games. Japanese doctors advised an immediate operation when he was stricken with severe appendicitis three days before his competition. The world record holder would not hear of it, nor would he accept their offer of pain-killing drugs. Instead his lower torso was packed in ice until the day of the race, when he emerged to win gold in a world record time.

➡ *Russia's Aleksandr Popov celebrates after winning gold in the 100m Freestyle at Barcelona 1992. He went on to win the 50m Freestyle as well to add to his gold-medal tally.*

Popov the marathon man

Aleksandr Popov, a 6ft 6in Russian, was a converted backstroke swimmer who remained at the top of the rankings at 100m Freestyle for a dozen years. His first great victory was at the 1991 European Championships, but it was at Barcelona 1992 that he drew gasps. His final 50 metres was the first sub-25-second length ever recorded. He won again in 1996, by which time he held the world record at 48.21, was second at Sydney 2000, and only missed out on the Athens 2004 final by a single place.

Apologetic champion

Rick Carey, a New Yorker, was so disgusted with the time that won him the 200m Backstroke gold medal in 1984 that he hung his head at the Victory Ceremony and expressed only anger. He had wanted to break his own world record. So vociferous was the criticism that greeted his attitude in the American press that Carey issued a formal public apology. 'I found it very difficult to smile when my performance didn't live up to my expectations,' he wrote.

Golden second chance

Duke Kahanamoku, a Hawaiian of royal ancestry, won the first two rounds of the 100m Freestyle at the 1912 Games in Stockholm comfortably but, like his two American team-mates, he believed himself through to the final. All three missed the semi-final round but were invited to swim off between them for two remaining final spots. Kahanamoku broke the world record to take one of them, and went on to win the final by two yards.

First black champion

Competitors of African origin were a rarity at one time in pools at the Olympic Games until, at Seoul 1988, Trinidad-born Anthony Nesty proved there was no reason for it. He won the 100m Butterfly, becoming the first person from the tiny South American country of Surinam, in which there was only one 50-metre pool, to win a medal at the Olympic Games in any sport.

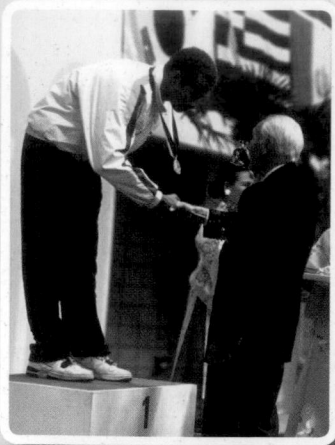

⬆ *A moment of Olympic Games history as Surinam's Anthony Nesty becomes the first African-American athlete to win a Swimming gold medal.*

Breaststroke loopholes

The most complex of strokes has had many techniques over the last 100 years, with the rules being inexorably tightened. Many loopholes were exploited in earlier days. In the 1930s, American swimmers began bringing their arms back above the surface, until in 1952 this was recognised as a new, different stroke, butterfly. And then in the 1950s the Japanese began swimming under-water because it was faster, but this was banned in 1956.

Unbroken record

No swimmer had a record to match that of Tamas Darnyi, a Hungarian who had lost all sight in his left eye when he was hit by an icy snowball as a boy. Between 1985 and 1992 he never lost a race at either Individual Medley distance. During that time he set numerous world records and won the 200m and 400m titles at both the 1988 and 1992 Games. Two of his world records came in finals: the 200m Individual Medley in 1988 and the 400m Individual Medley in 1992.

⬇ *Hungary's Tamas Darnyi was unbeatable in Individual Medley over both 200m and 400m, winning four gold medals between 1988 and 1992.*

Unlucky asthmatic

Rick DeMont, 16, from California, had been taking medication for asthma since he was four years old and listed those medications on an official form when he qualified for the United States team for Munich 1972. When he woke with a wheeze on the eve of the final he took his usual drug Marax, and thought nothing of it. Later that day he won the 400m Freestyle final, and received the gold medal, but three days later was told he had failed a drug test. US team doctors had omitted to clear his drugs, an act they publicly acknowledged only 29 years later.

Relay trend-setters

The USA won the first seven 4 x 100m Freestyle gold medals before Australia ended their run in unusual circumstances at Sydney 2000. Ian Thorpe had won the 400m Freestyle only 55 minutes earlier and had barely had time to complete the Victory Ceremony before he swam the final two lengths. After one length he was 0.6 seconds down on Gary Hall Jnr, bronze medallist in the individual event. Not only did he catch him but he finished with a 0.19 second lead for a world record.

One for mum

Pablo Morales expected a gold medal at the 1984 Olympic Games. He held the world record at 100m Butterfly and broke it in the final, only for German Michael Gross to swim even faster. A relay gold and another individual silver came as scant consolation. In 1988, after failing to make the US team, he retired, but when his mother, Bianca, died of cancer in 1991 he vowed to win gold in her memory. He returned to competition eight months before the 1992 Games in Barcelona and went on to win the gold he missed out on in 1984.

Hungarian fiddle

Hungarian swimming officials forgot to keep a record of their swimmers' times during 1996, so they 'invented' a fictional meeting in Budapest on 6–8 June, complete with results, to satisfy IOC regulations. Half of their eventual team at the Games qualified by this route, including Attila Czene, who took 200m Individual Medley gold and also broke the Olympic Games record.

Boy winner in a man's world

Andrew Charlton was always known as 'Boy' because of his extreme youth when he made his name at 16, beating a great Swedish swimmer, Arne Borg. On the long voyage to Europe for the 1924 Games in Paris, his coach Tom Adrian, a First World War veteran suffering from shell shock, tried to commit suicide by throwing himself overboard. He was rescued, and Boy Charlton, destrmined to make him happy, beat Borg again with a world record time to win the 1500m Freestyle.

London 2012

Fantastic Mr Phelps

Michael Phelps established his place in Olympic Games history when he rounded off his career in appropriate style by winning his record-extending 18th gold medal in the men's 4 x 100m Medley Relay on the final day of Swimming at the Aquatics Centre. Phelps, who first became an Olympian at Sydney 2000 aged only 15 (he finished fifth in the men's 200m Butterfly final, his only event), headed for retirement with six gold medals from Athens 2004, eight from Beijing 2008 and four from London 2012, twice as many as the next competitor in any sport in the history of the modern Olympic Games. Phelps also won two silver and two bronze medals during his career, giving him a total of 22, yet another record. Soviet gymnast Larisa Latynina had held the previous record of 18 medals since 1964, but the Phelps standard may last even longer than this 48-year gap. The capacity crowd at the Aquatics Centre, including Phelps's mother Debbie, afforded him a standing ovation and governing body FINA presented him with a lifetime achievement award. Phelps, born on 30 June 1985, in Towson, Maryland, holds a string of world records across the pool range plus an assessed 71 medals in all major international competitions, comprising 57 gold, 11 silver, and three bronze cumulatively in the Olympic Games, World Championships and Pan-Pacific Championships. Six times he had been voted World Swimmer of the Year and eight times American Swimmer of the Year Award. In 2008 he was named *Sports Illustrated* magazine's Sportsman of the Year.

⬇ *Ryan Lochte is all smiles after he won the men's 400m Individual Medley on the first day of competition at the London 2012 Olympic Games.*

⬆ *Michael Phelps set so many Olympic Games records in his career, but 22 medals, 18 of them gold, may be the most remarkable of all.*

Lochte shines bright

Ryan Lochte won five medals, fewer than had been predicted. But, given the brilliance of rival – and team-mate Michael Phelps – a proud achievement. Lochte opened by beating Phelps to win the men's 400m Individual Medley but that was his only individual gold; his other arrived as a member of the 4 x 200m Freestyle Relay team. He won two silver medals, in the 200m Individual Medley – behind Phelps – and the 4 x 100m Freestyle Relay and a bronze in the 200m Backstroke.

Phantom whistle almost eclipses Sun

Yang Sun smashed his own world record to win the 1500m Freestyle final and became the first man in 32 years to complete the men's 400m Freestyle/1500m Freestyle double. He won the longer race in 14:31.02, slicing more than three seconds off his previous world mark – though to do so he needed a little luck. Sun had tipped forward into the water after a spectator blew a whistle when the swimmers were crouched and waiting to go. He was given the starter's discretionary benefit of the doubt to stay in the race and secure a place of his own in swimming history.

World Record

Event	Name	Country	Record	Date
100m Breaststroke	Cameron van der Burgh	RSA	58.46	29 July
200m Breaststroke	Daniel Gyurta	HUN	2:07.28	1 August
1500m Freestyle	Yang Sun	CHN	14:31.02	4 August

Olympic Record

Event	Name	Country	Record	Date
400m Freestyle	Yang Sun	CHN	3:40.14	28 July
100m Backstroke	Matthew Grevers	USA	58.23	30 July
200m Backstroke	Tyler Clary	USA	1:53.41	2 August

Women's Swimming

Women's Swimming was staged for the first time at the 1912 Games in Stockholm with 27 competitors from eight nations contesting just two events: the 100m Freestyle and the 4 x 100m Freestyle Relay. At the London 2012 Games, there were 17 women's Swimming events.

Windmill in a hurricane

Janet Evans, despite a tiny frame of 1.66 metres and 46 kilograms weight, was years ahead of her time. Her 400m and 800m world records set in 1988 and 1989 lasted until 2006 and 2008 respectively, an astonishing achievement in a sport where records are broken frequently. She was swimming laps by the age of two and a year later could do both breaststroke and butterfly. She used an unusual straight-arm recovery in freestyle, saying: 'As I wanted to go down the pool the fastest, I figured the fastest way to get to the other end was to turn my arms over as fast as I could.' Evans won four gold medals over two Games and is still regarded as the premier female distance swimmer.

⬆ Janet Evans was always way ahead of her time and her 400m and 800m Freestyle world records lasted 18 and 19 years respectively.

Determined Durack

The honour of being the first Olympic Games women's Swimming champion went to Australia's Fanny Durack. She took the 100m Freestyle gold medal in 1912. The previous year, she had adopted the two-beat leg-kick for the Australian crawl and did not lose another race for eight years. However, the officials in charge of naming the Australian team believed it was wasteful to spend money on sending women to Sweden and refused to pay their fares. Eventually, Durack and her rival and close friend Mina Wylie were permitted to go if they raised the money themselves, and they did so by setting up a fund. In Stockholm, the pair finished first and second, after Durack had set a world record of 1 minute 19.8 seconds in the heat. Durack set 11 world records during her career from the distance of 100 yards to one mile.

⬆ Fanny Durack (left) holds the distinction of winning the first-ever women's Swimming gold medal at the Olympic Games. She eased to victory in the 100m Freestyle final at Stockholm 1912 with a 3.2-second winning margin.

⬋ Gertrude Ederle put any disappointment she suffered at the 1924 Olympic Games behind her by becoming the first woman to swim the English Channel.

Channel to stardom

Gertrude Ederle finished 'only' third in the 100m Freestyle at Paris 1924 and won gold in the 4 x 100m Relay. But two years later she earned international renown when she became the first woman to swim the English Channel. The American's time of 14 hours 31 minutes, helped by a wind-up gramophone playing popular songs on the accompanying boat, beat the men's record by almost two hours. An estimated two million people greeted her in New York, where she was welcomed by a ticker-tape parade. The city mayor described her achievement as being like 'Moses parting the Red Sea'. She recovered from a nervous breakdown in 1933 to live until she was 98, spending many years teaching deaf children to swim.

Holm over the limit

Eleanor Holm, winner of the 100m Backstroke in 1932, was favourite again in 1936. However, during the sea crossing to Europe, she outraged US officials by spending evenings carousing with other passengers and journalists and, despite a warning, drinking heavily. She was banned from competing in the Games by the US Olympic Committee led by its president, Avery Brundage, later the IOC president. Holm thus went to Berlin as a spectator and was lavishly entertained by the Nazis, despite being Jewish. Her highly publicised private life subsequently included two divorces, while her outspoken individuality was summed up in 1999, when, aged 85, she told Bill Clinton at a Washington reception: 'Mr President, you're a really good-looking dude.'

Fraser's historic hat-trick

Dawn Fraser became the first swimmer, male or female, to win three gold medals in the same event at the Games. Her victories in the 100m Freestyle from 1956 to 1964 led to her being voted in 1983 as Australia's greatest female Olympian. Her last victory, in Tokyo, was achieved despite her having been involved in a car crash in February 1964 which killed her mother and saw her spend more than a month in plaster because of a damaged vertebra. Fraser had frequent clashes with officials, climaxing at the 1964 Games in Tokyo when, together with two team-mates, she tried to steal the flag from the Emperor's Palace. Although she was arrested, the Emperor gave her the flag as a souvenir. However, the Australian authorities banned her for ten years.

⬆ *Dawn Fraser dominated the 100m Freestyle event, winning gold in 1956, 1960 and 1964.*

Brilliant Bleibtrey

A pioneer of women's swimming, Ethelda Bleibtrey won every race she could enter at the 1920 Olympics – the 100m, 300m and Freestyle Relay – to become the United States' first-ever Olympic Swimming champion. Bleibtrey, who took up the sport after suffering polio, was imprisoned for indecency in 1919, because she took off her stockings before swimming at Manhattan Beach. A public outcry prompted her release. Three years later, she was again arrested when she swam in the reservoir in Central Park in New York in an attempt to force the authorities to build a public pool.

Andersen out on her own

Greta Andersen not only won the 100m title at London 1948 but was an outstanding long-distance performer, completing a 50-mile endurance feat. The Dane also swam the English Channel six times, setting records for the distance and regularly beating men in races across the straits. Her ability to drive herself to exhaustion was shown in the 1948 Olympic Games in London, when she was pulled out of the water unconscious in the 400m Freestyle. Four years later, in Helsinki, she reached the 400m Freestyle Final, despite being able to use only one leg because she had undergone surgery on the other.

⬇ *Shane Gould poses with her medals after her successes in Munich.*

'All that glitters is not Gould'

Those were the words with which the American women's team emblazoned their T-shirts in 1972, in defiance of the expected supremacy of the 15-year-old Australian Shane Gould – who would set 11 world records in a top-class two-year career. These included all Freestyle events from 100 to 1500m and also the 200m Individual Medley. Although American rivals won the 100m and 800m in Munich, Gould won three titles and two further medals to become the first female swimmer to take five medals at a single Games. She retired in 1973 after setting a world record in 1500m. As fellow Australian and Olympic champion Mike Wenden said: 'Shane was like a high-decibel concert which had such an impact it left your ears ringing.'

Donna DeVarona

Blonde Californian Donna DeVarona won two gold medals in 1964, including the first ever 400m Individual Medley. She also became the cover girl for magazines such as *Sports Illustrated, Life* and *Time*. Between 1960 and 1964, she was the best all-round female swimmer in the world. Subsequently, she travelled extensively as a sports commentator and a campaigner for women in sport, co-founding the Women's Sports Foundation.

⬆ *Susie O'Neill (left) slipped to a surprise second in the 200m Butterfly final in front of her home crowd at Sydney in the 2000 Games.*

O'Neill, the unbeatable loser

Susie O'Neill was an Olympic champion at both 200m Butterfly (1996) and 200m Freestyle (2000), but she suffered one of the biggest upsets in Swimming history at the Games when she attempted to retain her 200m Butterfly title in Sydney. Not only was she competing before her home crowd, she had not lost at the distance for six years, had broken a 19-year-old world record and had just won the 200m Freestyle gold medal. The American Misty Hyman had been ill in the build-up to the Games, but won the final by 0.70 seconds.

The Mouse that roared

Krisztina Egerszegi was nicknamed the 'Mouse' by her Hungarian team-mates – Eger means 'mouse' in Hungarian – but there was nothing diminutive about her achievements. She won five Olympic titles, including three successive golds in the 200m Backstroke, emulating the feat of Australian Dawn Fraser. Yet she ranked her 200m Backstroke world record at the 1991 European Championships as probably her favourite moment. Her time of 2 minutes 06.62 seconds brought her a 10-minute standing ovation, and the mark lasted until 2008. She possessed a superbly smooth stroke, in which her long, purple-painted fingernails were also a trademark. In the later stages of her career, she opened a restaurant in Budapest, called The Mousehole.

America's record breaker

Natalie Coughlan won an individual gold medal in the women's 100m Backstroke at the Athens 2004 Games, was part of the United States' world record-breaking, gold medal-winning quartet in the women's 4 x 200m Freestyle Relay. Four years later, at the Beijing 2008 Games, she was one of the stars of the show, winning gold in the women's 100m Backstroke (to become the first woman in history to defend her Backstroke title at the Games), silver medals as part of the US women's 4 x 100m Freestyle Relay and 4 x 100m Medley Relay quartets and bronze medals in the women's 100m Freestyle, the women's 200m Individual Medley and the women's 4x200m Freestyle Relay. In doing so, she became the first female American athlete in modern history to win six medals at one Games.

Miss all-rounder

Tracy Caulkins was perhaps the most versatile swimmer in history – yet she competed in only one Olympic Games, at Los Angeles 1984, because the United States boycotted the 1980 Games. In 1978, aged only 15, Caulkins won five gold medals, including both medleys, at the World Championships, but she never really overcame being unable to compete in Moscow. Still, in 1984, she was named her country's Sportswoman of the Year when she won both Individual Medleys and also swam the breaststroke leg for the victorious Medley Relay quartet.

⬆ *Tracey Caulkins finally got her hands on an Olympic Games gold medal (three of them) at Los Angeles 1984.*

London 2012

High-speed teen

Shiwen Ye proved the latest young Chinese star to surprise the swimming world. The 16-year-old won two gold medals at London 2012, but her smashing of the women's 400m Individual Medley world record, with a time five seconds faster than her personal best, was astonishing. She won the first by covering the penultimate, freestyle lap of the 400m Individual Medley faster than Michael Phelps in the men's final, and her last lap quicker than Ryan Lochte in winning the male equivalent. Her time broke the world record, set by Stephanie Rice at Beijing 2008, by three seconds. Ye finished in 4:28.43. 'I was just trying my best to come from behind,' said Ye who won her second gold three days later in the 200m Individual Medley. She was fourth at the end of the first leg and third at the start of the final leg.

Ledecky lords it

American teenager Katie Ledecky scored a remarkable victory in the women's 800m Freestyle final at London 2012 that comprehensively ended home favourite Rebecca Adlington's hopes of repeating her Beijing 2008 success. Ledecky, at 15 the youngest member of the American team, commanded the entire length of the race to take gold in 8:14.63. She missed out on the world record in the longest event for women in the pool by half a second. She also finished an impressive four seconds clear of Spain's Mireia Belmonte Garcia who took her second silver of the Games after having finished runner-up in the 200m Butterfly two days earlier. Belmonte Garcia had promised to undertake a parachute jump if she won a medal at the London 2012 Games.

⬇ *Shiwen Ye broke both world and Olympic records with superb final sector swims in the 200m Individual Medley and 400m Individual Medley.*

⬆ *Rebecca Adlington won two of the four medals achieved by Great Britain at the Aquatics Centre at London 2012, both of them bronze.*

History for Adlington

Rebecca Adlington won Britain's only women's Swimming medals at London 2012, bronze medals in the 400m Freestyle and 800m Freestyle, events in which she had won gold at Beijing 2008. Adlington produced a remarkable performance to win bronze in the 400m Freestyle after struggling to qualifying eighth fastest. She made history as Britain's first female swimmer to win individual medals in successive Olympic Games and was consoled by an outpouring of public appreciation for her inspirational example. She responded with a grateful observation: 'People have sent me messages saying, "you made me get into swimming", "you made me get into sport" and that is the best reaction of all. If I can inspire just one person to get into the pool that is an amazing feeling.'

World Record

Event	Name	Country	Record	Date
400m Individual Medley	Shiwen Ye	CHN	4:28.43	28 July
100m Butterfly	Dana Vollmer	USA	55.98	29 July
200m Breaststroke	Rebecca Soni	USA	2:19.59	2 August
200m Backstroke	Missy Franklin	USA	2:04.06	3 August
4 x 100m Medley Relay	United States	USA	3:52.05	4 August

Olympic Record

Event	Name	Country	Record	Date
4 x 100m Freestyle Relay	Australia	AUS	3:33.15	28 July
100m Backstroke	Emily Seebohm	AUS	58.23	29 July
400m Freestyle	Camille Muffat	FRA	4:01.45	29 July
200m Freestyle	Allison Schmitt	USA	1:53.61	31 July
200m Individual Medley	Shiwen Ye	CHN	2:07.57	31 July
4 x 200m Freestyle Relay	United States	USA	7:42.92	1 August
200m Butterfly	Liuyang Jiao	CHN	2:04.06	1 August
100m Freestyle	Ranomi Kromowidjojo	NLD	53.00	2 August
50m Freestyle	Ranomi Kromowidjojo	NLD	24.05	4 August

Synchronised Swimming

A relatively new discipline to feature on the Summer Games Aquatics programme, Synchronised Swimming first appeared as an exhibition sport from 1948 to 1968, before gaining recognition as a fully-fledged discipline in Los Angeles in 1984. Known originally as 'water ballet', Synchronised Swimming, alongside Rhythmic Gymnastics, is the only exclusively female sport to feature at the Summer Games.

Making a splash in Hollywood

When the outbreak of the Second World War forced the cancellation of the 1940 Olympic Games in Tokyo, United States swimmer Esther Williams lost a chance to make a name for herself on the international sports stage. Instead her good looks and athletic ability saw her switch to performing alongside Olympian swimmer and screen star Johnny Weissmuller in Billy Rose's Aquacade – a music, dance and swimming show in New York. Williams went on to star in a number of Hollywood films in the 1940s and 1950s, performing elaborate swimming routines. *Bathing Beauty* was Hollywood's first swimming movie, and it created a new genre of 'aquamusicals' which helped popularise synchronised swimming. The best known was *Million Dollar Mermaid* (the nickname by which she would come to be known during her time at MGM) in which Williams portrayed the Australian swimmer Annette Kellerman.

First medals

In 1984, in front of a home crowd in Los Angeles, Tracie Ruiz and Candy Costie won the first-ever Olympic medals in the event, claiming gold in the Duet for the US. Ruiz went on to capture an additional gold medal a day later in the Solo event. Four years later, at Seoul, the 1984 Solo runner-up, Canada's Carolyn Waldo, reversed places with Ruiz to take the gold medal.

➜ *Canada's Sylvie Fréchette defied tragedy and controversy to share gold at Barcelona 1992.*

A sport is born

The sport of synchronised swimming evolved from the ornamental swimming and theatrical water ballets of the late 19th and early 20th centuries. Australian swimmer Annette Kellerman, who performed water acrobatics in a glass tank at the New York Hippodrome in 1907, is often referred to as the first under-water ballerina.

⬆ *Australian Annette Kellermann is credited with inventing synchronised swimming after her 1907 performance of the first water ballet in New York.*

Changing times

Introduced to the Olympic Games in Los Angeles in 1984 with Solo and Duet events, the Synchronised Swimming programme has evolved still further. After featuring in Seoul in 1988 and in Barcelona in 1992, the Solo and Duet events were replaced in Atlanta in 1996 by an eight-person Team event. In 2000 the Duet event was reintroduced to the programme, alongside the Team event. London 2012 will be a landmark Games for Synchronised Swimming. This is where the sport made its Olympic debut in 1948 as an exhibition event.

Barcelona tragedy

After exploding on to the world stage by winning the 1991 World Solo Championship, Canadian Sylvie Fréchette was an early favourite to capture Synchronised Swimming gold at Barcelona 1992. Days before her departure, however, Fréchette's fiancé and manager Sylvain Lake committed suicide. Despite her personal tragedy, she decided to compete, but there she was engulfed in sporting controversy. After a flawless performance by Fréchette, Brazilian judge Ana Maria da Silveira pressed the wrong button when scoring and awarded her an 8.7 instead of a 9.7. The error cost Fréchette the gold medal, which instead went to Kristen Babb-Sprague of the US. An appeal finally saw the gold medal shared.

Costume controversy

The Spanish Synchronised Swimming team was caught up in a swimsuit controversy at Beijing 2008, when their specially designed costumes were banned from the competition. The Spaniards had planned to wear custom-made suits that were embedded with battery-powered sparkling lights, but Games officials deemed them an accessory and, as such, in breach of the rules of the event.

⬆ *Spain's Synchronised Swimming team performs its routine at Beijing 2008 without their battery-powered swimsuits that were deemed to contravene competition rules.*

Consistent Japan

Until the London 2012 Games, Japan was the only country to have won at least one medal in Synchronised Swimming at every single Olympic Games since the discipline was first introduced in 1984. However, despite the impressive record, the nation has never managed to win a Synchronised Swimming gold medal at the Games and has to be satisfied instead with a haul of four silver and eight bronze medals.

Russian dominance

Russia has won more gold medals than any other country in Synchronised Swimming, a record partly inspired by Anastasia Davydova. For a decade she has been one of the sport's best-known competitors and also the most successful – with four Olympic Games gold medals and ten World Championships titles. At the Games, Davydova's success was emulated by another Russian, Anastasia Ermakova, who sharedher haul of four gold medals. The golden duet came to an end after the 2008 Games, when Ermakova decided on a career break. In 2009, reaffirming herself as the greatest athlete in the sport, Davydova, with new partner Svetlana Romashina, went on to win the Duet technical event at the FINA World Championships in Rome and also shared gold in the Team free event.

London 2012

China on the rise

Bringing in Japanese-born coach Masayo Imura has proved a significant decision by the Chinese in their determination to bring their synchronized swimmers up to the medal-winning level of their other aquatic stars. Imura, nicknamed the 'Mother of Synchro' used butterfly themes to bring the best out of her team. Chinese progress contrasted starkly with the failure of Japan to win a Synchronised Swimming medal for the first time since the sport was introduced at the Olympic Games in 1984. Britain finished a creditable sixth in their first Teams final with a Peter Pan sequence which delighted the home crowd and offered hope of further improvement by the time the Rio 2016 Games come around.

Back to the gold

A dangerous prehistoric lost world of dinosaurs and giant insects provided the inspiration for the Russian Federation synchronised swimmers, who collected a fourth consecutive Olympic clean sweep at London 2012. Spain, who won silver at Beijing 2008, slipped behind the Chinese, who moved up the rankings to underline their ever-improving status within Synchronised Swimming and claim their best result yet. The Russians, who had won every Duets and Teams gold since Sydney 2000, scored 98.93 points out of a possible 100 for their 'free' routine, a sequence which is not prescribed and in which swimmers show off their creative and technical skills. This, added to their outstanding routine in the Teams technical round, added up to a total of 197.03 points. The team threw head coach Tatiana Pokrovskaya into the pool in celebration.

⬇ *Natalya Ishchenko (left) and Svetlana Romashina won gold in the women's Duets competition and as part of the Russian Federation women's Teams squad.*

Water Polo

Water Polo was the first team sport to be contested in the Olympic Games, making its debut in Paris in 1900. Having evolved into two different forms, in the United States and Europe, it began as an inherently violent sport – largely because of the more brutal version preferred in the US, where outright violence, injuries and near-drownings were part of the game. Today, however, matches are played to European rules.

Clean sweep

The records show that, at the 1904 Games in St Louis, the United States won all the available medals in the Water Polo competition – gold, silver and bronze. That was because other nations refused to compete in the more violent version of the sport that was commonplace in the States and to which the event was due to be staged. In due course the International Olympic Committee adopted the more strategic, faster and less violent European style, which featured at the following 1908 Games in London, and which is practised universally today.

Hungarian domination

The Hungarians have been by far the greatest ambassadors of Water Polo at the Olympic Games. They won medals at every single one of the Games between 1928 and 1980, and between 1932 and 1976 won six of the ten gold medals available. In 2000 in Sydney, Hungary resurfaced as a powerhouse in the discipline, winning the seventh gold medal in their history. The country continued its dominance at Athens 2004 and Beijing 2008, when they claimed gold at both Games.

➡ *The Hungary team celebrates victory at the 1936 Olympic Games in Berlin. It was the second of an unprecedented nine Water Polo gold medals for the country, the latest of which was won at Beijing in 2008.*

Women's long wait

Women had to wait a full century before they contested Water Polo at the Games. In 2000 in Sydney, a full 100 years after the debut of the discipline, women's Water Polo made its first official appearance at the Olympic Games, with the Australian team claiming gold before an ecstatic home crowd.

⬅ *Australia became the first team to win women's Water Polo gold when they beat the United States 4–3 in the Final at Sydney in 2000.*

Blood in the water

Few sporting encounters have been more politically charged than when Hungary met the Soviet Union in the semi-final of the Water Polo competition at Melbourne 1956 – often referred to as 'the blood in the water match'. When the Hungarian team set off for Australia, the Soviet army had begun the invasion that would topple their country's reformist leaders. The match started with verbal taunts and soon became extraordinarily violent. With Hungary leading 4–0, blood staining the pool and the crowd on the verge of rioting, the match was brought to an early end, with Hungary declared the winners. They went on to claim gold.

Hungarian masters

Hungary's impressive record at the Games is evidence that they boast some of the most celebrated Water Polo players of all time. Among them was Oliver Halassy, who represented Hungary in 1928 1932 and 1936, winning two gold medals and a silver. His athletic ability is made even more remarkable by the fact that he had his left leg amputated below the knee as a child, following a traffic accident. Another great Hungarian player was Dezs Gyarmati, often hailed as the greatest ever water polo player. His record of winning a medal at five different Games from 1948 to 1964 (three golds, one silver and one bronze) has never been matched.

↑ *Hungary's Ervin Zador suffers a gashed eye in the famous 1956 Final.*

London 2012

Water torture

Hungarian fans could hardly believe their men's team failed to come up with Water Polo gold, a sport the country has dominated down the years and on which it has relied for medal delight. This time, however, the Olympic champions of Sydney 2000, Athens 2004 and Beijing 2008 came fifth after defeats by Serbia, Montenegro and Italy. Croatia, instead, were crowned men's Olympic Water Polo champions for the first time after seeing off Italy, the only non-Balkan semi-finalists. Hungary also failed to win a medal in the women's event, losing the bronze medal match 13–11 to Australia.

Sharp-shooter Steffens

Twelve years of near misses came to an end when the United States won the women's Water Polo gold medal to provide a career-ending high for veterans Heather Petri and Brenda Villa. The two had won medals for the Americans each time since women's Water Polo made its Olympic Games debut at Athens 2000. The star of their ultimate 8–5 defeat of Spain was 19-year-old Maggie Steffens who scored five goals in the final to finish with a total of 21. Unbeaten Spain   making their Olympic Games debut – had tied the United States 9–9 in the preliminary round, but never recovered in the final after Steffens scored three goals in six minutes to give the USA a 5–2 half-time lead.

↑ *Croatia ended Hungary's domination of the men's Water Polo competition winning the gold medal for the first time with a defeat of Italy 8-6 in the final.*

Chapter Three
Athletics

History relates that the most successful competitor in the Ancient Olympic Games was a runner – Leonidas of Rhodes, who won 12 running titles (both sprint and endurance) between 164 and 152 BC – and that track and field Athletics was at the centre of the modern Olympic Games as conceived by Baron Pierre de Coubertin in 1892. The first modern Games, four years later in Athens, featured 43 events, many now defunct such as one-handed weightlifting. Greek shepherd Spiridon Louis ensured Athletics earned peak attention by winning the Marathon.

The Athletics events are, for many, the centrepiece of the Olympic Games. At the London 2012 Games, the men's 100m was the most requested ticket, with more than 1.5 million applications. There were 47 Athletics events at London 2012, 24 for men and 23 for women – only the 50km Race Walk was not contested by women. However, the sprint Hurdles for women was over 100m (110 for men) and the multi-discipline competition was Decathlon (10 events) for men and Heptathlon (seven) for women.

Only one man has won the three sprint events 100m, 200m and 4 x 100m Relay in two Games, Usain Bolt of Jamaica, at Beijing 2008 and London 2012. Carl Lewis won the men's Long Jump four times, joining fellow American Al Oerter, who won Discus Throw gold four times between 1956 and 1968. In the early 20th century Standing Jumper Ray Ewry (USA) won eight gold medals. The most successful and enduring women's athlete was sprinter Merlene Ottey of Jamaica and Slovakia (the latter as Merlene Ottey-Page), who competed in seven Games, from Rome 1960 to Los Angeles 1984, and won a total of eight medals, three silver and five bronze.

Great Britain's Jessica Ennis won the women's Heptathlon at the London 2012 Games. A stress foot injury in 2008 meant that she missed Beijing 2008 and had to learn to jump off her 'wrong' foot.

🏃 Men's 100m

The shortest outdoor sprint race, but often the most spectacular and always the most watched, the men's 100m is the Olympic Games' blue riband event with the winner awarded the moniker 'The Fastest Man on Earth'. The event has been staged at every Games since Athens in 1896.

How it all started

The first man to be credited with a 100m world record, albeit in the years before the IAAF, the sport's governing body, was formed in 1912, was Britain's William MacLaren. He was given a time of 11.00 seconds as part of a run over 110 yards at Haslingden, in Lancashire, on 27 July 1867. It was seven years short of a century before the 100m was run in 10 seconds – Armin Hary of West Germany did so in Zurich on 21 July 1960. American Jim Hines was the first man to go under, winning gold in 9.95 at Mexico City 1968.

The legend of Jesse Owens

Winning the men's 100m at Berlin 1936 was only a start for Jesse Owens, a sharecropper's son who defied the racist Nazi propaganda of the time, in which the Americans were taunted over their use of 'black auxiliaries'. The German spectators, by contrast, offered him warm support throughout the Games as he went on to add further golds in the 200m, the Long Jump and the 4 x 100m Relay – an achievement his fellow American Carl Lewis replicated at Los Angeles 1984. Owens had managed an even more astonishing athletic feat the year before, when he broke five world records and equalled a sixth in the space of 45 minutes while competing for his university in Michigan.

Americans miss the bus

At Munich 1972 the men's 100m title was won by Valeriy Borzov, of the Soviet Union, whose time of 10.14 seconds saw him finish a tenth of a second clear of the field. Borzov had arrived at Munich as favourite – but who knows how he might have fared had Stan Wright, the US sprint coach in Munich, had the right bus timetable? Wright set off from the Olympic Village with his country's two top sprinters, Eddie Hart and Rey Robinson, accompanied by the third US 100m man Robert Taylor, in what he thought was good time for their second round of races on the evening of 31 August. But Wright was working to an out-of-date timetable, and rather than starting at 7pm, as he thought, the second round got underway at 4.15pm. While they waited for their bus, to their horror, the group saw a live TV transmission of the first race. Despite being rushed to the stadium in a TV car, Hart and Robinson, both of whom had clocked 9.9 seconds in the US Olympic trials, arrived too late. Taylor just made his heat, however, and went on to take silver behind the Soviet star.

⬆ *The Soviet Union's Valeriy Borzov raises his arm in celebration as he wins the men's 100m final at the 1972 Games in Munich.*

Old gold...

The men's 100m final at Los Angeles 1932 was so close that if current rules had been applied the silver medallist, Ralph Metcalfe, would have won, rather than compatriot Eddie Tolan. Both recorded a Games record time of 10.3, but the verdict went to the first man to cross the line. Today Metcalfe would get the decision as the first man to reach the line.

Starting over...

Nowadays, any athlete who false-starts in the 100m faces instant disqualification, but the rules have varied. Before the International Association of Athletics Federations voted in 2009 to bring in the current rule, one false start was allowed in any race without sanction, with anyone subsequently offending being disqualified. Before that the rule was that each athlete was entitled to one false start, but would be disqualified in the event of a second, a fate Britain's defending champion Linford Christie suffered before the men's 100m final at Atlanta 1996. Different rules applied in the modern Games' early years. The men's 100m final at Stockholm 1912, won by Ralph Craig of the United States in a time of 10.8 seconds, was marred by seven false starts, the first three of which came from the eventual gold medallist. Thirty-six years later Craig, then 59, reappeared at the Games as a member of the US Sailing team, and carried the US flag at the Opening Ceremony in Wembley Stadium. He only needed one attempt at this.

Brilliant Bolt

Usain Bolt improved his 100m world record to 9.58 seconds at the 2009 World Championships in Berlin. Bolt held the two previous marks too, having become the first man to break 9.70, at the Beijing 2008 Games, in a time of 9.69, which came less than three months after he had clocked 9.72 in what was only his fifth serious race at the distance.

➤ *Usain Bolt celebrates with panache his decisive victory in the final of the men's 100m at the Beijing 2008 Games.*

Bailey's speed double

Canada's Donovan Bailey reached a speed of 27mph during a 10-metre stretch in winning the men's 100m title at Atlanta 1996 in a new world record of 9.84 seconds. Both those measures of speed were topped by Jamaica's Usain Bolt, who won the men's 100m and 200m titles at Beijing 2008 in world records of 9.69 and 19.30 respectively, before adding world titles the following year in times of 9.58 and 19.19. In the latter 100m race, Bolt was clocked at 27.45mph.

Super achiever

Robert Hayes, who won the men's 100m title at Tokyo 1964 went on to spend nine years playing American football for the Dallas Cowboys as a wide receiver and is the only athlete to have earned an Olympic gold medal and a Super Bowl victory ring.

London 2012

The ultimate lightning Bolt

When the result of the London 2012 Olympic 100 metres final is reviewed in the future it will be noted that Usain Bolt retained the title of 'fastest man in the world' in an Olympic record time of 9.63 seconds by a margin of two metres. Even then this might appear straightforward for the greatest sprinter of his time. But this story had a lot more to it than the plain facts suggest.

The build-up centred around chinks in the invincibility of Bolt. Following a false start in the 2011 World Championship final which caused his exclusion, he was beaten by training partner and world champion Yohan Blake in the Jamaican trials and Bolt himself admitted to go into London 2012 not being 100 per cent fit. Meanwhile, Blake was looking sensational and Athens 2004 Olympic champion Jason Gatlin and Tyson Gay, recovered from injury, were also hugely competitive.

Astonishing to say after the event but it appeared to be an open race. The atmosphere in the Olympic stadium was spine-tingling. At 50 metres it was still wide open, with Bolt, Blake and Gatlin line abreast but this was when the great man came into his own. No one in history has been quicker in the third quarter of the 100m. Bolt won with something to spare against some of the fastest men in history. In those few seconds, by his own assessment, he was transformed from icon into legend.

⬆ *Usain Bolt affirmed his place as the greatest ever sprinter at London 2012.*

Olympic Record

Event	Name	Country	Record	Date
100m	Usain Bolt	JAM	9.63	5 August

Men's 200m and 400m

The men's 200m, contested at every Games since 1900, starts on the curve and finishes on the home straight. It attracts several competitors from the men's 100m and the 100m-200m double has been achieved on nine occasions at the Games – most recently by Usain Bolt. The men's 400m is contested over a single lap of the track and has been staged at every Games since Athens 1896.

The pride of Paris

The United States' John Tewkesbury won the first-ever men's 200m title, at Paris 1900, in a time of 22.2 seconds. It was his fifth medal of the Games (after taking gold in the 400m Hurdles, silver in the 60m and 100m Sprints and bronze in the 200m Hurdles).

Reynolds too late

In 1988, Butch Reynolds was the hot favourite to win the men's 400m title in Seoul, having recently beaten the 20-year-old world record of 43.86 seconds run by his fellow American Lee Evans when he took gold at Mexico City in 1968. Reynolds had no altitude advantage as he recorded his mark of 43.29 in the Zurich meeting. But in the final in Seoul, he left himself with too much to do after lying fifth with 100 metres to go and just failing to catch the winner, team-mate Steve Lewis, at the line and had to be content with a silver medal.

⬇ *A clean sweep of medals in the men's 400m final at Seoul 1988 for the US. From left to right: Butch Reynolds, Steve Lewis and Danny Everett.*

Frozen in history

Unlike his 200m record, Michael Johnson's men's 400m world record of 43.18, set at the 1999 World Championships in Seville, did survive Beijing 2008 and the 2009 World Championships. His 1999 time bettered the mark of 43.29 set 11 years earlier by fellow American Butch Reynolds.

Black power protest

The men's 200m final at Mexico City 1968 produced a world record run by Tommie Smith, who clocked 19.83 in the thin air. But the event is remembered more for what happened at the Victory Ceremony. As the American national anthem played, Smith and his US team-mate John Carlos, the bronze medallist, bowed their heads and raised black-gloved hands in a Black Power salute as a protest against racial inequality in the United States. Australia's silver medallist Peter Norman joined in their protest, wearing a civil rights badge they had given him. Both Americans were subsequently shunned by the US athletics establishment. Thirty-four years later, at Sydney 2000, Norman was conspicuous by his absence among past Australian medallists at the Opening Ceremony.

⬆ *Brothers in arms: Tommie Smith (centre) and John Carlos (right) make their infamous salute at the 1968 Games in Mexico City.*

Quick Cuban heels

Alberto Juantorena Danger of Cuba, winner of the men's 800m title at Montreal 1976 Games in Montreal in a world record time of 1:43.50, went on to win the men's 400m final in a time of 44.26 seconds. In so doing he became the first man to win the 400m-800m double – apart from Paul Pilgrim at the 1906 'Intercalated' Games. Juantorena was nicknamed 'El Caballo' – The Horse.

Fact and fiction

American Jackson Scholz, who won men's 200m gold at Paris 1924, later wrote sports fiction and published 31 novels. Another piece of fiction brought him to public attention at the age of 84. In the 1981 Oscar-winning film *Chariots of Fire*, Scholz is seen handing a religious message to Britain's Eric Liddell, a committed Christian, before the start of the men's 400m final, which Liddell won. Scholz, however, later said that the incident had never happened.

London 2012

Share in history

If the 100 metres was a showdown, the 200 metres was a chance to grab history. Usain Bolt could become the first man ever to complete the 'double-double', win both sprints at consecutive Olympic Games. Compatriot Yohan Blake, who had beaten Bolt in the Jamaican trials, was thought be his biggest rival. Both men eased to semi-final victories, in Blake's case almost going down to walking pace at the finish. In the final, Bolt made one of the best starts of his career, taking a clear lead at 100 metres . Blake appeared to close the gap, but just as in the shorter sprint Bolt pulled clear of his friend to etch his name into sporting legend.

Jamaican treble

Jamaica is a small place, a Caribbean island home to just under three million people but also home to some very special people. The whole world knew about Usain Bolt, most were aware of Yohan Blake but, apart from track and field fanatics, Warren Weir was not a name familiar to many. The appearance of the slight 22-year-old in the 200 metres as the third string Jamaican was a revelation. He received words of encouragement from Bolt at the start before the great man blasted past him inside 60 metres. Yet Weir did not wilt, surging instead in the straight to claim bronze. Apparently, the next great Jamaican sprinter had been unveiled.

↑ *Usain Bolt held off the challenge of training partner Yohan Blake in the 200m final at the London 2012 Games to retain both of his sprint titles.*

James breakthrough

Grenada is not famous for many things. The small Caribbean island, 100km north of Venezuela, is an occasional venue for international cricket, but it is also home to the world's best 400 metres runner – Kirali James. A brilliant junior career earned him a college scholarship in America and James was crowned world No.1 in 2011. At London 2012, he became Olympic champion with a consummate performance. His time of 43.94 was the first time a non-American had dipped under 44 seconds in the 400m and it was Grenada's first ever Olympic medal of any hue. The other medallists were also from the Caribbean – Luguelin Santos (Dominican Republic) won silver and Lalone Gordon (Trinidad & Tobago) bronze. Remarkably, no American made the men's 400m final, an event they have dominated in the past.

Proud Pistorius

Oscar Pistorius did not have to do anything other than turn up to make Olympic history. When the South African set off in the first heat of the 400 metres on 4 August he became the first double leg amputee to compete on the grandest stage in sport. It had been a rocky journey with disputes over whether Pistorius, who was born without fibula bones in his lower legs, gained any advantage from wearing his prosthetic 'blades'. The 'blade runner' came second in his heat, but he ran out of steam in the semi-final finishing eighth in 46.54.

→ *Kirali James celebrates his victory in the men's 400m, Grenada's first-ever medallist.*

Men's 110m and 400m Hurdles

The men's 110m Hurdles is staged over ten 1.067-metre-high hurdles and has been contested at every Games since 1896. The men's 400m Hurdles is staged over one lap of the track (over ten evenly spaced 0.914m-high hurdles) and has been contested since 1900.

Men's 110m Hurdles records tumble

The first official record holder in the sprint hurdles was Britain's Philip Norman, who was timed over the 120 yards (109.73 metres) hurdles at 18.00 seconds. The first IAAF world record holder was Forrest Smithson of the United States, who won gold at the 1908 Games in London in 15.00. In 1936, another American Forrest – Berlin gold-medallist Forrest Towns – became the first man to break the 14-second barrier, winning at Oslo in 13.7. Another American broke the 13-second barrier: Ronaldo Nehemiah, 12.93 at Zurich in 1981.

A drop of bad luck

As Boyd Gittens set off in the men's 400m Hurdles semi-final at the 1968 US Olympic trials, a pigeon dropping hit him in the eye and dislodged his contact lens before he reached the first hurdle. Happily he was able to take part in a run-off, where he secured his place in the United States squad for Mexico City. Sadly, a leg injury forced him to withdraw from his first-round heat.

Moses leaves world in the wilderness

In securing gold at Los Angeles 1984, Ed Moses extended an astonishing winning streak over 400m Hurdles. Having lost to Harald Schmid on 26 August 1977, the American got his own back a week later by beating the West German by a 15-yard margin and from then on he remained unbeaten all the way through the 1984 Games and until 4 June 1987, when his long reign was ended by fellow countryman Danny Harris.

← The highlight of Ed Moses' domination of the men's 400m Hurdles came with a gold medal at Los Angeles 1984.

That's what friends are for

Colin Jackson, the men's 110m Hurdles silver medallist at Seoul 1988, was favoured to go one better at Barcelona 1992, and he did finish the Games with a personal best time to his credit. Unfortunately for Jackson, his time of 13.10 seconds came in the opening round, and the gold went to Mark McKoy of Canada in 13.12 as Jackson, who had suffered a minor injury during the semi-final, faded to seventh in 13.46. Welshman Jackson's consolation after a stellar career was to have been crowned world champion twice, Commonwealth champion twice and European champion four times. The year before Barcelona 1992, Jackson had invited McKoy and his family to move in and they both trained under the guidance of Malcolm Arnold – who had guided John Akii-Bua to men's 400m Hurdles gold at Munich 1972. The year after the Games in Barcelona, McKoy beat Jackson to the world indoor title on home territory in Toronto after benefiting from a flying start. The two remain friends.

↑ Canada's Mark McKoy storms into the lead in the men's 110m Hurdles final at the 1992 Games in Barcelona. He held on to his lead to take gold.

Curtis and the calculated gamble

US athlete Thomas Curtis won the inaugural men's 110m Hurdles final at Athens 1896. Despite having qualified for the men's 100m final, Curtis chose not to contest it in order to concentrate on the sprint hurdles. His decision paid off.

Taking athletics to bed

Earl Thomson, the Canadian who won the men's 110m Hurdles title at Antwerp 1920 in a world record time of 14.8 seconds, took his sport very seriously. He used to tie his legs to the end of the bed so he wouldn't curl up and risk cramping.

Third referred

The first Games final result to be amended following a video replay was in 1932. American 110m hurdler Jack Keller was awarded the bronze medal after finishing in 14.8 seconds. But after viewing the race, judges revised the result and gave third place to Britain's Donald Finlay, also timed at 14.8. Keller sought out Finlay in the Olympic Village and passed the medal on.

London 2012

Favourite finishes first

The list of 'world leading' times and distances in each Athletics event issued before a major Games is the form guide. Thankfully, recent history does not always prove a reliable harbinger of Olympic fact. Favourites do not always win ... but the 110m Hurdles final was definitely an example of an instance when they did. It was written in the stars that American Aries Merritt would win and many thought the world record could be challenged by the only consistent sub-13 second hurdler this year. A slight headwind militated against that but 12.92 was far too good for everyone else, even world champion Jason Richardson. Merritt finished just 0.01 seconds behind Liu Xiang's Olympic record. Students of form had their champion.

⬆ *Felix Sanchez (left) turned back the clock in the men's 400m Hurdles final.*

Felix kept on running

The old cliche that yesterday's heroes should never come back was disproved, at least, in the 400m Hurdles. Felix Sanchez ruled this event in the early part of the 21st century. The man from the Dominican Republic won 43 straight races between 2001 and 2004, including the Olympic final in 2004. The shining light then faded somewhat as all the titles earned during that invincible period were lost. The London 2012 Olympic title, at the age of 34, seemed an impossible dream. His form was indifferent and others were way ahead of them on the ranking list. He progressed through the rounds then looked good in the semi-final. Even better, in the final Sanchez powered down the home straight to finish in exactly the same time he recorded at Athens 2004.

⬆ *Aries Merritt (red top with white side) was a favourite who delivered.*

More Achilles problems

China's Xiang Liu is an icon in the most populous country in the world. With that comes pressure to perform. He was catapulted to fame by winning the 110m Hurdles title at Athens 2004 and subsequent world titles and a world record enshrined his status. It all went wrong at Beijing 2008 when the anxiety to deliver a gold medal in a home Games made him rush recovery from an Achilles injury and he pulled out on the start line. At the London 2012 Games, there was a near shocking repeat. Liu again lined up for his heat with heavy strapping on his right Achilles. He sprang out of the blocks but ruptured the tendon as he tried to clear the first hurdle and fell.

Flying the flag

Javier Culson, like Felix Sanchez, was from a small Caribbean nation with little Olympic history. Puerto Rico had only ever won Olympic medals in boxing when Culson arrived in London but the whole island believed that Culson could bring home not just a first Athletics medal but gold itself. A World Championships silver medallist in both 2009 and 2011, he was the leading 400-metre hurdler in 2012. Culson, who was honoured with carrying Puerto Rico's flag at the Opening Ceremony, progressed through the heats and semi-final without difficulty and lined up as the favourite for the final. Coming home, it was between Culson and the Athens 2004 and Beijing 2008 Olympic champions, Sanchez and Angelo Taylor, respectively. Sanchez surged, Taylor faded, and Culson had to settle for bronze, behind the fast-finishing American Mike Tinsley. No gold, but Culson had not let his country down.

Men's 800m and 1500m

The men's 800m is the shortest middle-distance track event (run over two laps) and requires both speed and endurance. The men's 1500m is considered the premier middle-distance race and has produced some legendary champions at the Games. Both events have been contested at every Games since Athens 1896.

Maximum returns

London accountants Price Waterhouse granted their 22-year-old Australian employee Edwin Flack a month's holiday in 1896 so that he could compete in the first modern Olympic Games. He made the most of it, winning gold in the 1500m and, two days later, in the 800m – on the morning of which he had played in the Tennis tournament. He also took part in the Marathon.

Perfect champion

Heading into the 1960 Games, Herb Elliott had won 44 consecutive races at either 1500m or one mile, but despite opening up a 15-metre lead with a lap remaining in the men's 1500m final he did not allow himself to relax until he crossed the line in a world record time of 3:35.6. Time after time Elliott had practised for his biggest race by imagining an opponent on his shoulder who would be able to sense any weakness in him. 'I had practised a million times being challenged and winning that challenge,' said the Australian, who retired after his victory, unbeaten, and only 22.

⬇ *The 1960 men's 1500m medallists (from left to right): Michel Jazy (silver), Herb Elliott (gold) and Itsvan Rozsavolgi (bronze).*

British athletes Coe and Ovett get it wrong – and right

Even though the United States boycotted Moscow 1980, most observers were happy that the world's best two men's 800m and 1500m runners were present – the British pair of Sebastian Coe and Steve Ovett. Coe was widely expected to win the 800m (at which he held the world record), and Ovett the metric mile (in which he equalled Coe's world record of 3:32.1 on the eve of the Games and remained unbeaten in 42 races). Each left Moscow with a gold medal – but the 'wrong' gold. First Ovett took the 800m title with a characteristically bold flourish as Coe misjudged his tactics. But tactics favoured Coe in the longer final as East Germany's Jurgen Straub made a long run for home over the final 800 metres. Both Britons responded, but it was Coe who crossed the line in an agony of ecstasy. The ecstasy of redemption.

⬆ *The British trio of (from left to right) Steve Ovett, Steve Cram and Sebastian Coe hit the front during the men's 1500m final at Moscow 1980.*

Third time lucky

Algeria's Noureddine Morceli dominated 1500m and mile events between 1991 and 1996, but suffered the agony of finishing seventh at Barcelona 1992 in a slow, tactical race won by home favourite Fermin Cacho. Four years later, at Atlanta 1996, Morceli took men's 1500m gold, but only after the next rising star in the event, Morocco's Hicham El Guerrouj, had fallen. By the time of Sydney 2000, El Guerrouj dominated his distance as Morceli had done, but the Moroccan finished stunned and tearful after he was beaten to the line by Kenya's Noah Ngeny. Four years later in Athens, it all came right for El Guerrouj just as it had done for Morceli. He completed the men's 1500m-5000m double.

Not meant to be

At the 1968 Mexico City Games, men's 1500m world record holder American Jim Ryun finished second behind Kenya's Kip Keino. Four years later in Munich, Ryun – still world record holder – was expected to win gold, but he tripped and fell in his qualifying heat.

London 2012

Rudisha on fire

Kenyan 800m runner David Rudisha was one of the hottest favourites for Athletics gold in the Olympic Stadium. Even the legendary Usain Bolt had not been seen as such a certainty. Non track and field fans may have looked aghast at that statement but the fact is, for the past two years, the elegant Kenyan had utterly dominated the men's 800m. The London 2012 Games were witness to one of the greatest runs in Athletics history – the first time anyone had gone under 1.41. Rudisha set off from the gun like a man on a mission. He went through the bell in 48 seconds – an impossibly fast pace for the first 400m – but Rudisha was on his way to greatness and he breasted the tape in an incredible 1:40.91.

Teenage tearaway

The Olympic Games makes names. Previously unknown athletes leap to global attention in their respective sports. Botswana's 18-year-old Nigel Amos was recognised by those in the know – a time of 1:43.11 earlier in 2012 had been a national record. Amos was crowned World Junior 800m champion, his reputation embellished, but this time he was going in the big boys and the supreme talent of David Rudisha in particular. Amid the attention trained on Rudisha, Amos quietly qualified. In the final he set off in pursuit of Rudisha and appeared to actually be finishing quicker than the great man. His time of 1:41.73 equalled Sebastian Coe's old world record which had stood for 16 years and was the equal third fastest time ever. And he was only 18.

⬇ *Taoufik Makhloufi recovered from injury to win the men's 1500m title.*

⬆ *David Rudisha's world record triumph in the 800m was one of the iconic moments of the London 2012.*

Second time lucky

Taoufik Makhloufi created many column inches at London 2012 but not only as a gold-medal winner in the 1500m following in the rich tradition of North African middle distance performers. No Olympic Games proceeds without generating plenty of talking points and when Makhloufi powered down the home straight towards glory in the 'metric mile' his strength and focus created a sensation. He ran the final metres majestically clear of the field. Yet, only the previous day, injury had prevented him completing his 800m heat. Makhloufi had jogged the opening 150m of that race before pulling up and he was disqualified from the event for not trying hard enough. Later, on appeal, he was reinstated after a doctor's assessment supported the claim that he had not been 100 per cent fit.

Kiwi trapped on the bend

New Zealand's Nick Willis finished third in the Beijing 2008 Games 1500m final, but was elevated to silver medal position when race-winner Rashid Ramzi was disqualified for failing a drugs control test. A confident semi-final run raised Kiwi hopes that London 2012 could see Willis follow in John Walker's footsteps and rise to the gold standard. However, Willis got his tactics all wrong in the final. Boxed on the inside, he was unable to cover the break when Taoufik Makhloufi surged on the final lap and gave himself too much to do. Willis, who finished only in ninth place, probably wouldn't have caught the Algerian, but a clear run could have earned him another medal. Sadly, Willis may not have another gold-medal chance as he will be 33 by the time the Rio 2016 Games begin.

World Record				
Event	Name	Country	Record	Date
800m	David Rudisha	KEN	1:40.91	9 August

Men's 5000m and 10,000m

The track's longest distance races, the 5000m and 10,000m, challenge an athlete's speed and endurance. The two events were introduced at the 1912 Games in Stockholm and many athletes have competed in both over the years with the double achieved on eight occasions, most recently by Britain's Mo Farah at London 2012.

World records

Between the wars the men's 5000m world record was dominated by Finns, but the first great leaps were taken in the mid-1950s – the mark being reduced by 22 seconds in just three years. In 1987 Said Aouita ran the first sub-13-minute race. Vladimir Kuts, Ron Clarke and Haile Gebrselassie have each broken the record four times. The men's 10,000m has seen a more steady erosion of its record, although the current mark is over five minutes faster than the original standard set in 1912. The first landmark barrier, 30 minutes, was broken by Finn Taisto Maki in 1938, but the achievement of Emil Zatopek is unsurpassed. He lowered the record by more than 40 seconds over the course of five epic runs. No one has broken the men's 10,000m record on more occasions.

Nurmi the 'Flying Finn'

Finland produced a string of world-beating long-distance runners in the first half of the 20th century, but the greatest of them all was Paavo Nurmi. This phenomenon from the Baltic port of Turku won a record nine gold medals across five distances at three Games in the 1920s (1920, 1924 and 1928) and set 35 world records from 1500m to 20km. No wonder his fellow countrymen decided to set up a statue in his honour outside the Olympic Stadium in Helsinki. The only thing he did not achieve was the 5000m- 10,000m double at the same Olympic Games.

↑ *Finland's Paavo Nurmi crosses the finishing line to take gold in the men's 5000m final at the 1924 Games in Paris.*

Lasse brings it home

The enigmatic Finn Lasse Viren is the only man to retain the men's 5000m title at the Games and to achieve back-to-back 5000m-10,000m doubles (at the 1972 and 1976 Games). Even so, he is not as revered as other multiple gold medallists. A failure to produce performances of his medal-winning standard outside the Games, and a relative paucity of races internationally, created rumours and suspicion of his training techniques – although nothing was ever proven. What cannot be doubted, though, is his determination, as evidenced by his feat at Munich 1972, when he fell in the 10,000m final, losing 30 metres in the process, but recovered to win the race. Viren also finished fifth in the 1976 men's Marathon.

← *Finland's Lasse Viren is the only man in history to have completed the 5000m-10,000m double at two Games (at Munich 1972 and Montreal 1976).*

Heroes from the horn of Africa

Ethiopians have won six of the eight gold medals awarded for these classic long-distance track races since 1996. It took a while for the successors to Miruts Yifter to come through, but in Haile Gebrselassie and Kenenisa Bekele the East African state has produced two of the all-time greats. Gebrselassie burst on to the scene in the 1990s and progressed to become the pre-eminent marathon runner. Bekele took over his crown as king of the men's 10,000m in 2004 and four years later laid claim to being the best ever at half the distance. Bekele is also arguably the finest cross-country performer the world has ever seen.

Better late than never for Kuts

For a man who stumbled into the sport of athletics, Vladimir Kuts certainly made up for lost time. The Ukrainian, who ran under the Soviet banner in the 1950s, ran his first race at the age of 21. Just five years later he was the 5000m and 10,000m Soviet champion and within another 12 months he had broken the legendary Emil Zatopek's 5000m world record. Sporting immortality for the relentless Kuts was ensured at Melbourne 1956, when he became just the third man (after Zatopek and Hannes Kolehmainen) to claim the 5000m-10,000m double at a single Games.

London 2012

Go Mo! And he did...

The distance races on the track at the Olympic Games had been annexed by Africa for 20 years when 29 men lined up for the 10,000 metres final on the middle Saturday of the London 2012 Games. Now, for the first time, there was a credible challenger from elsewhere, albeit with roots in Somalia – Mo Farah. Farah, who, with his family, had moved to Britain at the age of eight, had won silver in the 2011 World Championships and then rubber-stamped his credentials with gold in the 5000m. With 500 metres to go, Farah made his move with four pursuers in tow. Union flags waved around the stadium and a deafening roar erupted from the 80,000 crowd as he surged clear. Farah was chased by the United States' Galen Rupp, but would not be denied as he won with a final lap of 53.48 seconds.

⬆ Mo Farah leads his American training partner Galen Rupp across the line at the end of the men's 10,000m at the London 2012 Games.

Out of time

Kenenisa Bekele is the latest in a long line of Ethiopian distance running legends, dating back to Abebe Bikila at Rome 1960. Bekele had won silver in the 5000m and gold in 10,000m at the Athens 2004 Games and went one better in Beijing 2008, completing the double. In 2009 he won a fourth straight 10,000m world title. For most that would be enough but Bekele wanted more. He battled back from injury to make the start line at the 2011 World Championships but had to retire after 10 laps. Perhaps it was that failure in Daegu that drove him: unfinished business. And, at the London 2012 Games, was in the shake-up with 200 metres to go in the 10,000m, but the old legs were just not up to Mo Farah's last-lap burst and Bekele eventually finished fourth. A great run for most, but failure for such a great champion.

Ethiopian legacy

To run for Ethiopia in distance events at the Olympic Games carries a heavy responsibility. No country concentrates its resources more not just on one sport but two specific disciplines within a sport as Dejen Gebrmeskel's homeland. Even the 22-year-old's name evokes memories of the legendary Haile Gebrselassie. Gebrmeskel, from the rural wilderness of Tigray, was Ethiopia's big hope in the men's 5000m. His country had won at least one men's distance event at each of the previous four Olympic Games, so there was extraordinary pressure on the frail-looking Gebrmeskel. It took an inspired Mo Farah to deny him after a run which, Farah aside, would have been feted as a perfectly executed race.

Then there were seven

Only six men had achieved the fabled 5000m/10,000m double in Olympic Games history, and none had been British. Mo Farah stood on the start line of the 5,000m with the chance to join the legends in that exclusive club: Hannes Kolehmainen, Emil Zatopek, Vladimir Kuts, Lasse Viren (twice), Miruts Yifter and Kenenisa Bekele. The race proceeded in a predictably cagey fashion, the pace not a factor until the closing laps. Farah moved to the front with two laps remaining and adopted the same policy as he had in the longer race a week earlier, gradually winding the pace up. One contender after another tried to pass Farah along the back straight and rounding the final bend, but the 10,000m gold-medallist would not give way. With 50 metres to go, Ethiopia's Dejen Gebrmeskel loomed up, but the driven Farah would not be caught, to delight of the vast British crowd.

➜ Farah acknowledges the crowd after his stunning run to win the men's 5000m.

🏃 Men's Decathlon and Steeplechase

The men's 3000m Steeplechase is an obstacle race run over seven-and-a-half laps, with each circuit involving four 0.914-metre-high hurdles and a water jump. It has been contested at every Games since 1920. The Decathlon consists of ten track-and-field events and (with the exception of London 1908) has been part of the Olympic programme since 1904.

Daley sees off teutonic titans to win gold

Arguably the most competitive Decathlon in history took place at Los Angeles 1984. It was billed as 'Daley versus the Germans', and with good cause as defending champion Daley Thompson was given a stern test by Jurgen Hingsen (the man who had taken the world record off him), Guido Kratschmer (another previous record holder), and Siggy Wentz. World-class performances from Thompson in the opening two events (the 100m and the long jump) laid down a marker, and Hingsen was unable to catch him; Wentz came third; and Kratschmer fourth. Thompson's tally of 8,798 points was recalculated as a world record a year later.

Brasher backed by rivals

London Marathon founder Chris Brasher claimed the spoils in the men's 3000m Steeplechase at Melbourne 1956 thanks to backing from his rivals after he was initially disqualified. The Briton had eased his way through on the inside on the final lap, nudging Norwegian Ernst Larsen in the process. The judges took a dim view, but Larsen and others protested that Brasher would have won anyway and he was reinstated as the race winner.

⬆ *Great Britain's Chris Brasher (226) leads the way in the men's 3000m Steeplechase final at the 1956 Games in Melbourne.*

Kenyans at a canter

Since 1968 the dominant force in the men's 3000m Steeplechase has been the East African state of Kenya. Other than the boycott years of 1976 and 1980, a Kenyan has won the title at every Olympic Games since Mexico City, often closely pursued by his team-mates. It was 1968 champion Amos Biwott who first showed the world at large the now-familiar leaping style of clearing the barriers, rather than the accepted one foot on, step off technique.

⬅ *Amos Biwott's victory in the men's 3000m Steeplechase at Mexico City 1968 sparked a run of ten gold medals (out of 12) for Kenya in the event, a run which continued in 2012.*

Steeplechase barriers broken

A world record for the men's 3,000m Steeplechase was not officially recognised by the athletics authorities until the mid-1950s, owing to inaccuracies with course distances and obstacles. Notable barriers broken through were 8:30, by Belgian legend Gaston Roelants in 1963, and 8:00 (the men's 3000m Steeplechase equivalent of the four-minute mile), by Kenya's Moses Kiptanui 32 years later.

Young master Mathias

Bob Mathias is the youngest ever Athletics gold medallist. At London 1948 he claimed Decathlon gold at the age of 17, and four years later in Helsinki he followed this up with another first by retaining the title.

A Cold War hero

Horace Ashenfelter, the men's 3000m Steeplechase champion at Helsinki 1952, not only won a gold medal on the track but was viewed as a propaganda weapon by the Americans. In the early years of the Cold War, the sight of Ashenfelter (who was an FBI agent at the time) chasing down Soviet star Vladimir Kazantsev was like gold dust for the PR men.

London 2012

Leaders of the pack

When it comes to one of the most physically demanding events in Athletics, the steeplechase, it has been a quadrennial procession for Kenya at the Olympic Games. On this occasion the man anointed to be the leader of the pack was Ezekiel Kemboi, the 2004 Olympic champion and winner of the past two World Championships. With a lap to go Kemboi was joined by Kenyan team-mate Abel Mutai in the lead but Mutai was unable to live with the nagging pace and Kemboi pulled clear on what was to be his glorious victory lap to regain the title he had ceded in 2008. Kenya had won the Steeplechase for the eighth straight Olympic Games.

↑ Ezekiel Kemboi rolled back the years to win a second gold medal in 2012.

Ever the silver

In 2008 Frenchman Mahiedine Mekhissi-Benabbad became only the third non-Kenyan to stand on the podium after the men's 3000m Steeplechase in six Olympic Games, claiming a valiant silver at Beijing 2008. The build-up to his London 2012 Games battle with the East Africans included retaining his European title at Helsinki and he carried that good form into the Olympic Stadium. The mark of a great competitor is to gain strength from adversity even self-inflicted ones. Mekhissi-Benabbad dug in on the final lap, chasing down Abel Mutai and earning another Olympic silvers; in this event that almost equals gold.

→ Ashton Eaton was unable to break the world record he set at the US Trials, but he did lead an American one-two in the Decathlon at London 2012.

Eaton all the way

Ashton Eaton arrived in London as the new Decathlon world record holder for the ultimate test of the all-round athlete. The man from Oregon had set the new mark of 9,039 points in winning the US Trials in front of a home state crowd in Eugene. The triumph was a huge psychological victory over the man who had defeated him in the 2011 World Championship in Daegu, Trey Hardee. The London 2012 Olympic Games gold medal would surely be a battle between the two Americans who had taken up the mantle of Jim Thorpe, Bruce Jenner and Dan O'Brien in this classic event. Eaton dominated from the off. His 10.35 seconds in the 100m was the fastest time ever recorded by a decathlete in that discipline. He came top in the long jump with a 8.03m leap, achieved a solid 14.66m in the shot put, tied second in the high jump with 2.05m and finished day one with the top time in the 400m of 46.90 – a full second faster than anybody else. Day two began with 13.56, but a narrow defeat by Hardee, in the 110m hurdles. A 42.53m throw in the discus further reduced his lead, but it was restored with the third-best pole vault of 5.20m. Eaton finished with a personal best throw of 61.96m in the javelin and a 150-point lead over Hardee. A time of 4.33.59 in the 1500m was almost a victory parade for Eaton, who ended on 8,869 points – 198 clear of his team-mate.

Men's 4 x 100m and 4 x 400m Relays

Relays are the climax of the Athletics programme at the Games. The aim is for a team of four athletes to carry a baton over a distance of either 400 metres (4 x 100m) or 1600m (4 x 400m), with the baton passed between competitors at the end of each 100m or 400m stint. Both events have been contested since Stockholm 1912.

Best for the test

Relay running is a team game, but talented individuals are required to make up a quartet good enough to claim gold. In 1924, Great Britain's men's 4 x 400m team was denied the services of the men's 400m champion, Eric Liddell, a religious man, because the final fell on a Sunday. Britain came third. In 1936, the United States curiously chose to leave out both the men's 400m gold and bronze medallists, Archie Williams and Jimmy LuValle, and were beaten by Great Britain. In 1948, Jamaica were favoured to win with newly crowned men's 400m champion Arthur Wint in their ranks. On the third leg Wint set out in pursuit of the Americans, but pulled a muscle and Jamaican hopes were dashed.

Americans forced to wait

Wembley Stadium in 1948 was the scene of the most long-winded Victory Ceremony in history, and probably the first instance of a decision aided by video. The USA men's 4 x 100m team won their event, but were initially disqualified for a faulty exchange. On reviewing film of the race, officials decide to reverse the disqualification. However, the final decision did not become official for three days.

⬆ *Avery Brundage (centre), President of the US Olympic Committee, talks to the disqualified US quartet at the 1948 Games. They were later awarded the gold medal.*

Gone in a Hayes...

At the 1964 Olympic Games in Tokyo anchor runner Bob Hayes ran arguably the fastest men's 4 x 100m Relay leg ever seen to come from fifth place to claim gold for the United States in a world record-breaking time of 39.0 seconds. Hayes' time is estimated between 8.5 and 8.9.

World records

The Usain Bolt-inspired Jamaica team in 2008 are just the second squad from outside the United States to hold the men's 4 x 100m Relay world record since 1968. Nesta Carter, Michael Frater, Bolt and Asafa Powell scorched around the Beijing track in 37.10 seconds to break the long-standing mark of 37.40 set by the USA's Olympic Games- and World Championship-winning quartets in 1992 and 1993. There have been a few twists and turns of the world record for the men's 4 x 400m Relay, but the one constant since 1960 is that a United States team has held it. In fact, a team from Jamaica in 1952 are the only non-USA side ever to hold the mark. It took 24 years for the altitude-enhanced first sub-three-minute time in the men's 4 x 400m, 2:56.16, set in Mexico City in 1968, to be bettered.

Blazing batons in Paris

The men's 4 x 100m Relay competition at the 1924 Games in Paris was about far more than just the final. This meet was the biggest step forward for the discipline. A bewildering set of races saw the old world record shattered four times inside two days. Harold Abrahams inspired Great Britain to clock 42 seconds dead in the first heat, and this was equalled by the Netherlands in the third. In the sixth race USA improved their old best time by a whole second – an astonishing margin for this event – and in the semis the Americans took it down to 41.0. Spare a thought for the Swiss team... They equalled the old record in each of their first two races, but were disqualified in the final.

⬆ *Harold Abrahams (number 419, winning gold in the 100m individual event) was part of Britain's silver medal-winning quartet in the 4 x 100m Relay at Paris 1924.*

London 2012

Bolt's double treble

The men's sprint relay was selected as the event to bring the track and field activity at the London 2012 Olympic Games to a close. It was an inspired choice, bringing a sensational meet to a rousing finish. Usain Bolt was aiming to bring the Jamaican baton home first to seal a so-called 'double-treble', having won the 100m, 200m and 4 x 100m Relay at Beijing 2008, and he stood on the brink of replicating that feat in London. But it was not a foregone conclusion, because the United States fielded a superb quartet, including former Olympic 100m champion Justin Gatlin and Tyson Gay, the second fastest man in history. Bolt received the baton with a fractional advantage over Gatlin, less than 10 seconds later it was metres rather than fractions as he flew across the line, stopping the clock in a remarkable world record of 36.84.

Double trouble

The 4 x 100m Relay is not about only speed but accuracy and discipline at the three baton changeovers. Most teams have their odd disasters; the implement falls to the track, is handed on too late or runners veer outside their lanes. In recent years, though, there has been one team who have been serial offenders – Great Britain. For the third major championship in a row, Great Britain were disqualified. This time the fault lay with a novice. The anchor leg runner, world junior champion Adam Gemili, went off too early and by the time team-mate Daniel Talbot had caught up with him, Gemili had crossed the yellow boundary and then stepped outside his lane; double trouble and a real chance of another British medal was over.

⬇ The men's 4 x 400m Relay had surprise gold medallists in the Bahamas.

⬆ Usain Bolt finishes off Jamaica's world record run in the 4 x 100m Relay.

Superpower no longer

At each Olympic Games it has almost become a given that the United States would win the men's 4 x 400m Relay. The United States have won the event 16 times, and often by wide margins. This time, though, chinks developed in their armour. Their number one, LaShawn Merritt, pulled up injured in his heat of the individual 400m, reserves Jeremy Wariner (a former world and Olympic champion) and Manteo Mitchell were also unavailable. That 28-year unbeaten run was in danger. The Americans have legendary strength in depth at the quarter mile but there was no Michael Johnson or Butch Reynolds to bring them home this time. Angelo Taylor led at the start of the final leg, but he faded badly in the last 100 metres and the United States had to settle for silver behind Bahamas.

Breeze for Bahamas

The beneficiaries of the weakness of the United States in the 4 x 400m Relay were Bahamas, who joyfully celebrated a first-ever male Athletics gold medal. Chris Brown put them in the lead on the first leg and Demetrius Pinder consolidated the advantage on the second leg. When Tony McQuay of the United States passed Michael Mathieu on the penultimate circuit it appeared that normal service would be resumed. Ramon Miller had to make up a three-metre deficit and overtake the experienced Angelo Taylor. Miller expertly paced his effort, drafting Taylor round the final turn and having enough in the tank to take the Bahamians to gold in a national record time of 2:56.72.

World Record

Event	Name	Country	Record	Date
Men's 4 x 100m Relay	Jamaica	JAM	36.84	11 August

🏃 Men's Race Walks

Men's Race Walks are road races that are staged over two distances: 20km (since 1956) and 50km (since 1932). Contestants are obliged to keep in contact with the ground at all times and must also keep their supporting leg straight until the body has passed directly over it. Failure to do so results in disqualification.

Walking 'sprint' finish classic

Soviet Union walker Vladimir Golubnichy regained the men's 20km Race Walk title in 1968 after the most dramatic finish in race-walking history at the Games. Golubnichy held off José Pedraza, who was roared on by 80,000 of his compatriots in the stadium in Mexico City, by a mere handful of metres after over 90 minutes of walking, with the Soviet Union's Nikolay Smaga only three seconds behind.

Korzeniowski the walking legend

Robert Korzeniowski has to be regarded as the greatest race walker of all time. He recovered from the bitter disappointment of being disqualified, when battling for the silver medal, close to the finish of the men's 50km Race Walk in his first Olympic Games at Barcelona in 1992 to become the only man to win both the men's 20km and 50km titles when he achieved the double at the 2000 Games in Sydney. After successfully defending the gold medal in the 50km Race Walk at Atlanta in 1996, the Pole claimed an unprecedented fourth Race Walk gold medal when he claimed his third consecutive men's 50km Race Walk gold at the 2004 Games in Athens.

↖ *Poland's Robert Korzeniowski reigned supreme in the men's 50km Race Walk, winning three successive gold medals between Atlanta 1996 and Athens 2004.*

Demise of the 'Hitler Oak'

Harold Whitlock, the men's 50km Race Walk champion at Berlin 1936, returned to Britain after the Games and ensured his name would not be forgotten by planting a tree at his old school in London. Whitlock, along with the other gold medallists, had been presented by Adolf Hitler with an oak sapling about 50 centimetres in height. The tree stood at Hendon School for 70 years and was nicknamed the 'Hitler Oak'. However, in 2007, by then 16 metres tall, it was chopped down after contracting a fungal disease.

↑ *Britain's Harold Whitlock took men's 50km Race Walk gold in 1936.*

The hero no one wanted

At Melbourne 1956 Norman Read won men's 50km Race Walk gold for New Zealand, having fought a battle to be recognised by the 'land of the long white cloud'. Born in Portsmouth, Read emigrated to New Zealand in 1954, but still tried to compete in a British vest at the 1956 Games. The AAA rejected his request, and so did their New Zealand counterparts – until he won the Australian Championship over the Olympic Games course in Melbourne, after which he was hurriedly accepted by the Kiwis.

Soviet walkers on top of the world

The first man to break through the one-and-a-half-hour barrier for the men's 20km Race Walk was the Soviet Union's Vladimir Guk in 1957. There has been a steady eroding of the mark since, with Sergey Morozov wiping 33 seconds off the previous record in June 2008 to take it below 1:17. Gennady Agapov was responsible for the greatest landmark performance in walking when the Soviet smashed the world record for the 50km Race Walk by over five minutes in 1965 to become the first man to go under four hours for the endurance test. Denis Nizhegorodov regained the record for Russia in 2008 at the expense of Australian Nathan Deakes.

Steam room Don sweats to victory

Don Thompson claimed Britain's only Athletics gold medal at the Rome 1960 Games in the 50km Race Walk after going to extreme lengths to prepare himself for the fierce Roman summer. The diminutive insurance clerk, who was dubbed 'Il Topolino' (The Mouse) by the Italians, trained in temperatures of up to 38° Celsius in the bathroom of his home by using a heater, kettles of boiled water and even a stove to turn it into a steam room.

← *Detailed preparation paid dividends for Great Britain's Don Thompson at the 1960 Games in Rome. He took 50km Race Walk gold in a new Games record time of 4:25.30.*

London 2012

First 'first' for China

China had never won a medal in the men's Race Walk, either 20km or 50km, prior to London 2012. In the 20km event, on a glamorous circuit, encompassing The Mall and Buckingham Palace, they won gold and bronze. At halfway, 12 walkers broke away, including the three Chinese, and disqualification of two of the other nine strengthened their hand. Ding Chen made his move on the penultimate lap and went to win in an Olympic record time of 1:18.46. Zhen Wang finished third, the Chinese split by Guatemala's first Olympic medallist, Erick Barrondo. Zelin Cai, China's third walker, finished fourth.

Record Russian

The men's 50km Race Walk was overshadowed by the exclusion of defending Olympic champion Alex Schwazer after the Italian failed a drugs control test. In his absence, at the 18km mark, a group of 10 had broken away, led by former world champion Sergey Kirdyapkin from the Russian Federation. The 2008 Olympic Silver medallist Jared Tallent, flying the flag for Australia, was also in the lead pack, with team-mate Nathan Deakes and Guatemala's 20km Race Walk runner-up Erick Barrondo also prominent, but Barrondo was later disqualified for lifting. Shortly after 35km, Tianfeng Si of China made a break, followed by three Russian Federation athletes and Yohann Diniz from France. Diniz inexplicably crashed into a barrier ending his chances of a medal. Kirdyapkin seemed to gain strength from this and launched a surge to catch Si. He finished 54 seconds clear of Tallent, with Si third, in an Olympic record time 3:35.59.

← *Sergey Kirdyapkin celebrates his 50km Race Walk gold medal.*

Olympic Record

Event	Name	Country	Record	Date
Men's 20km Race Walk	Ding Chen	CHN	1:18:46	4 August
Men's 50km Race Walk	Sergey Kirdyapkin	RUS	3:35:59	11 August

🏃 Men's Marathon

Named after the legend of Pheidippides, who, according to legend, ran non-stop from the battlefield at Marathon to Athens to announce victory over the Persians, only to drop dead having delivered the news, the Marathon is a road race run over 42.195 kilometres that has been contested at every Games since 1896.

⬆ *Ethiopia's Abebe Bikila, running barefoot, won the men's Marathon at Rome 1960 to become the first black African gold medallist in history.*

Bikila breaks the mould

When runners lined up for the men's Marathon at Rome 1960, almost no one outside his own country had heard of 28-year-old Ethiopian Abebe Bikila. He had been drafted into his country's team at the last moment only after Wami Biratu broke his ankle playing football. By the end of the race, he had claimed the first gold medal won by a black African in the Games' history – in bare feet, and in a world record time of 2:15.16. Four years later, he contracted appendicitis just six weeks before the Tokyo Games but jogged around the hospital to maintain his fitness. This was his first marathon in shoes, and he won in another record time (2:12.11), over four minutes clear of Britain's silver medallist Basil Heatley. In 1968, Bikila went to Mexico City attempting to clinch a hat-trick of gold medals. He kept a foot injury secret, but the pain was too much and he dropped out just short of half-way. In 1969, Bikila was involved in a car accident in Addis Ababa, which left him paralysed and he died four years later from a brain haemorrhage. His funeral was attended by 75,000 people and Emperor Haile Selassie proclaimed a national day of mourning. A stadium in the city is named in his honour.

➡ *Czech Emil Zatopek clinched a unique treble at the 1952 Games in Helsinki.*

Zatopek the Czech locomotive

When Czechoslovakia's Emil Zatopek claimed the men's Marathon title at Helsinki 1952 he set a record that surely will never be equalled: he had won gold in each of the classic distance races (5000m, 10,000m and Marathon) at the same Games. At London 1948, Zatopek had won the men's 10,000m and come second in the men's 5000m, but he went one better in Helsinki to achieve the double. Not content with that, the Czechoslovak followed up by running his first marathon – in the ultimate arena of the Games. World record-holder Jim Peters tried to burn off the track star by setting a scorching pace, but Zatopek stuck tenaciously to the Briton before going clear soon after the 15-kilometre mark and winning easily – and breaking the Games record in the process. Zatopek attempted to defend the men's Marathon title at Melbourne 1956, but a groin injury badly disrupted his training and he trailed in sixth.

In the footsteps of Pheidippides

The first Marathon of the modern Olympic Games, held in Athens in 1896, saw 17 runners trace the route of Pheidippides, the ancient Greek who in 490 BC, it is claimed, ran from the battle of Marathon to Athens (approximately 40 kilometres) as a messenger to proclaim the victory of the Athenians over the Persians. Legend has it that he collapsed and died after delivering the news. In 1896, only nine runners completed the 40km race, and the winner was a local man, Spyridon Louis.

Marathon that never was?

Hannes Kolehmainen, the first in a succession of great Finnish distance runners, surged to victory in the men's Marathon at Antwerp 1920 – but was it a 'marathon'? The official report from the Games states that the course was 42.75 kilometres, approximately 400 metres further than the classic distance. However, the Association of Road Racing Statisticians have estimated that the route was only 40km long, which casts doubt on whether Kolehmainen actually smashed the 'world best' by more than three-and-a-half minutes, as is claimed in many record books.

↑ *Italy's Dorando Pietri crosses the line to win men's Marathon gold at London 1908 ... or so he thought: he was later disqualified for having been helped to his feet by his manager while in a state of collapse.*

Pietri's place in history

It was the London 1908 Olympic Games which provided the event, previously run over 26 miles, with its idiosyncratic extra 385 yards. A lap of the track at the Olympic Stadium was included in addition to the 26-mile course, so that the finish could be in front of the royal box. If it wasn't for this, Italian Dorando Pietri would surely have won; as it is, he gained greater fame as the most gallant of losers. Pietri initially went the wrong way round the track and then proceeded to stagger to the finish line, falling to the ground with exhaustion several times. Officials helped him to his feet each time, but their actions cost Pietri the gold – American Johnny Hayes (who finished second) was later deemed to be the winner after the Italian was disqualified for accepting assistance.

Americans set the world pace

The first Marathon race over the now-accepted distance of 42.195 kilometres (26 miles 385 yards) was staged at London 1908. American gold medallist Johnny Hayes set the standard, but it was only six months before his effort was chalked off by compatriot Robert Fowler. The first sub 2:30 Marathon was recorded by yet another American, Albert Michelsen in 1925, but Haile Gebrselassie's epic in Berlin in 2008 (2:03.59) has lowered the mark by almost 20 per cent since Michelsen's performance to the brink of the magical two hours – a barrier generally considered unbreakable. No athlete has broken the world record as many times as Britain's Jim Peters (four).

London 2012

Ugandan springs Marathon surprise

The East African nation of Uganda has a limited athletics heritage, which is dwarfed by neighbouring Kenya. The 400m Hurdles at Munich 1972 was the only Olympic gold ever brought back to Kampala, until Stephen Kiprotich's glory run through the streets of London. Kenya's Wilson Kipsang Kiprotich, no relation to Stephen, came into the race as the fastest man, the leader of a three-man team selected from an amazing 248 Kenyans who had achieved qualifying standard.

Kipsang Kiprotich made the early pace, going through halfway at 1:03.15, sixteen seconds clear of the chasing pack. At the Tower of London, the 23-kilometre point on the second of three laps, past a string of famous landmarks, Kipsang Kiprotich was pursued by his team-mate, world champion Abel Kirui, Stephen Kiprotich and Ethiopian Ayele Abshero. Three kilometres later, with an estimated one million spectators lining the streets and producing an unprecedented level of support and atmosphere, Kirui and Stephen Kiprotich joined Wilson Kipsang Kiprotich.

On the final lap, at around the 36 kilometres mark, the two Kenyans made a what appeared to be a successful bid to drop the Ugandan. But, in an extraordinary twist, Stephen Kiprotich surged like a 1500m runner at the 35km marker, catching the Kenyan duo, overtaking them and, in the space of a kilometre, establishing a 20-metre lead.

Frequent glances over his shoulder as he ran alongside the River Thames told him that the gold was in the bag. The sight of Big Ben was welcoming in the 26-degree heat and Stephen Kiprotich could enjoy a solo cruise up The Mall to finish in 2:08.01 with the Kenyans in the minor medal positions.

↓ *An African men's Marathon 1–2–3 was no surprise, but the gold medal for Uganda's Stephen Kiprotich was a shock.*

Men's High Jump and Pole Vault

The men's High Jump and Pole Vault are two of 12 track and field events to have formed a part of the Athletics programme at every Games since Athens 1896. Both disciplines have benefitted enormously from advances in technique and technology over the years.

Osborn's double special

American Harold Osborn is the only athlete to have won an individual event in the Olympic Games as well as the men's Decathlon, having achieved the feat in the 1924 Games in Paris. A doctor of osteopathy, he was a leading high jumper from 1920 to 1936. He mastered the trick of pressing the bar back towards the uprights as he passed over them, a practice that was subsequently not permitted.

↑ *Harold Osborne (United States) took men's High Jump gold at the 1924 Games in Paris – ahead of compatriot Leroy Browne – with a leap of 1m98.*

Poles apart

The Pole Vault at Munich 1972 was marred by controversy over the use of a new type of pole, the Cata-pole. East Germany's Wolfgang Nordwig beat the American world record holder Robert Seagren. It was the first time a non-US athlete had won the event.

Talking the talk, walking the walk

Canadian Duncan McNaughton was a student at the University of Southern California (USC) in Los Angeles, the venue for the 1932 Games. However, Canada refused to include him in their team and it was only when he pestered officials that they finally succumbed. It was just as well. In the final jump-off, McNaughton faced his university team-mate Robert Van Osdel, who also trained under coach Dean Cromwell. McNaughton cleared the crucial height to take the gold, while Van Osdel secured silver.

Beau Brumel...

Ukrainian Valery Brumel and American John Thomas were friends, despite the political differences betwen their countries. However, both missed out on the men's High Jump title at Rome 1960 when another Soviet jumper, Robert Shavlakadze from Georgia, finished ahead of them. Then began a series of duels between the pair, in which Brumel was usually victorious. So it proved at Tokyo 1964, with Brumel winning on countback. However, a year later Brumel was severely injured in a motorcycle accident, breaking his right leg, and subsequently underwent about 20 operations. He cherished a well-wishing telegram from Thomas, who had hoped that the Ukrainian would jump again. He did, even managing to clear 2.12 metres, but he never competed at an elite level again.

Record-breaker Bubka

Sergey Bubka is the greatest ever pole-vaulter. He won six world titles and set 17 ratified world outdoor records, including the current 6.14 metres. Bubka, however, collected only one Olympic Games gold medal, at Seoul 1988, and he needed three attempts at the winning height of 5.90m. He did not register a height at Barcelona 1992, and was injured in the warm-up at Atlanta 1996.

Anything but a flop...

The 'Fosbury Flop' transformed the technique of the high jump. Developed by American Dick Fosbury, it involved clearing the bar backwards and landing head first on the inflated cushion. Disappointed by his results with the conventional straddle, Fosbury gradually evolved the 'Flop', and it was revealed to an international audience for the first time in Mexico City at the 1968 Games, when he cleared 2.24 metres on his final attempt to defeat his compatriot Edward Caruthers and take the gold medal. Subsequently Fosbury suffered a series of injuries, but he still won the US national collegiate title the following year. Within three years most leading jumpers had adopted his style.

↓ *The revolutionary technique that took Dick Fosbury (United States) to High Jump gold in 1968 was soon adopted by most leading high jumpers.*

London 2012

Where's my shirt?

The Olympic Games High Jump final is a high-stakes environment, but eventual gold medallist Ivan Ukhov unwittingly introduced an element of farce into the event as he prepared for an attempt at 2.33 metres. The Russian Federation jumper was seen scrambling around the floor and hurriedly rooting through his kit bag, having mislaid his competitor's vest. In desperation, he grabbed a T-shirt, pinned his number to it and rushed out with seconds to spare. He rose majestically above the bar with the unconventional attire flapping in the wind and went back to continue the search for the shirt. Having been reunited with his vest, Ukhov cleared 2.36 and 2.38 metres to clinch gold.

↑ Renaud Lavillenie added Olympic Games gold to his European title.

↑ Ivan Ukhov cleared 2.33 metres despite wearing a loose-fitting T-shirt.

Playing to the gallery

Sport is theatre and silver medallist Erik Kynard took that sentiment to heart during a passionate bid to beat Ivan Ukhov in the High Jump. The American college student urged the London crowd, who were cheering on home favourite Robbie Grabarz, to support him at every attempt. In an era of regulation team uniforms, it was novel to see Kynard wearing stars and stripes socks, adding to his antics which included grabbing the bar after each failed attempt and yelling at himself with a succession of shouts of 'Come on man!' He had achieved 2.33 metres, one centimetre short of his personal best, and tried to clear both 2.38 and 2.40 metres, but had to give best to the superior Ukhov.

Scaling the heights

The Pole Vault event is a compelling spectacle. The combination of speed, skill and nerve intrigues. The London 2012 final was a slow burner, with only three vaulters clearing 5.75 metres. One of these was France's Renaud Lavillenie, the pre-event favourite, thanks to a 5.97-metre effort in Helsinki in July 2012. His first failure came at 5.91 metres, by which time he was assured of a medal, along with Germans Bjorn Otto and Raphael Holzdeppe. Lavillenie elected to go to an Olympic record height, 5.97 metres, and was the only man to succeed, becoming the third French Pole Vault gold medallist, after Pierre Quinon and Jean Galfione. Six metres is pole vaulting's magical height, and Lavillenie tried to gild the lily by clearing 6.02 and 6.07, but he failed with three tries at those heights.

Australian anguish

Every Olympic champion wants to defend their title to the best of their ability. If someone else is better than them on the day, so be it. Sadly, this did not happen for pole vault king Steve Hooker at London 2012. The Australian, who had won every title available to him in the event, entered the London 2012 Pole Value competition at 5.65 metres (41 centimetres below his personal best). Afer two failures, the pressure was on, but a knee injury was eating into Hooker's self-confidence as he stood on the runway for his third attempt. He began his approach, stuttered and stopped. There was still almost a minute left for him to make his final try, but Hooker had had enough. He retired from the competition in despair.

Olympic Record

Event	Name	Country	Record	Date
Men Pole Vault	Renaud Lavillenie	FRA	5.97m	10 August

Men's Long Jump and Triple Jump

The men's Long Jump and Triple Jump are leaping events that rely on strength and speed. The former, the only known jumping event at the ancient Games, consists of a run-up followed by a single leap; the latter, a run-up followed by a 'hop, skip and jump leap'. Both events have been contested at each of the modern Games.

Hubbard's breakthrough

William DeHart Hubbard was the first black athlete to win an individual gold medal at the Games, when he captured the Long Jump title in Paris in 1924. Remarkably, his winning distance of 7.44m was less than that of another American, Robert LeGendre, who had reached 7.76m when coming third in the Pentathlon the previous day.

How Lewis emulated Owens

Carl Lewis saw himself as Jesse Owens' successor, and at Los Angeles 1984 he won the same four gold medals as Owens had in 1936 – the 100m, 200m, 4 x 100m Relay and Long Jump. But Lewis outdid Owens by winning gold in the same event, the Long Jump, at four consecutive Olympic Games. His narrowest victory was in 1992, when fellow American Mike Powell – who had broken Bob Beamon's world record with a leap of 8.96 metres in winning the 1991 World Championship – came within 3 centimetres of him. Lewis won again at Atlanta 1996, after which he scooped sand from the long jump pit to mark his departure from the sport.

Immortal Jesse Owens

Jesse Owens, one of the most celebrated names in international athletics, set a world long jump record of 8.13 metres, a mark which lasted for more than 25 years. It was one of a total of six world records (both metric and imperial) that he set within an hour on his 'day of days', 25 May 1935, at Ann Arbor, Michigan. Owens was clear favourite for the gold medal at the 1936 Games in Berlin the following year. However, the American's first two attempts were no jumps. Then Germany's Luz Long suggested he take off well behind the board to ensure qualification. Owens followed his advice ... and qualified by one centimetre. That afternoon, Long equalled Owens's best effort with a leap of 7.87m in the fifth round. However, Owens responded with two longer jumps, winning the title with 8.06m, and was congratulated by the German. The pair became friends, and although Long was killed in the war, Owens continued to maintain contact with his family until his own death in 1980.

⬆ *Germany's Luz Long (left) and Jesse Owens pose for the camera at the 1936 Games in Berlin. Owens beat the German to take Long Jump gold.*

Beamon the destroyer

The most publicised moment in long jump history occurred early in morning of 18 October 1968, when Bob Beamon, an unheralded American, leapt 8.90m to improve the world record by 55 centimetres, a performance that still resonates nearly half a century later. Although he was aided by the fact that those Olympic Games were held at altitude, thus reducing the air resistance, and the fact that the wind advantage was a maximum 2m per second, it was still an extraordinary feat and a record that stood for 23 years. Beamon's first-round effort completely demoralised the rest of the field, with Britain's Lynn Davies, the defending champion, saying: 'You have destroyed this event.' Beamon was so overcome by the experience that he had a cataplectic fit and did not jump again in Mexico City, and in subsequent competitions never jumped further than 8.21m. Still, his athletic immortality was assured. His autobiography was entitled *The Man Who Could Fly*.

⬅ *Bob Beamon leaps to the gold medal and immortality with his world record-breaking jump at the 1968 Games in Mexico City.*

London 2012

Greg the Great

Great Britain had not won the men's long jump title in any major global meeting since the Tokyo 1964 Olympic Games. Even with home advantage, there was no reason to assume that sequence would be broken at London 2012. Team GB had two men in the final and although neither was considered gold medal material, something was in the London air on the evening of 8 August. Sandwiched between victories for Jessica Ennis and Mo Farah, the unheralded Greg Rutherford leapt 8.21 metres to take the lead in the second round. Two jumps later, Rutherford extended his leading mark by 10 centimetres amid hysteria around the stadium. It was by no means an unreachable target but jumper after jumper failed to exceed it and Rutherford was left as one of the more surprising gold medal winners.

⬆ *Greg Rutherford leaps for glory in the London 2012 Games Long Jump final.*

Watt under pressure

Mitchell Watt was viewed as one of the best Australian hopes for a gold medal in the Olympic Stadium. Normally when the Athletics contests begin Australia are firmly established near the top of the Olympic medal table due to their strength in Swimming. Not this time, and when Watt took part in his final his country had just one gold to its name at London 2012. The pressure was on, but Watt fouled three of his first four attempts and failed to reach eight metres with the other. Round five saw the Queenslander edge into silver position by a centimetre. He lined up for the last time, the only man who could prevent Greg Rutherford from gold. It was good – but not good enough – 8.16 metres. In the context of Australia's opening week, though, a silver was a triumph.

Leaving it late

Christian Taylor was in a personal crisis approaching the middle of the London 2012 Triple Jump final. The American world champion had overstepped in each of his first two attempts and needed, literally, to make a line in the sand in order to go any further in the competition. He sprinted down the runway, planted his foot a half-metre behind the plasticine – first task completed. Hop, step, leap and he landed 17.15 metres away, more than enough to remain for the final three rounds. As he prepared for his fourth jump, he was 39 centimetres off his target, but this is when the cream came to the top. Taylor strung together the sequence of the night, out to 17.81 metres.

Impossible dream

Phillips Idowu should have been going toe-to-toe with Christian Taylor in the final of the Triple Jump at the London 2012 Games. The man who was brought up just a few miles away from the Olympic Stadium had been one of the host nations' biggest hopes for gold. He had won silver at Beijing 2008 and gold at the 2009 World Championship. However, the glorious uncertainty of sport was revealed once again. Idowu suffered a leg injury and pulled out of the European Championships at Helsinki, in what should have been a key warm-up event for him. He then failed to attend the Team GB athletics training camp in Portugal and there were communication issues between him and the national coaching staff. All in all, Idowu's attempts at recuperation did not go well and, clearly below-par, he failed to qualify for the final, achieving a longest leap of 16.53, almost 1.3 metres short of his personal best.

⬆ *Christian Taylor leapt a season's best 17.81 metres to win the Triple Jump.*

Men's Discus and Hammer Throws

The object of both the Men's Discus Throw (one of the events of the Ancient Pentathlon and contested at every Games since 1896) and Hammer Throw (part of the Olympic programme since 1900) is to throw the object further than the rest of the competitors in the field. The former is a 2-kilogram metal disc; the latter is a 7.257kg ball attached to a 1.215-metre chain.

Oerter the expert

In all of the four throwing events the greatest competitor in the history of the Games is Al Oerter, who won four successive gold medals and on each occasion defeated the world record holder at the time. He said: 'I beat inexperience in 1956, public expectancy in 1960, injury in 1964 and old age in 1968.' Probably his greatest feat was at Tokyo 1964, when he was suffering from disc problems in his back that forced him to wear a surgical collar, and then damaged his ribcage while practising. However, he was determined to compete, was given pain-killing injections and, although trailing, reached the fifth round, at which point he took off the collar, uttering the words: 'These are the Olympics, you die for them.' He then set a new Games record of 61.00 metres. In 1980, aged 43, he even took part in the US Trials – after the boycott of the Games had been announced – and finished fourth. If following the Trials the leading three Americans had gone to the Games, then at least one of them might have buckled under pressure and Oerter would have been on the team yet again.

⬇ *The greatest discus thrower of all time, Al Oerter defied to injury to produce a Games record-breaking throw to claim gold at Rome 1960.*

Champagne goes flat

The 1932 Games were held in Los Angeles at the height of Prohibition, so the French team brought its own supply of wine. During the men's Discus Throw event, Jules Noël used to leave the field after each of his efforts to have some champagne with fellow Frenchmen in the changing rooms. This seemed to inspire Noël and his fourth throw landed beyond the mark of the eventual gold medallist John Anderson. However, the attention of the officials was centred on the men's Pole Vault competition and they missed where the discus had landed. Noël was therefore awarded a further attempt, but he was unable to duplicate the effort and eventually finished fourth.

Sheridan's beat

Like several pioneers in the hammer, Martin Sheridan was born in Ireland but emigrated to the United States and became a New York policeman. He won his first men's Discus title at St Louis 1904, defeating Ralph Rose, the Shot Put champion, after both athletes had extra attempts. He then took men's Discus Throw gold at the 1906 Intercalated Games in Athens, as well as the Shot Put gold and three silver medals in other events, before winning a third men's Discus Throw title in London in 1908. Sadly, he died of pneumonia in 1918.

⬆ *An Irish-born New York policeman, Martin Sheridan won men's Discus Throw gold for the United States at St Louis 1904 and London 1908.*

Hal the hammer

American hammer thrower Hal Connolly, attracted international attention through his romance with Czech discus champion Olga Fikotova. Their relationship began at Melbourne 1956, when the Cold War was at its most intense. The pair returned to their own countries after the Games, both as gold-medallists, but in 1957, Connolly went to Prague and was allowed to marry Fikotova and take her back to America. However, they were divorced in 1973.

London 2012

Overcoming every hurdle

Robert Harting proved himself an unconventional discus thrower – at least when it came to celebrating. The German left it late to become a gold medallist at London 2012. His throw of 68.27 metres in the fifth round earned him the Olympic crown by nine centimetres. When his victory was confirmed, Harting set off on an impressive sprint, which surprised the ranks of the photographers, but that was not where it ended. As he proceeded down the home straight on a lap of honour Harting elected to take on the barriers set up for women's 100m Hurdles final, delighting the crowd as he showed impressive hurdling technique for a big man.

Propelled to success

The Islamic Republic of Iran had never won an Olympic Athletics medal when Tehran-born Asian champion Ehsan Hadadi stepped into the Discus Throw circle to launch his first attempt in the London 2012 final. Thirty seconds later Hadadi had propelled the discus 68.18 metres to set a benchmark which remained until the penultimate round. Throw after throw fell short and a sporting line in the sand appeared to be set, until Germany's Robert Harting took the prize away from Hadadi, who had one last chance to regain a place on the top step on the podium, but he just fell short. Nonetheless, Hadadi did receive unprecedented admiration.

Pars perfection

Until London 2012, Hungary's Krisztian Pars had been the nearly man of the Hammer Throw. He finished fourth at the Beijing 2008 Games but was briefly elevated to silver medallist after two athletes who had finished ahead of him were disqualified. They appealed and were reinstated, so Pars had the precious medal wrenched from his grasp. In Daegu, Pars at last earned a podium finish, winning silver at the 2011 World Championship. He went one better at the 2012 European Championship. At London 2012, he achieved the minimum required to qualify, but the final would surely require an 80-metre heave of the implement. In round three Pars propelled the hammer to 80.59 metres. After eight major championships with no gold medals, he had won two in succession, including the biggest of the lot.

KO for Kozmus

Primoz Kozmus has been a trailblazer for Slovenia athletics for a decade. After serving his apprenticeship at the highest level of hammer throwing, Kozmus came through in 2007 to earn silver at the World Championships and was victorious at both Beijing 2008 and 2009 Berlin World Championships. He opened up the London 2012 final with an effort of 78.97 metres, but Krisztian Pars soon overtook him by 17 centimetres. Kozmus had three chances to regain his lead and retain the title, a feat achieved only twice before in Olympic Hammer Throw history ... but fell short, his fifth throw going 79.36 metres.

Men's Shot Put and Javelin Throw

Men's Shot Put competitions have been held at the Olympic Games since their inception in 1896 and use a 7.26-kilogram shot. Men's Javelin Throw events (which have been staged at every Games since 1908) are used with spears measuring 2.6–2.7 metres in length and weighing 800 grams.

One-way traffic

At 1.98 metres in height and weighing more than 120 kilograms, American Ralph Rose was physically a forerunner of modern competitors, although he had a rudimentary technique and lacked the explosive speed of modern-day competitors. He took the men's Shot Put title in front of his home crowd at the 1904 Games in St Louis – with a world record of 14.81 metres – and retained his title in London four years later, when he was handed the honour of carrying the US flag at the Opening Ceremony. In the London final he defeated Irishman Denis Horgan, who in 1907 had nearly been killed in a brawl while working as a New York policeman. At Stockholm 1912, Rose lost his title to another New York policeman, Patrick McDonald, who was a point duty traffic officer in Times Square.

The Zelezny and Backley show

The Czech Republic's Jan Zelezny and Britain's Steve Backley dominated men's Javelin throwing for more than a decade. Backley won four European titles but never a world or Olympic title, frequently beaten only by Zelezny, who won Games gold medals in 1992, 1996 and 2000 and three World Championship titles too.

United States revolutionary

American Parry O'Brien always remembered the words of his coach Jesse Mortensen: 'The orthodox is another word for the obsolete.' Whereas previously the accepted shot put technique was a sideways glide across the circle, O'Brien's method was to crouch, facing backwards to begin the movement, allowing him to push the weight for longer and propel the shot farther. He took gold at the 1952 and 1956 Games and won 116 successive competitions during that period. His world record of 19.33 metres in 1960 was finally overhauled by compatriot Bill Nieder, who went on to beat O'Brien into second place at the 1960 Games, and at Tokyo 1964, his fourth successive Games, O'Brien could only finish fourth. However, his revolutionary technique was adopted by most shot-putters, until the arrival of the spiral style, in which athletes turn as they cross the circle, before releasing the weight.

⬆ *Bill Nieder headed an American one-two-three in the men's Shot Put final at Rome 1960 with a new Games record throw of 19.68 metres – compatriots Parry O'Brien and Dallas Long finished second and third respectively.*

Timmermann's title

East German shot putter Ulf Timmermann was a supreme exponent of the glide technique. He broke the world record for the first time in 1985 (with a throw of 22.62 metres) and, in the build-up to Seoul 1988, became the first shot putter in history to break the 23m barrier (with a throw of 23.06m). And as the men's Shot Put final in Seoul progressed, it soon became clear that Timmermann was the man to beat: he hit the front of the 12-man field as early as the third round (with a throw of 22.16m), extended his lead in the fourth round (21.09m) and, after increasing it yet again in the fifth round (with a Olympic record-breaking throw of 22.29m) seemed set for gold. But the USA's Randy Barnes had other ideas, producing a throw of 22.39m to take the lead. It was now or never for the East German … and he duly lived up to the sense of occasion, producing a throw of 22.47m to take gold.

← *East Germany's Ulf Timmermann won the men's Shot Put final at Seoul 1988 with his final throw – a new Games record of 22.47 metres (eight centimetres ahead of United States' Randy Barnes).*

London 2012

Golden fractions

The men's Shot Put had the honour of being the first Athletics event to be decided and the final developed into a fascinating contest. It is a discipline which has traditionally been ultra-competitive and the London 2012 edition was no exception. Defending champion Tomasz Majewski from Poland was bidding to become the first man for 56 years to retain the title, and his biggest rival was thought to be Christian Cantwell, who had produced a season's best 22-metre throw a month earlier. Majewski propelled the shot 21.87 metres in round three to edge into a one centimetre lead over Germany's David Storl. The American Cantwell was not at his best on this night and finished fourth, behind Storl and compatriot Reese Hoffa. Majewski sealed his victory by improving by two centimetres with his last attempt. Big men, small margins ... the Pole won by little more than a fingernail.

↑ Among the rewards showered on Trinidad and Tobago's Javelin Throw gold medallist Keshorn Walcott was having a lighthouse named after him.

Teenage tornado

Think of Caribbean athletics and sprinting comes to mind. Except for a handful of power athletes from Cuba, field events have been barren territory for the islands. Now, though, there is Keshorn Walcott. The 19-year-old from Trinidad and Tobago announced himself on the global stage by becoming the 2012 World Junior champion, but the Olympic Games event is supposed to be about experience. In the first round of the final, Walcott threw a personal best of 83.51 metres and improved his new national record by 1.07 metres with his second attempt. Competitors stretched every sinew to topple the newcomer but all fell short. History was looming, as no non-European had won the men's Javelin Throw for 60 years, and there had never been a teenage champion. Walcott became that man.

↑ Tomasz Majewski won his second Shot Put gold medal by three centimetres.

Storl stymied

Germany's David Storl came agonisingly close to gold at London 2012. Storl, who celebrated his 22nd birthday on the day the London 2012 Games opened, had been hailed as the present and the future in the Shot Put. He won the World Championship in 2011, having set a ream of records at Junior level. He took an early lead but saw Majewski deny him in torturous fashion and had to settle for silver. In another era he would have been part of the East German system, hailing from the small town of Rochlitz in Saxony. Instead Storl, born nine months after the fall of the Berlin Wall, was in the vanguard of the first tranche of world-class athletes from a reunified Germany.

No fun for Finns

In contrast to Trinidad & Tobago, which has a new-found love for the Javelin Throw, Finland is the world capital of javelin throwing. The discipline is followed with a fervour in the Scandinavian nation. Seven times a Finn had been crowned the Olympic champion, but not once since Seoul 1988. They had three hopes at the final at London 2012 – 2007 world champion Tero Pitkamaki launched an 82.68-metre effort in round two to move into second place but could only marginally improve and finished fifth. Antti Ruuskanen's late 84.12 metres was good enough for bronze, but not good enough to live up to the rich tradition cultivated in Helsinki and all parts of the Finnish peninsula. Ari Mannio trailed in 11th. The wait goes on for their next javelin hero.

Women's 100m

As is the case in the men's competition, the women's 100m is considered the blue riband event of the women's Athletics programme. It was one of only five Athletics events that women contested at the 1928 Games in Amsterdam, the first time women's events were included at the Games.

Ashford's breakthrough

The 11-second barrier remained impenetrable in women's 100m competition at the Olympic Games until Evelyn Ashford finally broke the hoodoo in a gold medal-winning time of 10.97 in Los Angeles in 1984. In all, Ashford broke the barrier on no fewer than 30 occasions in the course of a glittering career.

↑ *Evelyn Ashford (centre) took women's 100m gold after recording a new Games record time of 10.97 seconds at Los Angeles 1984.*

Queen Merlene

Jamaican-born sprinter Merlene Ottey has earned the title 'Queen of the Track' for a remarkable career which, by the age of 50, had included competition at seven different Olympic Games. Inspired to take up running by a radio commentary on the Montreal 1976 Games, she won a bronze medal in the women's 100m four years later in Moscow. Further medals in the women's blue riband event would elude Ottey for 16 years before she took silver at the Atlanta 1996 Games and a second bronze medal followed at Sydney 2000, when she competed at the age of 40. At Beijing 2008, aged 48, having become a Slovenian national in order to qualify again, Ottey failed by just 0.28 seconds to reach her eighth Olympic Games.

↑ *Merlene Ottey picked up her third Olympic Games medal in the women's 100m (bronze) at Sydney 2000 at the tender age of 40.*

Clock watching

Fully automatic timing (to a hundredth of a second) only became the IAAF's accepted method in January 1977. At the Olympic Games, the gold medal-winning performances by American Wyomia Tyus in 1968 and East German Renate Stecher in 1972, both in 11.07 seconds, were the fastest recorded fully electronic 100m races to that time and were declared world records.

Zero to heroes

Jamaica's rise to the top of sprinting at the Olympic Games was nothing short of meteoric. Prior to Beijing 2008, the nation had never won a gold medal. However, one day on from the sensational track exploits of compatriot Usain Bolt, Shelly-Ann Fraser led home a clean sweep of the medals for the Reggae Nation in the women's 100m final. Fraser, who clocked a personal best time of 10.78 seconds, was followed home by team-mates Sherone Simpson and Kerron Stewart, who both finished in a time of 10.98 and were awarded silver medals – completing the first sweep of medals in the women's 100m by any nation at any Olympic Games or World Championships.

Golden debut

Elizabeth 'Betty' Robinson of the United States was the inaugural winner of the women's 100m at the 1928 Games in Amsterdam. She proved that inexperience was no barrier to success, claiming the gold medal in only her fourth competition, at the tender age of 16. In just her second race she had equalled the world record and she emulated that feat in the final in Amsterdam. Three years later she came 'back from the dead' following a plane crash. A man found her unconscious in the wreckage and wrongly thought she was dead. He put her in his car boot and drove her to an undertaker's, where she was diagnosed as very much alive, albeit in a coma that would last for seven months. She was unable to walk properly for more than two years but, remarkably, would perform again at the Games – in the women's 4 x 100m Relay at Berlin 1936.

Fabulous Flo-Jo

The women's 100m world record has stood for more than 20 years now. The time of 10.49 seconds was set by the late Florence Griffith-Joyner, during the US Olympic trials in July 1988. In the mid-1980s she became popularly known as Flo-Jo and was instantly recognisable for her extremely long and colourful fingernails. The record-breaking performance aroused controversy as witnesses questioned whether it was wind-assisted. What was never in doubt was Flo-Jo's speed, and she duly won the gold medal at Seoul 1988 in a time of 10.54. The inspirational effect of the Games competition may be judged by the fact that her best time, before that 1988 season, had been 10.96. Griffith-Joyner retired after her Seoul triumphs – she won two golds and a silver – and died 10 years later at the tragically young age of 38.

↑ *Florence Griffith-Joyner was the class act of the women's 100m final field at Seoul 1988: her margin of victory was 0.29 seconds.*

Gail force

American sprinter/hurdler Gail Devers was as famous for her own Flo-Jo-style fingernails as for winning blanket finishes. At the Barcelona 1992 Games, Betty Cuthbert of Jamaica had to settle for silver after finishing one hundredth of a second behind her. Then, at Atlanta 1996, another Jamaican, Merlene Ottey, was even closer, recording the same time as the American but the photo finish gave gold to Devers, who thus emulated compatriot Wyomia Tyus (in 1964 and 1968) by winning consecutive Olympic 100m titles. Devers did not win any Olympic hurdling medals, but did reach four semi-finals.

London 2012

Jamaican double double

Usain Bolt was not the only Jamaican to defend an Athletics 100m title at the London 2012 Games. Shelly-Ann Fraser-Pryce had triumphed at Beijing 2008 and spearheaded the female challenge from the remarkable Caribbean hotbed of sprinting at London 2012. The 1.52m 'pocket rocket' had shown herself to be in top shape during the Jamaican trials, posting the year's fastest time, a searing 10.70. She was joined in the 100m team by defending 200m champion Veronica Campbell-Brown and Kerron Stewart, joint silver-medallist at Beijing 2008.

Inevitably, their sternest opposition would come from the 'big sister' to the north – the United States. Carmelita Jeter certainly proved that by recording back-to-back clockings of 10.83 to be the fastest qualifier in both the heats and semi-finals. Fellow Americans Tianna Madison and Allyson Felix were also in the mix and Nigerian Blessing Okagbare was a fast-finishing threat. The final, which Stewart missed by 0.03 seconds, would be a race to savour but was held in a surreal atmosphere of almost joyous apathy.

With no British representation in the race, the vast majority of the crowd were more concerned with celebrating three gold medals in an hour for the host nation than concentrating on the battle to be crowned fastest woman on the planet. Fraser-Pryce made a sensational start. Jeter pursued but failed to gain any ground and the crown remained with the Jamaican. Just 0.14 seconds covered the first five in a remarkably competitive race, Campbell-Brown managing to edge out Madison and Felix in the battle for bronze. Amazingly, six runners beat the 11-second mark. Okagbare was a disppointing last, but her time was only 0.26 seconds behind Fraser-Pryce; she crossed the line in 11.01.

↑ *Shelly-Anne Fraser-Pryce (right) retains her Olympic title just ahead of Carmelita Jeter (lane 4) and Veronica Campbell-Brown (top) in the women's 100m final.*

Women's 200m and 400m

Part of the Games programme since 1948 and 1964 respectively, the women's 200m and 400m have spawned some legendary champions, including Fanny Blankers-Koen and Florence Griffith-Joyner, but only one woman in history has claimed the 200m-400m double: France's Marie-José Pérec at the 1996 Games in Atlanta.

The face of the games

In September 2000, the world focused on the women's 400m final in Sydney to watch Cathy Freeman, an Australian Aborigine, who had become the face of the Games, after lighting the Olympic Flame at the Opening Ceremony. Freeman duly won gold, becoming the first Australian Aboriginal track and field Olympic champion. On her victory lap she carried both the Aboriginal and Australian flags, and throughout the competition she had the words 'Cos I'm Free' tattooed mid-way between her shoulder and elbow. Freeman later represented Oceania, carrying the Olympic Flag at the Opening Ceremony of the next Winter Games, in Salt Lake City, alongside world dignitaries including Archbishop Desmond Tutu, John Glenn, Lech Walesa and Steven Spielberg.

From podium to studio

Valerie Brisco-Hooks was the leading women's track and field athlete at Los Angeles 1984. She accomplished what no other man or woman had ever done by completing a double in the 200m and 400m at the same Games, before winning a third gold medal as part of the United States' winning 4 x 400m Relay team. Two years later she achieved another kind of stardom, appearing on television with Bill Cosby as a guest in an episode of *The Cosby Show*, entitled 'Off to the Races'.

Marjorie's the governor

Marjorie Jackson-Nelson, AC, CVO, MBE, sits high in the annals of Australian track and field achievement at the Olympic Games. She finished her sporting career with an impressive haul of nine Olympic Games and Commonwealth Games gold medals, having broken ten world records and held every Australian State and National title she contested for a four-year period. Her zenith came at the 1952 Games in Helsinki, when she completed the women's 100m-200m double, to become her nation's first Athletics gold medallist since 1896. At the Opening Ceremony of the 2000 Games in Sydney, Jackson-Nelson was one of eight flag-bearers given the honour of carrying the Olympic Flag. She later became Governor of South Australia, a position she held until 31 July 2007.

Two by two

The event has been staged on 16 occasions, but only two women have successfully retained their women's 200m crowns at the Games. The first to do so was East German sprinter Bärbel Wöckel (née Eckert), who struck gold at the 1976 Games in Montreal and again four years later in Moscow. Her achievement was emulated in 2008 by Jamaican athlete Veronica Campbell-Brown, who had previously won the event at the 2004 Games in Athens.

↑ *Australia's Marjorie Jackson surged to women's 200m gold at the Helsinki 1952 Games some 0.5 seconds ahead of her nearest competitor.*

← *Veronica Campbell-Brown (right) held off the challenge of Allyson Felix to retain her women's 200m crown at the Beijing 2008 Games.*

London 2012

Felix wrap-up

A race in which history beckoned for a trio of reigning champions saw Allyson Felix come through to win her first Olympic title. Felix had been a three-time world champion at 200m, but the only Olympic gold the Californian had to show for her glittering career was in the 4 x 400m Relay at Beijing 2008. She had come second at both Athens 2004 and Beijing 2008. Felix flowed round the turn, but was behind 100m queen Shelly-Ann Fraser-Pryce as they came into the straight. Speed endurance will always win against pure speed in the 200m and Felix strode away with the gold, although Fraser-Pryce maintained her form to clinch the silver. For Felix the medal collection was now complete.

⬆ Allyson Felix was the only runner to go under 22 seconds in winning the 200m final at the London 2012 Games. Carmelita Jeter (left) won bronze.

End of an era

Veronica Campbell-Brown (or VCB as she is known throughout athletics) had ruled the Olympic 200m since 2004. The strong and compact Jamaican powered her way to victory at Athens 2004 and Beijing 2008, now was the chance for her to become the first track athlete to win three consecutive golds in the same event. This time, though, was probably the most competitive women's 200m final in history and VCB had not even won the Jamaican trials. Her domestic rival Shelly-Ann Fraser-Pryce gained significantly in the first 80 metres, pressuring VCB to ignite her trademark finish. It was in vain as Allyson Felix, whom VCB had beaten to the gold twice before, gained revenge. This was the first Olympic final defeat for a great champion.

No solace in silver

Christine Ohuruogu is a big race performer. Some athletes find major championships overwhelming and cannot replicate the form they show at lesser meetings. Not so Ohuruogu, who won gold at the 2007 World Championships and Beijing 2008 Olympic Games without showing an inkling of form in between. London 2012 was the ultimate for her; she was born and raised just down the road from the brand new stadium built for the event. If ever there was a time when stage fright could catch hold of her it was now. It didn't. As normal, she ran an even race, refusing to be rattled for those who stormed off inside and outside her. Ohuruogu finished the fastest but it was not quite enough as Sanya Richards-Ross took gold. She said she was disappointed with silver, the mark of a champion.

Supreme from Sanya

Jamaican-born American Sanya Richards-Ross arrived in London desperate for Olympic recognition in the 400m. She could boast six relay gold medals at global level with United States squads plus an individual world title in 2009, but she had come away from Beijing 2008 with just the bronze. To win she had to dethrone the reigning Olympic champion in her own backyard. A few stars and stripes were dotted around the stadium, but the final was played out in front of a sea of Union flags and fans roaring on local girl Christine Ohuruogu. The Russian Federation's Antonina Krivoshapka went off at an impossible pace to sustain over a full lap and paid for the effort in the final 100 metres. Richards-Ross, however, paced her race perfectly, and had enough in hand to hold off a trademark Ohuruogu rush to the line.

⬇ Sanya Richards-Ross overturned Beijing 2008 form by beating Christine Ohuruogu in the women's 400m final.

Women's 100m and 400m Hurdles

Women's Hurdles events are contested over two distances – 100m (10m shorter than the men's equivalent) and 400m – and have been part of the Games programme since 1972 and 1984 respectively. Remarkably, no woman in history, in either event, has been able to defend her crown.

Changing times

The East German athlete Annelie Ehrhardt competed at a time of transition for the women's sprint Hurdles contest. The event had been a part of the Games programme since Los Angeles 1932, but had been raced over 80 metres until Ehrhardt's inaugural success over 100m at the 1972 Games. Her new electronic world record performance of 12.59 seconds in the final also came during the transition between hand and electronic timing, and a year later she set the last recognised hand-timed world record for the 100m hurdles of 12.3 in the East German national championships at Dresden.

Olympic ideal in action

While an Olympic Games gold medal is regarded by many as a form of heroism, Athens 2004 women's 100m Hurdles champion Joanna Hayes has targeted a different level of success at grass-roots level. Hayes is the daughter of Los Angeles homeless advocate Ted Hayes but was primarily raised by her mother. Following her crowning moment on the track, during which she set a new Games record time of 12.38 seconds, she has established the Joanna Hayes Foundation, whose aim is: 'To open the eyes and broaden the horizons of children living in the most challenging situations and help them see new options and prepare for new futures.'

↑ *Joanna Hayes edged to women's 100m Hurdles gold by 0.08 seconds (ahead of the Ukraine's Olena Krasovska) at the Athens 2004 Games.*

Devers disaster

The Athletics track at Barcelona 1992 was the setting for one of the biggest shocks in the history of track and field at the Olympic Games. The final of the women's 100m Hurdles was expected to be the defining moment in American superstar Gail Devers' career. However, she had not reckoned on the surprise element in Greek competitor Paraskevi ('Voula') Patoulidou, the first woman to represent her nation in a track final at the Games. Devers, the red-hot favourite for gold, tripped on the last hurdle, allowing Patoulidou to join her on the finishing line in a time of 12.64 seconds. Voula immediately celebrated her silver-medal achievement – and then learned that she had in fact won gold, making her the first Greek woman in history to do so. Her victory inspired a nation, and subsequent Greek athletes have referred to Patoulidou's triumph as the catalyst for their ambitions.

↑ *Gail Devers crashes to the track after hitting the final hurdle in the women's 100m Hurdles final at the Barcelona 1992 Games.*

Records, records

The women's world 100m Hurdles record of 12.21 seconds was set during what proved a glorious 1988 for Bulgarian sprinter Yordanka Donkova. She had come to prominence during 1986, when she broke four world records and became European champion, but in 1988 she set the world record just one month before the 1988 Games in Seoul. Although she failed to better that time, she set a then Games record time of 12.38 in winning the gold medal.

Newcomers' glory

Jamaica's domination of sprinting events at the Games is a relatively recent track and field phenomenon. Deon Hemmings (at Atlanta 1996) was the first Jamaican woman to win a gold medal when she won the women's 400m Hurdles. No champion has successfully defended her title in this event at the Games, but Hemmings came closest when she won the silver medal behind Russian Irina Privalova at Sydney in 2000.

London 2012

Pearson pinches it

Sally Pearson's triumph in the women's 100m Hurdles at London 2012 marked the climax of two seasons of outstanding form. The queen of Australian track and field arrived at the Olympic final having lost just one race across the 2011 and 2012 campaigns, and had the hopes of a nation on her slim shoulders. Pearson started well and with 20 metres to go it seemed a foregone conclusion, but reigning champion Dawn Harper produced a blistering finish to make it very close. After an agonising wait, Pearson let out a piercing scream of delight as her name flashed up on the giant scoreboard above the Olympic flame, confirming her gold medal, and reversing the result with Harper from Beijing 2008. There can be little doubt that Pearson's prize was richly deserved.

Out in front in defeat

Lolo Jones was one of the more famous faces in the United States team for the London 2012 Games, but she did not figure among their gold medal prospects. For Jones, who was the favourite for the event at Beijing 2008 until a late stumble in the final, reaching the podium in the women's 100m Hurdles would have been a victory. She had achieved her fame through popular culture rather than sport, with public statements about her private life and glamour photos adding to her legend among bloggers and Twitter users. In the London 2012 100m Hurdles final Jones just missed out on a medal, finishing fourth. Many Olympians will return to virtual anonymity, but Jones's life is already public property.

↑ *Sally Pearson (centre) took the 100m Hurdles gold medal by 0.02 seconds*

Rosolova's final chance

Qualifying for track athletics finals appears a simple task: just run as hard as you can, look at the clock and then it is in or out. But Czech 400m hurdler Denisa Rosolova found the challenge anything but simple. Rosolova finished third in 54.87 in her semi-final, good enough to get through as a fastest loser. But she was then disqualified for allegedly running outside her lane. Four years of training appeared to have been ruined by a misplaced foot. On appeal, however, Rosolova was reinstated and took her place in the final. A seventh place finish was not a glorious end to a traumatic 24 hours but thanks to video analysis at least Rosolova had the chance to try.

Speed pays for Antyukh

Natalya Antyukh won a bronze medal at the Beijing 2008 Games in the 400m. Natural speed was not a issue when she switched disciplines to the 400m Hurdles – just the obstacles on the track. Antyukh bolted from the gun, but she could not make any impression on world champion Lashinda Demus. At 250 metres they were level but Antyukh was clearly moving the better entering the end of the turn. Demus stuck to her task but Antyukh led by three metres. Russian Federation nerves were frayed as the far-from-natural hurdler stuttered preparing to meet the final hurdle. The more fluid Demus gained but Antyukh's flat speed saw her through in an exciting finish. When victory, in a personal best time of 52.70, was confirmed she sank to her knees and offered a personal prayer.

◀ *Natalya Antyukh's switch from 400m to 400m Hurdles paid off at London 2012 with a gold medal.*

Olympic Record				
Event	Name	Country	Record	Date
100m Hurdles	Sally Pearson	AUS	12.35	7 August

Women's 800m and 1500m

The women's 800m was first contested at Amsterdam 1928 and, after a 32-year break, at every Games since Rome 1960; the women's 1500m has been staged since 1972. Three women – Tatyana Kazankina (1976), Svetlana Masterkova (1996) and Kelly Holmes (2004) – have achieved the 800m-1500m double.

Long-distance champion

For many years it seemed Karoline ('Lina') Radke-Batschauer would stand alone as the only ever winner of the women's 800m at the Olympic Games. With assistance from her husband and coach Georg Radke, she trained hard for the 1928 Games in Amsterdam and set a world record of 2:16.8 en route to the final. She went on to win the gold medal, but the race was overshadowed by concerns for several of her competitors, who finished it completely exhausted, and the IOC banished the event from its programme, fearing that women did not have the constitution to compete over such a distance. The women's 800m did not return to the programme until the 1960 Games in Rome.

Brilliant Bragina

Unlike the men, who have raced over 1500m since the first modern Games in 1896, women did not compete in the 'metric mile' until the 1972 Games at Munich. Soviet athlete Lyudmila Bragina dominated the inaugural event, shattering the world in all three rounds and taking the gold medal in 4:01:38.

↗ Mozambique's Maria Mutola, women's 800m champion at Sydney 2000, made the last of her six appearances at Beijing 2008.

Magic Mutola

Between the 1990s and 2000s, no women's 800m event was complete without Maria Mutola. Mozambique's superstar athlete competed in her sixth Olympic Games in Beijng, making her only the fourth athlete to accomplish this feat. After previous near misses, the 'Maputo Express' had her moment of glory when she won gold in Sydney in 2000. She was appointed an honorary United Nations youth ambassador in 2003, and now her Lurdes Mutola Foundation aims to bring more young Mozambicans to sport and help them achieve their sporting and educational potential.

Kenya catch-up

While Kenya's male athletes had long been admired in middle- and long-distance track and field events, it was not until 2008 that the women matched that success. Pamela Jelimo became the first Kenyan woman to win a gold medal at the Games when she won the women's 800m. A few days later Nancy Langat won the women's 1500m to make it a double celebration for Kenya.

Golden girl

The Soviet Union's Nadezhda Olizarenko became a national heroine when she won gold in the women's 800m at the 1980 Games in Moscow, ahead of compatriots Olga Mineyeva and Tatyana Providokhina. Her world record time of 1:53.43, set later that year, has only once been bettered once, by Jarmila Kratochvílová, in 1983.

Kelly Holmes at the double

Kelly Holmes came to full-time athletics at the late age of 22. Having been an outstanding junior athlete, she joined the British Army where she continued to compete, even running against the men over 800 metres. Sebastian Coe's exploits at the Games had inspired the young Holmes, and in 1992, after watching the Games in Barcelona, she returned to the sport full-time. Her career was continually beset by injuries, but she arrived at Athens in 2004 injury free and duly won gold in both the women's 800m and 1500m, becoming Britain's first double gold medallist at the same Games since 1920. A year later she became a Dame Commander of the Order of the British Empire.

← Double delight for Kelly Holmes as she completes the women's 800m-1500m double at Athens 2004.

London 2012

Style and glory ... and gold

The women's 800m at London 2012 was a highly competitive race which allowed the cream to come to the top, with the Russian Federation's Mariya Savinova proving herself to be No.1 and complete her set of gold medals in the event, having won European and world titles in 2010 and 2011 respectively. American Alysia Montano took the field through the first lap in 56.31 seconds, and the urgent pace was taken on by Kenya's defending Olympic champion Pamela Jelimo down the back straight. All the time Savinova was confidently moving through the gears. She caught Jelimo at the perfect place, rounding the final bend and elegantly galloped to victory in 1.56.19. This is how gold medals should be won, with masses of ability and plenty of style.

⬆ *Mariya Savinova of the Russian Federation took the women's 800m gold medal, holding off the fast-finishing South African Costa Semanya.*

Silver for Semenya

When 18-year-old Caster Semenya burst on to the 800m scene at the 2009 World Championships in Berlin, the athletics world did not know what to make of it. The muscularly built South African was a class apart from her competitors at such a young age. Intense media scrutiny led to a messy saga of a teenager being subjected to gender testing for the best part of a year. She was cleared as a bona fide woman, regrouped and won a silver at the 2011 World Championships in Daegu. At London 2012 she eased into the final where she was content to stick at the back of the pack for the first 500 metres. As others wilted off a searing pace, Semenya gained ground but her impressive effort was too late to catch winner Mariya Savinova.

Uceny takes another tumble

The 1500m often throws up a hard-luck story because so many athletes remain bunched together for a major portion of the race. Staying out of trouble on the outside or at the front is not always a practical option. Morgan Uceny of the United States was one of those in the pack and her race was ended just after the ball when a tangle of legs sent her tumbling to the ground. Not for the first time. At the 2011 World Championship final in Daegu, Uceny lost her footing with 500 metres left, again unintentionally tripped up. Uceny must now build for the 2013 World Championships and hope that it's a case of third time lucky.

History for Turkey

The women's 1500 metres final was looking likely to be one of the least satisfactory Athletics races of the London 2012 Games. A slow early pace turned the event into a virtual 600 metres event, finished off with a last lap timed at 58 seconds. The woman who made it exciting and prevailed was Asli Cakir Alptekin, who thus became Turkey's first track and field gold medallist. She made her presence felt internationally in 2011 and 2012, winning the European Championship a month before the Olympic Games. Alptekin had smart race plan when others appeared to have none. She kicked with 200 metres to go, clocking a sensational 14 seconds for the 100 metres to the top of the home straight, from where she could ease to victory.

⬅ *A blistering final 100 metres took Turkey's Asli Cakir Alptekin to the women's 1500m gold medal at the London 2012 Olympic Games.*

Women's 5000m and 10,000m

Women's long-distance track events are relatively new to the Games programme: strangely, the women's 10,000m came first – at Seoul 1988 – and the women's 5000m did not make its debut until the 1996 Games in Atlanta. Only one woman, Ethiopia's Tirunesh Dibaba at the Beijing Games in 2008, has achieved the accolade of claiming the 5000m-10,000m double.

Ethiopian dominance

The Oromo ethnic group found in Ethiopia must be one of the most athletically blessed on earth. The list of long-distance running champions it has produced includes Haile Gebrselassie, Abebe Bikila, and Sileshi Sihine, as well as the Dibaba sisters and Derartu Tulu.

Wang Junxia's Chinese revolution

China's Wang Junxia dominated the world of women's long-distance running for a short but memorable period in the mid-1990s. Having won the women's 10,000m world junior championship in 1992, she claimed the world senior title for the 25-lap distance a year later in Stuttgart. In 1993, at the Chinese National Games, Junxia set her iconic women's 10,000m world record of 29:31.78 which was also the first ever sub-30-minute performance by a woman. Although she never improved on her peak form of 1993, Junxia went on to win the inaugural women's 5000m gold medal at the 1996 Games in Atlanta (ahead of Kenya's Pauline Konga) and also claimed the silver medal in the women's 10,000m event (when Portugal's Fernanda Ribeiro won the gold medal).

➜ *China's Wang Junxia surged to a comfortable victory in the first-ever women's 5000m final at the Atlanta 1996 Games.*

Hand in hand

Following her dramatic victory in the women's 10,000m final at Barcelona 1992, Ethiopia's Derartu Tulu waited at the finish line for her opponent Elana Meyer, a white South African, and the two set off hand in hand for a victory lap that came to symbolise new hope for Africa. At Sydney 2000, having regained her form of eight years earlier, Tulu again won gold in the women's 10,000m event, becoming the first woman to win two gold medals in long-distance races at the Games and the only woman to win 10,000m gold twice.

⬆ *Ethiopia's Derartu Tulu (left, the gold medallist) and South Africa's Elana Meyer (right, silver) celebrate after the women's 10,000m final at the Barcelona 1992 Games.*

Barefoot and controversial

Zola Budd – born, brought up and awarded star status in South Africa – attracted headlines of controversy in 1984 when she was then awarded British citizenship on the strength of a British grandfather. Her subsequent decision to run for Britain at Los Angeles 1984 caused uproar among those who deemed the move as a convenient way to bypass the ban that had been imposed on South African athletes as a result of apartheid. The controversy pursued her all the way into the Games, in which, in the women's 3000m, she collided with the American favourite Mary Decker, who fell and failed to finish the race. The following year, Budd smashed the women's 5000m world record, running the race barefoot in 14:48.07 – 10 seconds faster than the previous record. In fact, the race was really her second women's 5000m world record, but the first could not be recognised because it was set during a race in South Africa.

Szabo finds her métier

After flirting with gymnastics and swimming in her younger years, Romania's Gabriela Szabo switched to track and field events when it became apparent that she would not be good enough to make it professionally in the other disciplines. In 1996, after failing to qualify for the women's 5000m final, Szabo won silver in the women's 1500m competition. Then, four years later at Sydney 2000, Szabo ran a world record of 14:40.79 in the women's 5000m final to win the gold medal.

London 2012

Patience pays for Defar

Meseret Defar's misfortune has been in running in the same era as arguably the greatest female distance athlete ever seen – Tirunesh Dibaba, her Ethiopian team-mate. There had been an Olympic gold medal at Athens 2004 and four world indoor titles but despite all that Dibaba's name was pre-eminent. A slow first two-thirds at the women's 5000m final at London 2012 played into Defar's hands and she had the power when it came to the closing stages. Dibaba pushed it on from four laps out, gradually accelerating and trying to run the finish out of her rival with consecutive 68-second laps. With 800 metres to go it was a predictable Ethiopia–Kenya battle with Defar biding her time. The bell came and went, Dibaba went for home, but could not break her team-mate rounding the final bend. Defar went for it, the gold was hers, and Kenya's Vivian Cheruiyot beat Dibaba for silver.

A race too far

Tirunesh Dibaba came into the 5000m final at London 2012 off a hard race in the 10,000 metres and the signs of wear and tear were showing. A tell-tale, hardly inconspicuous, navy blue strapping along her left hamstring must have given her rivals great hope. Dibaba was trying to complete the distance double but more than that she was aiming for a Bolt-esque double-double. Even the all-time greats from her country – Yifter, Gebrselassie and Bekele – had never won four Olympic gold medals. A slow-run race did not suit her 10,000 metres endurance; it was left to the great champion to make her own pace. This time it was time, tactics and fatigue that beat her – and an exceptionally good team-mate in Meseret Defar.

⮌ Meseret Defar crosses the line clear of her rivals to win the women's 5000m final at the London 2012 Games, her third medal in the event after winning gold at Athens 2004 and bronze at Beijing 2008.

Striking a blow for the Gulf

The presence of Shitaye Eshete in the women's 10,000m final was a reminder of the growing power of the Gulf states in Olympic sport. Eshete was born in Ethiopia but has run for Bahrain since she was 19. Away from the hothouse of distance competition in the land of her birth, Eshete has accumulated honours for her adopted country at Asian level, claiming the 10,000m title in 2011. The Olympic final was a huge step up for her, competing against her idols. Eshete fell off the pace in the closing laps but still finished sixth in a personal best of 30.27.45 as the first non-East African representative.

➜ Tirunesh Dibaba shows off the gold medal she won at London 2012, her second in the women's 10,000m.

Queen by a distance

Ethiopian star Tirunesh Dibaba successfully defended her 10,000m Olympic title in majestic style at London 2012, winning both the tactical and physical battle and her country's arch rivals Kenya. After a quiet opening 3,000 metres, the East Africans moved to the front and began to dominate. It was a formula seen at so many major distance finals. Gradually the contenders were whittled down by the winding up of the pace to just Dibaba and a pair of Kenyans. Three laps to go and Sally Kipyego moved to the front, Dibaba went with her with world champion Vivian Cheruiyot in third. Dibaba calculated that a lap-and-a-half from the finish was the time to put the foot on the accelerator. The Kenyans had nothing left and Dibaba strode round on a victory lap.

Women's Heptathlon and Steeplechase

The women's Heptathlon consists of seven events – 100m hurdles, high jump, shot put, 200m, long jump, javelin throw and 800m – and has been contested at every Games since Los Angeles 1984. The women's 3,000m Steeplechase was staged for the first time at Beijing 2008.

Heptathlon breakthrough

The image of women athletes in the Olympic Movement has undergone a startling evolution. Whereas in the early days they were considered to be delicate creatures, who needed to be restricted from competing in endurance events, they are now regarded as hardened athletes. The former impression prevailed until 1964, when the women's Pentathlon was first admitted to the programme in Tokyo. The five-event formula was replaced by the current Heptathlon in 1984, comprising seven events over two days: on the first day the 100m hurdles, the high jump, the shot put and the 200m run; on the second day the long jump, the javelin throw and finally the gruelling 800m.

→ *Women's Heptathlon gold medallist at the 1988 Games, Jackie Joyner-Kersee made a successful defence of her title at Barcelona 1992.*

Evolving event

The women's Heptathlon replaced the Pentathlon at the Olympic Games from 1984, but it may, in time, be replaced by a women's Decathlon (over ten events). Decathlons have become more common recently and the IAAF has started to keep records for the event but, in the meantime, the Heptathlon is still the standard.

J-K a class apart

In the pantheon of Olympic Games Heptathlon greats, Jackie Joyner-Kersee stands alone as the greatest competitor. Having won the silver medal at Los Angeles 1984, she became the first woman to score over 7,000 points at the Goodwill Games in 1986 and bettered that with her gold medal-winning and world record score of 7,291 points at the Seoul 1988 Games. Joyner-Kersee remains the only woman to retain her title, capturing a second gold at Barcelona 1992. Not content with Heptathlon competition, the gifted American set a Games record of 7.40 metres in the women's Long Jump in Seoul and later played professional basketball for the Richmond Rage. Joyner-Kersee was voted the Greatest Female Athlete of the 20th Century by *Sports Illustrated for Women* magazine.

↑ *Carolina Klüft's domination of the Heptathlon climaxed with a gold medal at Athens 2004.*

Klüft coronation

Carolina Klüft dominated the women's Heptathlon in the early years of the 21st century. The Swede was unbeaten in 22 heptathlon and pentathlon competitions between 2002 and 2007, winning nine consecutive major championship gold medals, including three World Championships and the Olympic Games gold medal at Athens 2004, where she won by a Games record margin of 517 points. Her personal best score of 7,032 points, achieved at the 2007 World Championships in Osaka, Japan, sits second on the all-time list behind Jackie Joyner-Kersee.

Unique Australian

The first Heptathlon gold medallist was Glynis Nunn, the only Australian to win a multi-discipline Athletics event at the Games. The former physical education teacher had quit her job and gone on the dole in order to concentrate on preparing for Los Angeles 1984. It was a desperately close competition, which was sealed by the long jump. American Jackie Joyner-Kersee, a long-jump specialist and Nunn's closest rival, set a disappointing distance with her only legal leap and it left her with a narrow lead before the last discipline, the 800m. Nunn's time was 2.46 seconds faster than Joyner-Kersee's, and she won gold by five points with a final total of 6,390.

London 2012

Ennis reaches her Olympic pinnacle

A visit to London leading up to the 2012 Olympic Games made it impossible to avoid one particular face around almost every street corner. Heptathlete Jessica Ennis was the poster girl of the London 2012 Games. Supremely talented, good looking and with an engaging personality, she was a marketing executive's dream. However, with prominence comes huge pressure. Only gold would be good enough. The 2009 world champion, who had missed the Beijing 2008 Games because of a foot injury – which forced her to change her long jumping technique – had failed to defend the title at the 2011 World Championships in Daegu and needed a good start at London 2012.

Before an ecstatic 80,000 crowd she ran 12.54 seconds in the 100m hurdles – the best time ever recorded for the discipline in a Heptathlon. Average performances in the high jump and shot put caused Ennis to lose the lead to Lithuania's Austra Skujyte, but a scorching 22.83 seconds in the 200m gave Ennis the overnight lead she craved. Day two opened with an excellent 6.48 metres in the long jump and she followed that with a solid 47.49 metres effort in the javelin. The crowd roared but that noise was nothing compared to the concluding 800m.

All but assured of gold, Ennis could afford to coast round in midfield, but the overwhelming support dragged her tired body round the track and she won in the grand manner with victory over two glory laps. This was a British version of Cathy Freeman's memorable 400m triumph on home soil in Sydney 12 years before. It will be remembered as one of the great moments in the history of the Olympic Games.

↑ One for Europe as the Russian Federation's Yuliya Zaripova won 3000m Steeplechase gold at London 2012; African athletes filled the next five places.

Zaripova zips to glory

The Olympic cycle occasionally throws up teams and individuals who achieve pre-eminence in between the Games, but who fail to sustain their form when it really matters on any given date every four years. Yuliya Zaripova, the Russian Federation steeplechaser, could have gone that way but didn't. She had been crowned European and World champion in between Beijing 2008 and London 2012, and from the start of the final she appeared to be a woman on a mission. Three Ethiopians, a pair of Kenyans and Tunisia's Habiba Ghribi stayed with Zaripova as she gradually extended herself. With less than 1,000 metres remaining, the unfit defending champion and world record holder Gulnara Galkina pulled out, Zaripova demanded more of her pursuers and it was too much for them. It was a classy performance from a true champion.

Silver again for Ghribi

Women's sport in the Arab world is fast improving. The presence of female competitors from Saudi Arabia at the Olympic Games for the first time was a massive step forward and nations who led the way have been seeing world-class performances year-on-year. Tunisia fetes steeplechaser Habiba Ghribi, who was voted Arab sportswoman of the year in 2009 and benefited from Eastern European expertise in coach Constantin Nourescu, but Ghribi was left still waiting for an elusive first major title after silver at the 2011 World Championships in Daegu and silver again at London 2012. On both occasions, she was beaten by Yuliya Zaripova on the big stage.

← A look of serene bliss is on Jessica Ennis's face as she completes the 800m knowing that the London 2012 Games Heptathlon gold medal was hers.

Women's 4 x 100m and 4 x 400m Relays

The first women's 4 x 100m Relay at the Games was held in 1928, 16 years after the first men's event in 1912. Women had to wait even longer to compete in the 4 x 400m Relay, which was introduced in 1972, a massive 60 years after the men's event. But it was worth the wait, as the women's Relay races brought some of the world's greatest sprinters together in formidable teams, such as the 1988 USA team, which featured the mighty Evelyn Ashford and the fastest woman in history, Florence Griffith-Joyner.

Evelyn Ashford

Evelyn Ashford of the United States claimed three of her four career Olympic Games gold medals in the women's 4 x 100m Relay, winning three consecutive titles between 1984 and 1992. In the 1984 final in Los Angeles, Ashford ran an anchor leg of 9.77 seconds, the fastest ever, to win her second gold medal of the Games following her success in the women's 100m final. During the final of the 1988 Games, Ashford recovered from a sloppy handover with Florence Griffith-Joyner to overcome her long-time rival Marlies Göhr of East Germany in the anchor leg.

Quick wrap-up

The sprint events at Seoul 1988 belonged to one American, Florence Griffith-Joyner, known to her fans as 'Flo-Jo'. Hailed as the fastest woman of all time (as long-term holder of records for the women's 100m and 200m), Flo-Jo capped off a remarkable Games by helping the US team to victory in the women's 4 x 100m Relay. In the final, Griffith-Joyner came into the passing area first in her leg of the race, and anchor Evelyn Ashford, in spite of their poor handover, completed the win for the American team in 41.98 seconds, giving Griffith-Joyner her third gold medal of the Games. Her bid for a fourth gold fell short as the United States took silver in the women's 4 x 400m Relay. Griffith-Joyner, born in Los Angeles, was the wife of triple jumper Al Joyner and the sister-in-law of heptathlete and long jumper Jackie Joyner-Kersee. She first came to prominence when finishing fourth in the 200m at the inaugural World Championship in 1983.

← *Florence Griffith-Joyner won her third gold at Seoul 1988 in the women's 4 x 100m final.*

The Flying Housewife

As the Relay Races are among the final track running events at the Olympic Games, many of the best sprinters have used these events to cap off individual solo successes. At 30 and a mother of two, Dutch athlete Fanny Blankers-Koen was dismissed by many as being too old in the run-up to the 1948 Games in London, before the 'Flying Housewife' went on to win four gold medals in the women's sprint events. Blankers-Koen began her haul with the women's 100m, which she won in 11.9 seconds, and continued with wins in the 80m Hurdles – in a then Games record time of 11.2 – and the women's 200m. She then completed her sweep in the women's 4 x 100m Relay, running the anchor leg. The Netherlands took the gold medal in a time of 47.5.

↑ *Fanny Blankers-Koen anchors the Netherlands to victory in the women's 4 x 100m final at London 1948.*

US dominance

The United States women's teams have dominated the relay events at the Olympic Games. The American women won 10 women's 4 x 100m Relay titles out of the 20 contested between 1928 and 2012. Meanwhile, in the women's 4 x 400m Relay, they have also continued to claim more honours than any other team, winning six of the 11 titles on offer between 1972 and 2012, including five consecutive victories between 1996 and 2012.

London 2012

Inroads on history

The benchmark for the women's sprint relay was set in the mists of time. The 1980s East German squads, whose validity to hold records has been called into question by revelations since German re-unification, set Olympic and world records that have never been approached ... until now. Perhaps it was the competition with Jamaica, but the United States 4 x 100m Relay team were in inspired form at London 2012. Tianna Madison ran one of the great lead-off legs in history to set the tone. Next up was 200-metre champion Allyson Felix, who glided down the back straight and then Bianca Knight bustled around the turn to hand Carmelita Jeter a five-metre lead. Jeter powered down the straight as the clock seemingly struggled to keep up. It stopped at 40.82, more than half-a-second inside a mark which had stood for 27 years.

↑ The United States women's Relay teams were utterly dominant. Whilst the 4 x 400m Relay team broke no records, they won the race by 3.34 seconds.

⬇ Carmelita Jeter's final leg not only sealed women's 4 x 100m Relay gold at London 2012 for the United States, the team shattered the world record.

Jamaica have to settle for silver

Jamaica were always going to be up against it in the final of the women's 4 x 100m Relay at London 2012, but the big surprise was that they effectively lost the race on what should have been their strongest suit. Shelly-Ann Fraser-Pryce had retained her 100m title earlier in the week, so Jamaica would have expected to be ahead after the first leg, particularly as the champion was up against a converted long jumper in Tianna Madison. However, Fraser-Pryce could make no impression on Madison and, in fact, lost ground. Sherone Simpson was no match for Allyson Felix on the second leg and the battle was lost. Even the great Veronica Campbell-Brown had too much to do on her trademark curve. Consolation came from a time of 41.41 – the fastest in Jamaican history.

United States by a distance

The final women's event of the London 2012 Olympic Games was also one of the biggest anti-climaxes. Excellence is to be treasured in sport, but the 4 x 400m relay relies on closely fought battles to create a spectacle. After 500 metres of the women's 4 x 400m Relay at London 2012 the result was a foregone conclusion. America's DeeDee Trotter, bronze medallist in the individual 400m, ran 49.5 and Allyson Felix, going for her third gold of the Games ran ever faster – 48.8. It was game over, and it was left to Francena McCorory and 400m champion Sanya Richards-Ross to bring the baton home for the United States fully 30 metres clear of the silver medallists. The dominance recalled the East German displays in the long form of the women's relay in the 1980s but in a very different context.

Silver solace for Russian Federation

The Russian Federation and Jamaica were always resigned to the pressure from the challenge of pursuing the seemingly uncatchable Americans in the women's 4 x 400m Relay at London 2012. From well before the halfway mark the teams settled into a straight fight for silver. Tatyana Firova got the better of Shericka Williams on the third leg, which is usually the pivotal circuit of this relay – unless you have someone good enough to win bronze individually on the opening leg. The Russians had 400m Hurdles gold medallist Natalya Antyukh on the anchor lap and that made the difference. Antyukh was able to use the strength and resilience she uses over the barriers to ensure that Novlene Williams-Mills would not get past her.

World Record

Event	Name	Country	Record	Date
Women's 4 x 100m Relay	United States	USA	40.82	10 August

Women's Road Events

Although the Marathon has been contested by men at every Games since Athens 1896, the first women's Marathon did not take place until Los Angeles 1984. The women's 20km Race Walk has been part of the Games programme since Sydney 2000.

Oldest Marathon champion

At 38 years of age, Romania's Constantina Tomescu won the 2008 women's Marathon in Beijing in 2:26:44, beating her nearest rival by 22 seconds. Her gold medal triumph not only made her the oldest Marathon champion ever, male or female, but also the oldest Marathon medallist in the history of the Games.

⬆ *Romania's Constantina Tomescu heads the women's Marathon field at Beijing 2008.*

Women make their point

In 1966, after not being granted an official entry into the Boston Marathon, Roberta Gibb joined the race from behind a bush – and finished in an unofficial time of 3:21:25. The following year, K.V. Switzer entered the Boston Marathon and it wasn't until two miles into the race that officials realised the runner was a woman, Kathrine Switzer. Despite the officials' best efforts, 20-year-old Switzer finished the race, and the following day the national papers propelled the issue of women's long-distance running into the public eye. Switzer went on to lobby for the inclusion of a women's Marathon at the Olympic Games and was instrumental in the IOC's decision in 1981 to introduce the event.

Debut drama

Perhaps the most dramatic scenes at the inaugural women's Marathon at Los Angeles 1984 – and indeed of the entire Games – came after the medals had been decided. Entering the stadium around 20 minutes after winner Joan Benoit, Swiss competitor Gabriele Andersen-Scheiss had spectators gasping in horror when she staggered on to the track, painfully exhausted. Cheered on by the crowd, she stumbled and limped towards the finish line in clear distress, before collapsing into the arms of waiting medics. Her courageous effort placed her 37th of 44 finishers, with a time of 2:48:42, and immortalised Andersen-Scheiss in Games folklore as a symbol of courage and determination.

History girl

The women's Marathon was finally introduced to the Olympic Games programme at Los Angeles 1984, marking the day that women runners had long been campaigning for. American runner Joan Benoit was one of 50 competitors from 28 nations who started the first women's Marathon, and she went on to be the first champion, winning on home soil in 2:24:52. Norwegian Grete Waitz finished second and Portugal's Rosa Mota third.

First for Japan

Naoko Takahashi created history at the 2000 Olympic Games in Sydney, becoming the first Japanese woman to collect a track and field gold medal when she won the women's Marathon. She joined the record books in style, setting an Olympic record time of 2:23:14. Afterwards she went on to become the first woman to break the magical 2:20 barrier, running 2:19:46, the world's fastest time, at the 2001 Berlin Marathon.

➡ *Japan's Naoko Takahashi takes women's Marathon gold at Sydney 2000.*

⬆ *A moment of quiet despair for Paula Radcliffe after she pulled out of the Marathon at Athens 2004.*

Remarkable Radcliffe

Paula Radcliffe is synonymous with female Marathon running. The British runner enjoyed massive success on the big-city marathon circuit, with multiple wins in London, New York and Chicago. Following an impressive track career, Radcliffe's Marathon debut in London in 2002 set a best time (2:18:56) for a women's-only race, a European record and the fastest ever debut over the 26-mile distance. After she had smashed the world record by 1:29 in Chicago later that year with a time of 2:17:18, it was on home soil that Radcliffe set her incredible world record of 2:15:25 at the 2003 London Marathon – a time not bettered by any British male in that year. Radcliffe's dream of Olympic Games gold was shattered at Athens 2004. Having gone into the race a firm favourite, she pulled out at the 23-mile mark. Her disappointment at the Games continued at Beijing 2008, when she struggled to a 23rd-place finish.

Time out…

Paula Radcliffe confirmed her place in marathon folklore in 2005 with a 15-second toilet stop on the side of the road five miles from the finish of the London Marathon. She duly powered to her third London title in 2:17:42.

World record

Vera Sokolova broke the world record in the women's 20km walk at the 2011 Russian Federation national championships, shaving 33 seconds off the previous record set by fellow Russian Olimpiada Ivanova in 2005.

Walking in

The women's Race Walk has only recently been welcomed into the Olympic Games programme. After being introduced as a 10-kilometre event in 1992, it was then replaced by a 20km walk in 2000. At the 2008 Olympic Games in Beijing, Olga Kaniskina won the gold medal and set a then Games record for the fastest women's 20km Race Walk in a time of 1:26:31, smashing the previous record of 1:29.05 set by Wang Liping at Sydney 2000.

London 2012

Lashmanova is 'The One'

Women have only one Race Walk at the Olympic Games, the 20km event, so all available talent at the sport has only one chace of glory. At the London 2012 Games, the defending champion from Beijing 2008, Olga Kaniskina, set the pace on the 10 circuits around some of the city's best-known tourist attractions and at 14 kilometres she had a 33-second lead, but Elena Lashmanova cut that to 17 seconds with two kilometres to go. Lashmanova, surged up and down the hill alongside Buckingham Palace and, with less than 200 metres to go, caught her Russian Federation team-mate, going on to win by seven seconds in a world record 1.25.02.

Never mind the rain

Marathon runners do not mind the rain so London – which hosts a popular and well-supported annual event each spring – is a favourite venue. Heavy rain greeted the starters of Olympic Games Marathon but, by halfway, the rain had subsided. Africans, as is often the case, dominated the race, but there was a strong Eastern European presence too. It was an Ethiopian, Tiki Gelana, who seized the moment, powering to victory in a time of 2.23.07. Kenya's Priscah Jeptoo held off the Russian Federation's Tatyana Arkhipova to claim silver.

⬆ *Tiki Gelana of Ethiopia splashed through the London rain to win the women's Marathon in the fastest time ever recorded in the Olympic Games.*

World Record

Event	Name	Country	Record	Date
Women's 20km Race Walk	Elena Lashmanova	RUS	1:25:02	11 August

Olympic Record

Event	Name	Country	Record	Date
Women's Marathon	Tiki Gelana	ETH	2:23:07	5 August

Women's High Jump and Pole Vault

The High Jump was one of five events – along with 100m, 800m, 4 x 100m Relay and Discus Throw – to be contested by women at the Amsterdam 1928 Olympic Games (and the 800m was then dropped for 32 years). In contrast, the women's Pole Vault is relatively new to the Olympic Games: it was staged for the first time at Sydney 2000.

Rolling and diving

High jumping has long been regarded as an event open to experimental technique, the most prominent example being the introduction of the Fosbury Flop by US athlete Dick Fosbury at Mexico City 1968. However, in 1932, when Babe Didrikson leaped to a new world record of 1.67 metres, tying with her US compatriot Jean Shiley in Los Angeles, it was Shiley that was awarded the gold medal. Didrikson had used the Western Roll technique, which at the time was regarded as 'diving', so was awarded silver.

Test of time

In 1987, Bulgaria's Stefka Kostadinova set a women's high jump world record of 2.09 metres. It remained one of the longest-standing world records in modern athletics and was one of seven world records (both indoor and outdoor) that Kostadinova set in a glittering career. Having won a silver medal at the 1988 Games in Seoul, Kostadinova went one better at Atlanta 1996, winning the gold medal with a Games record of 2.05m. Later she became President of the Bulgarian Olympic Committee.

⬇ Bulgaria's Stefka Kostadinova leaps to gold in the women's High Jump at Atlanta 1996. She had won a silver medal in the event at Seoul 1988.

Saskatoon Lily

The women's High Jump competition at the Games began with a touch of glamour at Amsterdam 1928. The winner, Ethel Catherwood, broke the world record with a height of 1.59 metres, becoming the first (and still the only) Canadian female athlete to have won individual gold in track and field at the Games. Her natural good looks did not go unnoticed and a *New York Times* correspondent labelled her the 'prettiest girl athlete', while she earned the nickname 'Saskatoon Lily'. After her success Catherwood became embroiled in scandal, with two failed marriages conducted in the media spotlight. She later moved to California and admitted she was really an American, having been born in Hannah, North Dakota.

← *Ethel Catherwood became the first Olympic Games' women's High Jump champion at Amsterdam 1928.*

Csak's special celebration in Berlin

Hungarian high jumper Ibolya Csák won one of the closest women's High Jump competitions ever seen at the Games, at Berlin 1936. Three competitors cleared 1.60 metres, but all failed to clear 1.62m, until Csák succeeded at the fourth attempt. As a Jew, her victory had extra poignancy, coming at a time of increasing anti-Semitism in Germany. Two years later she became European champion in bizarre circumstances, after the winner, Dora Ratjen, was disqualified for being a man; his participation was a ploy by the Nazis.

Meyfarth the mighty

Ulrike Meyfarth went into the record books as the youngest and then the oldest women's High Jump champion at the Games. The German's first gold medal came in 1972 at her home Games in Munich. The 16-year-old was among athletes who had already and eagerly adopted Dick Fosbury's technique and her enterprise saw her win the gold medal with a world record-equalling height of 1.92 metres. After that her career went into decline, but in 1982 she returned to set a new world record (2.02m), becoming European champion for good measure. The absence of Soviet bloc competitors at Los Angeles 1984 enabled Meyfarth to reclaim her title 12 years on, this time as the oldest woman ever to win the High Jump.

London 2012

Chicherova on a high

The high jump has a fascination all of its own. No equipment is needed, just a human being reaching for the sky. The women's final of the High Jump at London 2012 was of a higher all-round quality than the men's with four athletes clearing two metres, the benchmark of world-class in the event. The reigning world champion was Anna Chicherova of the Russian Federation, and she was in the heart of the battle. She was the only competitor clear at the first attempt at all heights through to 2.03 metres. After her first failure at 2.05 metres, Chicherova's clearance at the second attempt was enough to secure gold as both American Brigetta Barrett and Chicherova's team-mate Svetlana Shkolina both failed to achieve a clearance in three attempts at that height.

↑ *Russian Federation's 2011 world champion Anna Chicherova was again the best and most consistent in the field of the women's High Jump at London 2012, winning the gold medal with the only clearance at 2.05 metres.*

When losing is winning

In some cases the biggest battle is just making the Olympic Games. India is still finding its feet in Olympic sport and has yet to achieve the success that its huge population potentially provides. High jumper Sahana Kumari hails from a tiny village in the deep south and was the last Indian athlete to earn a passport to London, setting a national record of 1.92 metres. In qualifying for the women's High Jump at London 2012 she cleared 1.80 metres but bowed out when 1.85 metres proved insurmountable. Athletes like Kumari are trailblazers. India has no tradition in high jump but through her efforts she has put her country on the international stage.

Tough assignment for Isinbayeva

In the short history of the women's Pole Vault at the Olympic Games one name stands above all others. Elena Isinbayeva of the Russian Federation is, unquestionably, the greatest exponent of the art the world has seen. Her world record of 5.06 metres has been untouchable, no one else has even cleared five metres. The weather is a great leveller in her sport, though, and Isinbayeva battled the wind and rain to try to win her third Olympic title, but could only clear 4.70 metres. She used her experience to pass a third attempt at 4.75 metres, going on to 4.80 metres instead. On a fair day it should not have been a problem, but this was anything but and Isinbayeva ceded her crown. Even legends can have their off-days.

Suhr makes sure

London's weather is variable and in the summer of 2012 never was the phenomenon seen more than during the Olympic fortnight, where daytime temperatures swung from 12 to 32 degrees, clear skies to intense cloud, sunshine to rain and from still to windy conditions. A strong headwind is not ideal for pole vaulters but that was what the women faced for their final. Only four cleared a modest 4.55 metres and the winning height was just 4.75 metres. American Jennifer Suhr emerged victorious after just three successful leaps and three failures at 4.80 metres. It was good enough for gold on count back, due to fewer misses. This was not vintage competition but for Suhr the gold medal was all that mattered.

← *Jennifer Suhr battled unhelpful weather conditions and adapted better than all her rivals in the women's Pole Vault final to win the gold medal.*

Women's Long Jump and Triple Jump

The women's Long Jump has been part of the Games programme since London 1948. Remarkably, no woman has retained her title, although Germany's Heike Drechsler took gold in 1992 and 2000. The women's Triple Jump was staged for the first time at Sydney 2000.

↑ *Mary Rand won the women's Long Jump at the Tokyo 1964 Games to become Britain's first female track and field gold medallist.*

Kick-start for Niger

Chioma Ajunwa set the standard for female athletes across Africa in 1996, when she became the first African woman to win an Olympic gold medal in a field event. Ajunwa had already represented Nigeria at football, but it was her success in the women's Long Jump at Atlanta 1996 that ultimately led to the police officer being made a Member of the Order of Niger. In the final, she jumped 7.12 metres to secure gold – as well as a chieftaincy title from her home state Imo.

Dominant Drechsler

Across three decades East Germany's Heike Drechsler was a name to fear in women's Long Jump or sprint races. During 1986, she twice equalled the women's 200m world record, but is perhaps best remembered for her Long Jump exploits. Drechsler is the only athlete to have won two women's Long Jump gold medals at the Games and, in 1983, she became the inaugural world champion. Her first gold medal came at Barcelona 1992; that same year Drechsler jumped 7.63 metres at altitude in Sestriere, a distance 11 centimetres further than the current world record. She won a second gold medal at Sydney 2000, at which point it was claimed she had won more than 400 Long Jump competitions with jumps over 7 metres.

↓ *Heike Drechsler leaps to women's Long Jump gold at the Sydney 2000 Games. Following her win in 1992, she is the event's only two-time winner.*

The gifted Mary Rand

Great Britain's women have a long and successful history in track and field events at the Games. It all started with Mary Rand, who took the gold medal in the women's Long Jump competition at Tokyo 1964. A successful pentathlon competitor, Rand had disappointed in the women's Long Jump at Rome 1960, but four years later in Tokyo, she jumped 6.52 metres in the qualifying round, to set a new Games record. In the final, Rand broke the world record with a leap of 6.76m and followed up with a silver medal in the Pentathlon and a bronze in the women's 4 x 100m Relay. Her room-mate Ann Packer, who won the women's 800m gold medal in Tokyo, later paid tribute to Rand : 'Mary was the most gifted athlete I ever saw. She was as good as athletes get; there has never been anything like her since. And I don't believe there ever will.'

Lebedeva's long wait

At Athens 2004, Russian athlete Tatyana Lebedeva went into the women's Long Jump final with a frustrating succession of Olympic Games silver and bronze medals behind her. She had already twice been a triple jump world champion, but now she had been thwarted three times in her bid for Olympic Games gold after being hot favourite for that event. In Greece, fortunately, compensation was at hand in the women's Long Jump. Her leap of 7.07 metres took her to the gold medal by just two centimetres, ahead of her Russian team-mates Irina Simagina and Tatyana Kotova. It is the only time the event has seen a clean sweep of the medals by one nation.

London 2012

Reese all clear

The halcyon days of the Long Jump at the Olympic Games, when Jackie Joyner-Kersee, Heike Drechsler and Galina Chistyakova battled to be queen of the sand with consistent seven-metre leaps, are long gone but there was a spark that something big may be around the corner in Brittney Reese's progress to the gold medal at London 2012. Reese, the two-time world champion both indoors and out, failed to pass the magic seven in finishing fifth at Beijing 2008, but she made a mark no one else could match in the first round at London 2012 with a 7.12-metre effort. This was just 40 centimetres off Chistyakova's 24-year-old world record.

⬆ *Olga Rypkova won the women's Triple Jump final with 14.98 metres in the third round. Her fifth attempt, at 14.86, would also have been good enough.*

⬇ *Brittney Reese had only two legal leaps in the women's Long Jump final, but her second-round effort was enough to bring her the gold medal.*

Rypakova prevails

The women's Triple Jump was the domain of veteran athletes at London 2012. Both Tatyana Lebedeva and Yamile Aldama were competing at ages nearer 40 than 30, but it was the relative youngster, 27-year-old, Olga Rypakova who clinched gold for Kazakhstan after an exciting final. Rypakova took the lead in the first round with a 14.54-metre effort but the response was swift with Hanna Knyazyeva edging ahead in the second round by two centimetres for Ukraine. In the third round Colombian Caterine Ibarguen made a mark of 14.67 metres but Rypakova resumed leadership shortly afterwards with 14.98 metres. It was to prove to be the winning performance. The standard was not on a par with previous major championships but the former heptathlete had proven her competitive instincts when it mattered. Aldhama, who turned 40 nine days after the final, was fifth, and 36-year-old Lebedeva finished 10th.

Out of focus

One of the most disappointed competitors on a sultry evening in London on 8 August was British No.1 Shara Proctor. She could hardly be termed as a familiar figure to home fans, having been born and brought up on the Caribbean island of Anguilla, but with the British overseas territory not having its own National Olympic Committee, her only route into the Games was as a member of Team GB. And, as a British passport holder, she was perfectly eligible to wear the red, white and blue. Proctor finished top of the qualifying list for the final of the women's Long Jump, raising hopes of a fourth gold medal for the hosts, but failed to build on a below-par opening effort of 6.55 metres. 'I lost my focus,' she admitted afterwards.

Saladuha misses out

Olha Saladuha is one of the outstanding athletes to emerge from Ukraine since the country gained independence from the old Soviet Union. Born before the split, in the industrial region around Donetsk, she put industrial concentration into her athletics career and broke through at top international level by winning triple jump gold at the European Championship in Barcelona in 2010. Gold followed in the 2011 World Championships in Daegu and the European Championships in Helsinki in June 2012, with a personal best of 14.99 metres. These previous successes should have been the springboard for Olympic gold in the women's Triple Jump at London 2012, but Saladuha had an off day and claimed only a bronze with her final leap of 14.79 metres.

Women's Discus and Hammer Throws

The women's Discus Throw is one of four events to have been contested by women at every Olympic Games since Amsterdam 1928. The women's Hammer Throw, on the other hand, is a relatively new event: it has only been part of the Games programme since the Sydney 2000.

Renaissance girl

The lineage of French athlete Micheline Ostermeyer suggested that she might be artistically inclined. The great-niece of author Victor Hugo was also the niece of composer Lucien Paroche so, unsurprisingly, Ostermeyer's formative years were spent playing the piano. The outbreak of the Second World War saw Ostermeyer return to her family home in Tunisia, where she began to participate in sports. On returning to France, she became a formidable athlete, and at London 1948 won the women's Shot Put and the Discus Throw – having only picked up a discus for the first time a few weeks before. Afterwards, at the French base, she provided her team-mates with an impromptu performance of piano music by Beethoven.

↑ *Micheline Ostermeyer won women's Discus Throw gold at London 1948.*

Prescription for success

Aksana Miankova's hopes of competing at the Olympic Games could have been dashed in her formative years. The 2008 gold medallist came from a family of doctors in Belarus, and such was her mother's disapproval of her daughter's athletic aspirations that Miankova had to attend training while her mother was at work. She was introduced to the hammer aged 15 and began to win regional titles before stepping into international competition. Her crowning moments came in 2008, when first she achieved her personal best throw of 77.32 metres and then, in Beijing, won the gold medal with a Games record throw of 76.34m.

Discus delight

Only East German Evelin Jahl has won successive women's Discus Throw titles at the Games. She beat world record holder Faina Melnyk at Montreal 1976 and beat her for gold again at Moscow 1980.

Lost century

The men's Hammer Throw contest has been contested since the 1900 Games, but it took another 100 years before a women's competition was established. The IAAF started to ratify women's marks only from 1995, and the first major event was the 1999 World Championships, with Sydney playing host to the first Olympic Games competition a year later.

➡ *Nina Ponomaryova won women's Discus Throw gold at the Helsinki 1952 Games.*

Prize pole

Halina Konopacka's success in the first women's Discus Throw event at the Games, at Amsterdam 1928, made her Poland's first Olympic Games champion. This was the first women's gold-winning track and field event in the Olympic Games and Konopacka broke her own world record with a throw of 39.62 metres. After she retired from sport, Konopacka became a renowned poet and painter, releasing a collection of poems in 1929 called *Someday*. She later moved to the United States, became a member of the Board of the International Women's Sports Federation and played a role in the Polish Olympic Movement.

Soviet starter

Nina Ponomaryova's story is a remarkable tale of glory in an era of heightened world tension. Ponomaryova competed at four Olympic Games, twice winning the gold medal in the women's Discus Throw. However, her gold medal at Helsinki 1952, where she set a new Games record of 51.42 metres, has the distinction of being the first gold medal for any Soviet athlete. It was the first time her country had competed at the Games since 1912. Her huge strength and fitness earned her the nickname the 'Iron Lady'. She followed up with a second gold medal at Rome 1960. Ponomaryova's rise to prominence was remarkable given that she lived in one of Stalin's gulags until the age of six, when her parents moved to a Cossack village in Southern Russia.

London 2012

⬆ *Croatia collected six medals from six different sports at London 2012, inlcuding Sandra Perkovic's gold in the Discus Throw.*

Sharing the glory

Sandra Perkovic's gold medal-winning performance in the women's Discus Throw was greeted warmly by the London 2012 crowd. The Croatian benefited from the all-enveloping feel-good factor in the Olympic Stadium on the middle Saturday when her own triumph was sandwiched between the glories of three British gold medals. Not that Perkovic minded. She celebrated with a smile as wide as all the other winners that night, happy also that she had won with a winning throw of 69.11 metres, a national record. The Russian Federation's silver medallist, Darya Pishchalnikova, could not match her world-leading 2012 effort of beyond 70 metres set at her national championships.

Li off course

Discus throwing is a hit or miss affair. Get it right and the disc can whiz through the air beyond 70 metres, get it wrong and it ends up in the netting alongside the circle. China's Yanfeng Li had such a final competition at the Olympic Stadium at London 2012. After an initial no throw, she propelled the discus to 67.22 metres to go into the lead, only for eventual gold medallist Sandra Perkovic to take it off her. Li failed to register a throw in rounds three and four, and although she got it right in round five, it was only 63.64 metres. She had one last chance to defend what was now the bronze medal position, but she fouled out. Li recorded only two legal throws and won bronze, but was a gold medal almost literally thrown away?

Spot the difference

For the majority of athletics fans the hammer is a worthy if unglamorous event. The women's title, a relatively new addition to the track and field roster, rarely dips above the radar but the London 2012 Olympic final was an extraordinary contest featuring 'the throw that never was'. With the naked eye, Betty Heidler's fifth round effort landed beyond 75 metres and was challenging for second place. The judges declared via the scoreboard that it was only just in excess of 70 metres. Heidler was confused. China's Wenxiu Zhang, whose best throw was 76.34 metres, ran off celebrating a bronze but then Heidler was informed that the judges had re-measured her throw, this time correctly, at 77.12 metres, and she was promoted to third place.

Lysenko back with a bang

Tatyana Lysenko missed the Beijing 2008 Olympic Games, but the former world record holder proved a force back on the Olympic stage at London 2012 for the first time in eight years. To prove a point, the Russian Federation thrower opened her competition in the women's Hammer Throw by breaking the Olympic record, set at Beijing 2008, with 77.56 metres. She held onto her lead and made sure of victory by adding 62 centimetres in round five with a new Olympic record of 78.18 metres. Lysenko had first set a world best in 2005, and her gold-medal throw was only 1.24 metres short of Betty Heidler's world record set in 2011.

⬇ *Tatyana Lysenko broke the Olympic record with a 78.18-metre effort in the Hammer Throw final. World record-holder Betty Heidler settled for bronze.*

Olympic Record

Event	Name	Country	Record	Date
Women's Hammer Throw	Tatyana Lysenko	RUS	78.18	10 August

Women's Shot Put and Javelin Throw

Two of the more established events on the women's Athletics programme, women's Javelin Throw and Shot Put have been staged since Los Angeles 1932 and London 1948 respectively. Both disciplines have been dominated by Eastern European athletes over the years.

↑ *East Germany's Ruth Fuchs defended her title with a throw of 65.94 metres at the Montreal 1976 Games.*

Talented Babe

The women's Javelin Throw was contested at the Games for the first time at Los Angeles 1932. The first winner was fittingly an American, Mildred 'Babe' Didrikson, who threw 43.69 metres to claim gold and then went on to achieve a second success in the women's 80m Hurdles. This, however, represents only a fraction of her achievements: Didrikson reached All-American status at basketball, played organised baseball and softball, was an expert diver, roller skater and bowler and even recorded records as a singer and harmonica player. Outside the Olympic Games, however, Didrikson's main exploits were in golf. Having been denied amateur status, she competed against the men in the Los Angeles Open – a PGA event – in 1938. No woman would repeat this for another 60 years. 'The Babe' was named the tenth Greatest North American Athlete of the 20th Century by ESPN, and the ninth Greatest Athlete of the 20th Century by the Associated Press.

↖ *A woman of many talents, Babe Didrikson won women's Javelin Throw gold at the 1932 Games.*

Gale force Fuchs

Only two women have made a successful defence of their titles in women's Javelin Throw at the Games, the first being East German Ruth Fuchs. During the 1970s Fuchs broke the world record six times, but her defining moments came at the 1972 and 1976 Games. She later became a Member of Parliament in the unified Germany.

Six of the best

Soviet athlete Natalya Lisovskaya is almost certainly the greatest shot-putter in the history of the sport. She set the first of her world records in 1984, aged 21, with a throw of 22.53 metres. Her mark of 22.63m in 1987 remains the world record, but perhaps the clearest demonstration of her dominance came at Seoul 1988. Lisovskaya not only won the gold medal, but also every one of her six throws was good enough to win the competition.

Kiwi crowning

When Valerie Vili threw 20.56m in the women's Shot Put final at Beijing 2008, she won New Zealand's first track and field gold medal since John Walker's won the 1976 men's 1500m. Vili received the 2008 New Zealand Sports Award for her success and was crowned world champion in 2009.

Eastern effort

For over two decades Soviet bloc countries dominated the women's Shot Put event at the Olympic Games. Nadezhda Chizhova of the Soviet Union won three consecutive titles from 1968, including the gold medal at the 1972 Games in Munich. In a glittering career, Chizhova also set seven world records and became the first woman to break both the 20-metre and 21-metre barriers.

Winning words

Czechoslovak javelin thrower Dana Zátopková was as formidable a character in her press conferences as she was a competitor at the 1952 Olympic Games in Helsinki. Remarkably, her husband Emil Zátopek won men's 5000m gold barely an hour before she won the women's Javelin Throw competition with a throw of 50.47m. At the press conference that ensued, Emil suggested his victory had inspired his wife, to which she replied, 'Really? OK, go inspire some other girl and see if she throws a javelin 50 metres!' She became the oldest woman (at 35) to set a world record, with a throw of 55.73m in 1958, and two years later won a silver medal at the Olympic Games in Rome.

London 2012

What a difference a day makes

New Zealander Valerie Adams is a novelty in her event. Shot Put has a reputation of being a European domain and the facts bear that out. Adams, who won the event at Beijing 2008 as Valerie Vili, is one of only two non-Europeans to win this particular gold. She confirmed her status with world titles in 2009 and 2011. At London 2012, Adams took the lead in the women's Shot Put with her first throw of 20.61 metres only to be overtaken by Nadezeya Ostapchuk of Belarus. Adams learned, only the day after the Closing Ceremony, that she had been promoted to gold after Ostapchuk was disqualified by order of the International Olympic Committee having failed a doping control test.

Crying Games

The Russian Federation's Evgeniia Kolodko was one of the many competitors at London 2012 who contributed to a record-breaking flood of tears, created by both defeat and victory. Kolodko burst into tears after moving up into medals contention in the women's Shot Put with the very last of her six throws of 20.48 metres, just 22 centimetres behind Adams. Later Kolodko was promoted from bronze to silver. That throw was also a personal best for the former European under-23 champion who had first made her international mark on that occasion in Ostrava. The 22-year-old had never before competed at the Olympic Games.

↓ *The Czech Republic's long tradition of success in the Javelin Throw was continued by Barbara Spotakova in the women's event at London 2012.*

↑ *Valerie Adams successfully defended her Olympic Games Shot Put title at London 2012, but only after the original winner failed a doping control test.*

Spotakova's special delivery

Success breeds success and Czech javelin-throwing has been riding a wave of triumph ever since Jan Zelezny was breaking records and regularly picking up gold medals in this dramatic throwing event. The heiress to the great Zelezny's throne is Barbara Spotakova, who came to London as the defending Olympic champion and world record holder in the women's javelin. Spotakova took the lead with her first throw of the competition, 66.90 metres, a position she would not relinquish. With her second and third efforts Spotakova peppered the 66-metre mark without improving. In round four she unleashed a 69.55-metre throw, the best in the world in 2012, and that was that. The favourite had justified her standing; over four metres (a chasm at this level) separated her from the silver medallist.

Pride in a personal best

Athletics is a genuinely global sport, with world-class competitors involved from every region of the world – from the Caribbean to East Asia and Scandinavia to Oceania. One of the outposts, Iceland, sent only two male and one female athletes to London 2012. Javelin-thrower Asdís Hjalmsdottir was that woman and she fully justified her elite status in Icelandic sport with a qualifying throw of 62.77 metres – a new national record – to make the women's Javelin Throw final. She would have to go a similar distance to ensure a top eight finish but her opening effort of 59.08 metres was the best she could muster. An 11th place finish, but Hjalmsdottir is true to the Olympic motto that it is not the winning which counts as much as the taking part, and she also had the satisfaction of achieving a personal best at the London 2012 Games.

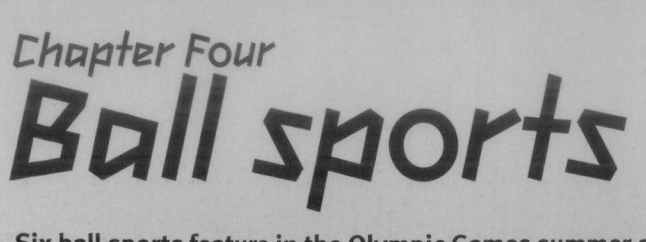

Chapter Four
Ball sports

Six ball sports feature in the Olympic Games summer schedule for London 2012 compared with eight in Beijing after which Baseball and Softball fell by the wayside.

Football was the first to come aboard, at the second of the modern Games in Paris in 1900. It has been present ever since, with the exception of Los Angeles in 1932. Up until 1928 in Amsterdam, the Olympic Games tournament was considered the unofficial world championship, but then the sport launched its own World Cup and that tournament quickly established pre-eminence.

London 1908 saw Hockey accepted to the Games programme, with Basketball and Handball 'arriving' in Berlin in 1936. Volleyball had to wait until Tokyo 1964, with the most recent addition being Beach Volleyball. This was a demonstration event at Barcelona 1992 and confirmed as a medal sport in 1996 in Atlanta.

The women's versions of the first four sports endured long waits for equality with Football needing the prospect – fulfilled – of a United States victory to join the Games in Atlanta in 1996.

Hockey produced the most bizarre twist in the equality tale. Its first women's tournament coincided with the boycott-hit Moscow Games of 1980. A makeshift Zimbabwe team – selected only the weekend before the Opening Ceremony – carried off the gold medal.

Jennifer Kessy (right) tips to ball over the net as Kerri Walsh Jennings defends during the women's Beach Volleyball final at the London 2012 Games. The all-United States final saw Walsh Jennings and Misty May-Treanor prevail over Kessy and April Ross in two sets.

Basketball

Men's basketball was contested for the first time at Berlin 1936, with the United States beating Canada (19–8) in the final. It was a sign of things to come: the United States have been the event's dominant team, winning gold on 13 (out of 16) occasions. It has been a similar story in women's Basketball, with the United States winning five of the seven tournaments contested since 1976.

Schmidt, Gaze and Cruz

Only three men have played Basketball at five different Games – and two of them lead the overall rankings for points scored. Brazil's Oscar Schmidt scored 1,093 points in the 1980, 1984, 1988, 1992 and 1996 tournaments, and his average of 28.8 per match is also a record. Second is Australia's Andrew Gaze, with 789 points spread across the 1984, 1988, 1992, 1996 and 2000 events – he also had the honour of carrying the host nation's flag at Sydney 2000's Opening Ceremony. His father Lindsey Gaze had played Basketball for Australia at the 1960, 1964 and 1968 Games and coached the team in 1972, 1976, 1980 and 1984. Puerto Rico's Teofilo Cruz was not only the first Basketball player, but also the first athlete in any team sport, to compete at five Olympic Games (1960, 1964, 1968, 1972 and 1976).

➔ *Australia's Andrew Gaze in action against Russia at his record-equalling fifth-and-final Games at Sydney in 2000.*

Undying hurt

After seven consecutive gold medals and an unblemished record in 63 matches, the first United States Basketball team to be denied the top prize at an Olympic Games felt so upset by their 51–50 defeat to the USSR, that they refused to accept the silver medals they were due. Four decades on from the dramatic Final at Munich in 1972, the silver medals still remain in the possession of the International Olympic Committee.

◀ *The tip-off at the 1972 Olympic Games Basketball Final that saw the United States lose for the first time.*

Moving homes

The Basketball finals at the London 2012 Games were played at the 20,000-seater North Greenwich Arena. The early qualifying rounds of the Basketball tournament were played in the temporary 12,000-capacity Basketball Arena, which was located in the Olympic Park. Once Basketball moved to Greenwich, the Basketball Arena became home to the men's and women's Handball finals, the earlier rounds which had been staged at the Copper Box, also in the Olympic Park, but it had only 7,000 seats

➔ *Former NBA star John Amoechi was part of the London 2012 bidding team.*

American dream

'Like Elvis and the Beatles put together' was how US Basketball coach Chuck Daly described the excitement and impact of his country's so-called 'Dream Team' at the Barcelona 1992 Olympic Games in Barcelona. A change in the rules made three years earlier meant that this was the first Games at which professional players were allowed to compete. Household names such as Earvin 'Magic' Johnson, Michael Jordan and Larry Byrd starred in a scintillating side whose average winning margin was as high as 43.8 points. The final against Croatia was their tightest game of the tournament – and yet they still cruised to a 117–85 win ... a margin of 32 points.

Five games, four golds

Teresa Edwards became the first – and, to date, only – female basketball player to compete at five different Games, when she won a gold medal with the United States team at Sydney 2000. She also won golds in 1984, 1988 and 1996, and a solitary bronze in 1992. The triumph in 1984, when aged 20, made her the youngest woman to win a Basketball gold medal at the Games – and the 2000 success made her the oldest, at 36.

↖ *Teresa Edwards is the only woman to play at five different Games.*

London 2012

Seven-up for Americans

American women have proved even more dominant in Olympic Basketball in the 21st century than their male counterparts. Their 85–50 crushing of France at London 2012 was their fifth gold medal in a row and seventh in all since the discipline entered the Games at Montreal 1976. The USA had constructed a decisive 12-point lead by halftime and then added a further 19 points without reply to by 30 in the third quarter after a French side appearing in the final for the first time. Candace Parker fulfilled a personal golden dream in scoring 21 points while Sandrine Gruda and Edwige Lawson-Wade claiming 12 points each for France. Australia claimed the bronze with an 83–74 victory over Russia, successors to the Soviet winners from Montreal 1976, Moscow 1980 and Barcelona 1992.

→ *Kobe Bryant (10) soars to the basket during the United States' 107–100 defeat of Spain in the men's Basketball final at the London 2012 Olympic Games.*

Dream on

The latest version of the 'Dream Team' brought gold home to the United States in the men's Basketball at London 2012, but their victory over Spain was anything but a points procession in a rematch of the Beijing 2008 final. Spain lost, in the end, by 107–100 in front of a thrilled 20,000 crowd at North Greenwich Arena. Kevin Durant, with 30 points, led the way for the Americans, supported by Kobe Bryant and LeBron James. They had been only 83–82 ahead going into the fourth quarter. Pau Gasol, who had won two NBA titles as a team-mate of Bryant at the Los Angeles Lakers, inspired a far tougher challenge than any before to the USA who had won all their previous seven matches by an average margin of 35 points.

Football

The FIFA World Cup is the only rival the Olympic Games has for the title of the world's pre-eminent sporting event. While most footballers regard the World Cup as their sport's top prize, the Olympic Games Football tournament has achieved its own niche after introducing a new rule in 1992, limiting the tournament to under-23s except for three over-age players per squad.

Future generations

Many players who have appeared in the Football tournament at the Olympic Games have gone on to become FIFA World Cup winners, including: Brazil's Dunga, Taffarel, Bebeto, Romario, Ronaldo and Roberto Carlos; Italy's Fabio Cannavaro, Andrea Pirlo, Daniele De Rossi and Gianluigi Buffon; France's Patrick Vieira, West Germany's Andreas Brehme and Jürgen Klinsmann, and Spain's Xavi Hernandez and Carles Puyol.

Far, far away...

Los Angeles may have been the official Host City for the 1984 Games, but the Football tournament was played in two venues situated more than 3,200 kilometres away: the Navy-Marine Corps Memorial Stadium in Annapolis, Maryland; and the Harvard Stadium in Boston, Massachusetts.

Africa calling

An injury-time winner by Emmanuel Amuneke not only gave Nigeria victory over Argentina in their 1996 Final showdown, but also secured Africa's first Football gold at the Games. Four years earlier, Ghana had finished third to become the continent's first Football medallists.

⬇ *Celebration time for Nigeria after they beat Argentina 3–2 in the 1996 final.*

Pioneering champions

Before the first FIFA World Cup was held in 1930, the four-yearly Olympic Games Football tournament was considered an equivalent world championship. Uruguay, who would both host and win the 1930 World Cup, went into the tournament having clinched Football gold in both 1924 and 1928 Games. José Nasazzi, José Andrade, Hector Scarone and Pedro Petrone played in all three winning teams.

⬆ *Uruguay's 1928 gold medal-winning team line up before the Final.*

Water works

Unusually, two breaks for water were allowed during the Football Final between Argentina and Nigeria at the 2008 Games, played on a baking hot afternoon in Beijing's Bird's Nest Stadium. With the temperature at 42° Celsius, the Argentina side, including Lionel Messi and winning goal-scorer Angel Di Maria, ultimately prevailed, winning 1–0 for the country's second successive Football gold medal.

➡ *Argentina's Lionel Messi takes a water break during the 2008 Final against Nigeria.*

Prolific women

Women's Football was introduced at the 1996 Games in Atlanta – and the United States have won four of the five tournaments held, finishing runners-up only at Sydney 2000. Brazil, like their men's team, have never won an Olympic gold medal, despite having some outstanding players. They reached the semi-finals in all of the first four tournaments, but lost in the final at both Athens 2004 and Beijing 2008. Brazil's brightest stars have been Cristiane and Marta, the latter five-times FIFA Women's World Player of the Year. Cristiane is the all-time leading scorer in women's Football at the Olympic Games with a total of 12 goals to her name.

← *Joy Fawcett (left) and Carin Gabarra celebrate the United States' victory in the final at the Atlanta 1996 Games.*

London 2012

USA bank on Lloyd

The United States won their fourth women's Olympic Football title in their fifth Final and, in doing so, avenged their defeat by Japan in the 2011 FIFA Women's World Cup final. Experienced goalkeeper Hope Solo played a key role in securing a 2–1 win but midfielder Carli Lloyd played the most decisive role. Lloyd had scored the Americans' extra-time winner in the gold medal-game victory over Brazil at Beijing 2008 but then missed a penalty in the shoot-out defeat by Japan in the 2011 FIFA Women's World Cup final. At Wembley, in front of a European women's record crowd of 80,203, she scored both USA goals. Canada, who had beaten debutantes Great Britain in the quarter-final, took the bronze medal after defeating France 1–0.

➡ *Carly Lloyd stoops to head home the United States' first goal as they beat Japan 2–1 to win gold.*

Brazil still waiting

Olympic gold continued to elude Brazil in the men's tournament at London 2012, as the favourites – featuring many of the stars expected to lead their FIFA World Cup bid in 2014 – lost 2–1 to Mexico at Wembley Stadium. Football attendances totalled a quarter of the London 2012 aggregate, and a crowd of 86,162 saw the Mexicans seize control with goals in each half from forward Oribe Peralta. Mexico thus won their first Olympic Football gold while Brazil salvaged 'only' a third silver. They have also twice won bronze. Great Britain, appearing at the Olympic Games in the event for the first time in 52 years, had been knocked out in the quarter-finals by the Republic of Korea. The Koreans went on to win bronze, beating Japan 2–0, at Cardiff's Millennium Stadium.

Handball

Men's Handball made its debut as at the Games at Berlin 1936 but did not feature again until the 1972 Games in Munich. Russia (in its various guises) have been the most successful team, claiming gold on four occasions. Women's Handball has been a regular feature of the Games since Montreal 1976 and Denmark lead the way with three victories.

There and back again

Like Basketball, Handball was introduced as a competitive sport at the 1936 Games in Berlin – but, unlike Basketball, which was back 12 years later, it had to wait another 36 years before returning. Romania went into the 1972 Olympic Games in Munich as favourites for Handball gold – and as reigning world champions – but were surprised in the final by the ultimate winners Yugoslavia. Women had to endure another four-year wait before making their Handball debut at the 1976 Games in Montreal. The game is played by 31 million people across 183 different countries, according to the International Handball Federation, but nothing gives it more exposure than its four-yearly place in the Olympic Games.

Celluloid heroines

The Republic of Korea's women's Handball team just missed out on gold, in agonising circumstances, at Athens 2004. Their final against Denmark went to extra time twice, before a penalty shoot-out finally separated the teams and gave Denmark a third championship in a row. But the epic efforts of the Korean team, after coming into the tournament with little fanfare or expectation, inspired a film called *The Best Moment of Our Lives*, which went on to become a hit with the country's cinema-goers.

⬇ *Tears all round for the Republic of Korea after their agonising final defeat to Denmark in 2004.*

Great Danes

The gold medal in the women's Handball events at the Games has been a Scandinavian monopoly since 1996, when Denmark won the first of three consecutive titles. Their triumphant run only came to an end at the 2008 Games in Beijing, when they were knocked out in the quarter-finals and neighbours Norway took the top prize instead. Recent Scandinavian dominance should come as no surprise – Denmark and Sweden were among the countries where the game was pioneered in the late 19th century, though the first official rules were published in 1917 by Germans Max Heiser, Karl Schelenz and Erich Konigh. The International Amateur Handball Federation was founded 11 years later, to coincide with the 1928 Olympic Games in Amsterdam – although it would be another eight years before Handball was contested at the Games for the first time.

Opening gold

Croatia's 27–26 victory over Sweden in the men's Handball Final at the 1996 Olympic Games in Atlanta gave the newly independent Balkan state their first ever Games gold medal. They went on to win gold again in 2004 – having failed to even qualify for the Handball tournament at the 2000 Games.

Talented talant

Talant Duyshebaev has won men's Handball medals at the Games for two different nations. The Kyrgyzstan-born player represented the CIS at the 1992 Games, helping his side take gold while finishing as tournament top scorer with 47 goals. After moving to Spain and taking Spanish citizenship, he represented his new nation at the 1996 and 2000 Games – winning bronze each time.

⬆ *Spain's Talant Duyshebaev in action at Athens 2004; 12 years earlier he had won bronze with Kyrgyzstan.*

↑ *Sweden's Magnus Wislander shoots during the Sydney 2000 Handball final against Russia.*

So near and yet so far

Sweden could claim to be the near-invincibles, with their men's Handball team winning every match at three consecutive Games – except, on each occasion, the final. Their last-ditch conquerors were the post-Soviet Confederation of Independent States (CIS) in 1992, Croatia in 1996 and Russia in 2000. Each of these Swedish sides featured the 'World Handball Player of the Century', as Magnus Wislander was dubbed in 1999 by the International Handball Federation. Wislander represented his country for 19 years, following his debut in January 1985, and played not only at the 1992, 1996 and 2000 Games, but also in 1988, when Sweden finished fifth. Although the gold medal eluded him, Wislander did help Sweden become world champions in 1990 and 1999 and European champions in 1994, 1998, 2000 and 2002.

On thin ice

Handball gave the world its final sight of Olympic Games sporting action in 2008 when France's 28–23 victory over Iceland in the men's Final was the last of the 302 events to be completed in Beijing. Iceland are still waiting for their first-ever gold, at either the Summer or Winter Games. The country's President Olafur Ragnar Grímsson described 24 August 2008 as the biggest day in Iceland's sporting history. Although they fell short of gold, clinching silver was Iceland's best achievement at any Olympic Games for 52 years.

↓ *France celebrate their 28–23 victory over Iceland at Beijing 2008. It was the last of the 302 events to be completed at the Games.*

London 2012

French double up

World champions France celebrated a remarkable double/double at London 2012 in becoming the first men's Handball team to defend their Olympic title. Their narrow 22–21 win sentenced Sweden to a fourth final defeat on their first appearance at the Games since Sydney 2000. Thierry 'Titi' Omeyer, France's former world player of the year and semi-final match-winner against Croatia, was in top form in goal as France repeated their 29–26 win from the group stages. Four goals in the final six minutes proved to be just too little too late for the Swedes, with Luc Abalo scored twice for France with just under 60 seconds remaining. That was described as a 'magic moment' by relieved team-mate Nikola Karabatic who had to sit out a two-minute suspension at the end.

↑ *Bertrand Gille acrobatically shoots at the Swedish goal during France's dramatic 23–22 victory in the final, but Johan Sjostrand made the save.*

Norway make their point

Norway's women's team reacted to some harsh early criticism from their own media to come through to win gold and justify their status as world and European champions. They had to come back from six goals down early in the second half against Brazil in the quarter-final then lifted up their shirts, at the subsequent press conference, to reveal T-shirts labeled 'Norges Lagand' (Norwegian team spirit). Norway went on to defeat Montenegro 26–23 in the final, a result which still left the Balkans with their first Olympic medal. 'It's remarkable,' said coach Dragan Adzic, 'I think we have only 100 female players in the entire country.' Spain won bronze.

Hockey

One of the oldest team sports on the Games roster, men's Hockey has been played at every Olympiad since London 1908 (bar 1912 and 1924). India were the event's early powerhouses, winning six consecutive gold medals between 1928 and 1956, although their dominance waned with the advent of astroturf pitches at Montreal 1976. Women's Hockey has been contested since Moscow 1980 and Australia have been the event's most successful team, with three victories.

← *England on the attack during their 8–1 victory over Ireland in the first-ever men's Hockey Final in 1908.*

India and Pakistan

The roots of hockey stretch back 4,000 years to 'stick-and-ball' games in Egypt. The sport first appeared at the Olympic Games with a men's competition at London 1908, since when it has featured at every Games except for those of 1912 and 1924. Hockey was dominated by India and Pakistan, where the sport is followed most fanatically, until the 1970s. India won all six gold medals at the Games from 1928 to 1956 and either they or Pakistan continued to be the teams to beat until 1972, when hosts West Germany took gold. Even since then India and Pakistan have never failed to qualify for a men's Hockey competition at the Games, although Pakistan boycotted Moscow 1980. The two countries' relative demise may be connected, as some believe, with the switch to artificial turf at the 1976 Games in Montreal, but India still managed to take gold again four years later and Pakistan four years after that. Women's Hockey first appeared on the Olympic Games programme at Moscow 1980, where Zimbabwe snatched a surprise gold.

Out ... and in

Men's Hockey was removed from the Games schedule at Paris 1924 owing to the lack of an international sporting structure. This led to the formation of the International Hockey Federation, and the sport became a permanent feature from 1928 onwards.

Women under way

Women's Hockey became full-medal sport at the Moscow 1980 Olympic Games (some 72 years after the men's Hockey competition had made its first appearance at the Games), but the outcome was one that few could have predicted as Zimbabwe (who had not trained together as a team in the build-up the event) snatched a surprise gold, pipping Czechoslovakia to finish at the top of the Championship Pool by a single point. Their victory chant was 'Forward with the rooster' – Robert Mugabe's party slogan. Their minister of sports promised each squad member a gift of an ox when they arrived home.

Independent success

In 1948, a year after gaining independence, India came to the post-war Games in London as reigning men's Hockey champions. The team had lost some players of English descent and a number of Muslims, who had moved to the new nation of Pakistan. These included Ali Dara, who in 1936 had played for India but in 1948 was Pakistan's captain. Nevertheless India reached the Final, where they beat Great Britain 4–0 to win gold. India outscored the competition in their five games, ending with a 25–2 aggregate.

Record success

The widest winning margin in a men's Hockey Final at an Olympic Games was seven goals. In 1908, England beat Ireland 8–1 in London, and in 1936 India beat Germany in Berlin by the same score. The highest margin of victory in any men's Hockey match at the Games was achieved by India at the 1932 Olympic Games in Los Angeles when they beat the United States 24–1.

Hat-trick hero

Dhyan Chand is arguably the greatest player the game of hockey has ever known. He won three gold medals as a centre-forward for India at the Games of 1928, 1932 and 1936. His birthday, on 29 August, is India's national sports day.

↑ *Dhyan Chand (standing on the back row, second left) led India to men's Hockey gold at the 1928, 1932 and 1936 Olympic Games.*

Pakistan breakthrough

Pakistan ended India's streak of six straight gold medals and 30 consecutive victories by winning the 1960 men's Final in Rome 1–0. India had outscored their opponents during those 30 games by 178 points to seven. The defeat ended India's streak of invincibility at the Games.

Pitching in

Synthetic pitches are mandatory for all international tournaments and for most national competitions. While hockey is still played on grass fields at some local levels and in lesser national divisions, it has been replaced by synthetic turf almost everywhere in the western world. Over the years, the game has become quicker, more skilful and, with the development of new techniques such as the Indian dribble, more exciting to watch.

Hawkes makes history

Australian midfielder Rechelle Hawkes competed in the Olympic Games for the first time at Barcelona 1988 and won the first of her three women's Hockey gold medals as Australia beat the Netherlands 3–2 in the semi-finals and then hosts the Republic of Korea by 2–0 in the final. At Barcelona 1992, Hawkes experienced a contrasting low point in her career when the Australians were upset 1–0 in the preliminaries by Spain. She then led her country back to the top at Atlanta 1996. Australia reached the final on the back of a 38-game unbeaten streak and again beat the Koreans, this time 3–1. Four years later, in Sydney, Hawkes recited the Athletes' Oath at the Opening Ceremony ... and duly ended up with another gold medal. She is the only female Hockey player to win three medals (let alone three gold medals) and the only one to win medals 12 years apart.

➔ *Gold medals in 1988, 1996 and 2000 earned Rechelle Hawkes a place in the history books.*

London 2012

Walsh toughs it out

One of the bravest displays of London 2012 came from Great Britain's women's Hockey skipper Kate Walsh. She broke her jaw in the first match, had surgery the next day and returned five days later to eventually lead her side to Olympic bronze for only the second time in 20 years. Walsh had a plate inserted into her jaw after being struck by a stick in Team GB's opening game against Japan. She missed two subsequent matches but led by example in the bronze medal match, setting up two penalty corners in a 3–1 win over New Zealand. Walsh said: 'I loved every minute of being out there. I love leading this team and that's all my thoughts were on once I had fractured my jaw – getting back. I wasn't nervous. I wanted to win that badly.'

Hat-trick for Weise

Germany overcame a slow start to retain their Olympic men's Hockey crown after defeating favourites Australia 4–2 in the semi-finals and then Netherlands 2–1 in the final at London 2012. The Dutch team badly missed midfielder Klaas Vermeulen who had been injured in the semi-finals. The German victory extended the remarkable record of coach Markus Weise who had thus won three successive gold medals, once with Germany's women's team and then twice with the men. Australia took bronze after a 3–1 win over a Great Britain team striving to regain the pride badly dented in a 9–2 defeat by the Netherlands. That had been their highest-ever defeat and a record beating in an Olympic semi-final. Fourth place was still their best finish since gold-medal success at Seoul 1988.

← *Kate Walsh (left) wore protective headgear after undergoing surgery to repair her broken jaw.*

Volleyball

Volleyball (both men's and women's tournaments) has been contested as an indoor sport at the Olympic Games since 1964. The United States and former Soviet Union lead the way in the men's tournament (with three wins apiece), while the latter are the only four-time winners in the women's event.

Tournament format

The Volleyball tournament format at the Olympic Games originally paralleled the one still employed in the sport's World Cup. All teams played against each other and then were ranked by wins, set average and points average. One disadvantage of this round-robin system is that medal winners could be determined before the end of the games, prompting a loss of focus on the outcome of the remaining matches. To cope with this situation, the competition was split into two parts by the introduction of a knock-out phase, consisting of quarter-finals, semi-finals and final. Since its creation, at Munich 1972, this system has become the standard for the Volleyball tournament at the Games, and is usually referred to as the 'Olympic format'.

➜ *The Soviet Union made a successful defence of their men's Volleyball crown at the 1968 Games in Mexico City.*

Eastern glory

The first two editions of the men's Volleyball tournament, at the Games of 1964 and 1968, were won by the Soviet Union. Four years later it was third time lucky for Japan, and in 1976 the introduction of a new offensive skill, the back row attack, helped Poland strike gold.

More and more

The number of teams involved in the Olympic Games has grown steadily since the first men's Volleyball tournament in 1964. From 1996 onwards, both men's and women's indoor events have involved 12 nations. Each of the five continental volleyball confederations has at least one affiliated national federation involved in the Games.

Taking turns

At Moscow 1980, many of the strongest teams belonged to the Eastern bloc, which meant that the boycott, led by the United States, did not have as great an effect on men's Volleyball as in some other sports. Not surprisingly, the Soviet Union won again, this time beating Bulgaria 3–1 in the Final. The roles were reversed in 1984, when the United States confirmed their new domination of the sport in the west by sweeping past Brazil. This time the Soviets were absent.

↑ *Karch Kiraly shows his power at the net at the men's Volleyball tournament at Seoul 1988.*

Kiraly's double

'Karch' Kiraly of the United States is the only person to have won medals in both the indoor and beach versions of Volleyball at the Games. Known as the 'Thunderball in Volleyball', he was a fixture on the national team through much of the 1980s as a passer/ outside hitter in the 'two-man' or 'swing hitter' serve reception system. Kiraly was in the USA teams that won gold medals at the 1984 and 1988 Games, the latter as team captain. He was also named the International Volleyball Federation's top player in the world in 1986 and 1988. In 1996, he won a gold medal in men's Beach Volleyball at the Atlanta Games. The nickname 'Karch' could be derived from the Hungarian 'Karcsi', which can be translated as 'Charlie'. It is a common derivative of Karoly, which is Charles. His last name, Kiraly, means 'King'.

Brazil out in front

Brazil have featured in more men's Volleyball competitions at the Games than any other country, having appeared in all 13, followed by Italy and the United States on 10 each. Eleven nations have made just one appearance, the latest of them being Great Britain, who took part as the host nation in 2012. The team, ranked No. 92 in the world. lost all five first-round group matches and finished joint 11th overall.

Giba's the man

Brazilian star Giba – full name: Gilberto Amaury de Godoy Filho – is arguably the most recognised men's Volleyball player among fans all over the world. Although by modern standards he is not that tall, at 6ft 4in, his charisma, skill and energy have more than made up for his lack of reach. After Brazil lost in the Final at Beijing 2008 some volleyball fans thought their run of success had come to an end. But, in 2010, Giba led Brazil to the world title – the perfect preparation for London 2012.

⬆ *The most famous name in men's volleyball, Brazil's Giba led his country to victory in every major competition in the game: eight South American Championships, three World Championships and to Olympic Games gold at Athens 2004.*

London 2012

Resilient Russians

A thrilling fight-back saw the Russian Federation recover from the jaws of defeat, after losing the first two sets, and wreck Brazil's dreams of gold in the men's Volleyball final at London 2012. The Russians were twice match point down in the third set but eventually won 3–2 to upset the favourites and world's top-ranked nation. Hero for the winners was 7ft 2in Dmitriy Muserskiy who sparked the Russian resistance which eventually upset the Brazilians' rhythm and cohesion at the net. This was the first time a team had come back to win the final from two sets down. Russia, stronger and taller, triumphed in the deciding set by six clear points to bring a first Olympic men's Volleyball gold home to Moscow since the Soviet Union won at Moscow 1980.

Escape to victory

Brazil's women's Volleyball team have never failed to reach the Olympic Games Volleyball semi-final since finishing sixth at Seoul 1988. They reminded everyone of their powerhouse status by defeating the United States 3–1 to retain the title they won four years earlier at Beijing 2008. The Americans, top of the world rankings, commanded the first set but Brazil, who had saved six match points in their quarter-final win over Russia, refused to lose heart. Jacque (Jaqueline Carvalho) top-scored with 18 points as they rolled out the three subsequent sets by 25–17, 25–20 and 25–17. Victory sealed a notable revival after Brazil had teetered on the brink of early elimination after defeats by the United States and the Republic of Korea.

⬆ *Three Brazilians leap trying to block the spike of Sergey Tetyukhin during the Russian Federation's dramatic victory in the men's Volleyball final.*

Beach Volleyball

Beach Volleyball originated in southern California and Hawaii around the 1920s but is now popular as far afield as eastern Europe, even in countries not known for their beaches: for example, landlocked Switzerland won the men's Beach Volleyball bronze medal in 2004.

Where it all began

At international level, the elite nations are the United States, Brazil and China. Along with Australia, they are the only winners of gold medals at Olympic Games in either men's or women's Beach Volleyball. The original purpose of the sport was to give bored surfers something to do when the surf was down. The major differences now between beach and indoor volleyball are that the former is played on sand instead of a hard floor and has two players per team rather than six. Plus, most players, even when not playing competitively, when the rules require it, prefer to play the beach version barefoot.

Class of his own

Ron Von Hagen is regarded as the Babe Ruth of men's beach volleyball. Von Hagen established standards and set records at a time when the sport was just beginning. He played in 54 tournaments from 1966 to 1972, never finishing lower than third place in any tournament he entered.

Trebling up

Kerri Walsh and Misty May-Treanor are the only pair to successfully defend their Olympic Games women's Beach Volleyball title, adding the London 2012 gold medal to their successes four and eight years earlier and being named 'the greatest beach volleyball team of all time'. They beat China's Tian Jia and Wang Jie 21–18, 21–18 at Beijing 2008. The victory was also the 100th of Walsh's career and the team's 19th consecutive tournament and 108th consecutive match win. Walsh became the fastest player, man or woman, to reach the 100-win milestone, having done it in just 141 career tournaments, eclipsing even May-Treanor, who had achieved the feat in her 153rd tournament.

← Misty May-Treanor (left) and Kerri Walsh (right) won in Olympic Games gold medals in 2004, 2008 and 2012.

New arrival

Beach Volleyball was introduced into the Barcelona 1992 Olympic Games as a demonstration event, becoming a medal sport four years later. A total of 24 teams participate in each tournament. Teams qualify on the basis of their performance in FIVB events over the course of approximately 18 months leading up to the Games. There is a limit of two teams per country, and one spot is reserved for the Host Country and another for a randomly chosen wildcard country. In the event that any continent is not represented, the highest ranked team from that continent also qualifies for the tournament.

→ Karch Kiraly took his indoor Volleyball form to the sand to help the United States to the inaugural Beach Volleyball title at Atlanta 1996.

Kiraly crosses over

Talk about versatility. Widely regarded as one of the best indoor men's volleyball players ever, leading the United States to gold in 1984 and 1988, 'Karch' Kiraly is considered the Michael Jordan of the sport, beating performers half his age. He has won at least one tournament in 24 of the 28 seasons he has played, spanning four different decades. He was the first person in the history of the Olympic Games to have won three men's Volleyball gold medals, but the first to have struck gold in both versions of the sport, having been part of the United States' indoor teams in 1984 and 1988 before winning on the sand in 1996 in Atlanta with Kent Steffes. Kiraly grew up in Santa Barbara, California, and learned the game from his father, Dr Laszlo Kiraly. He has claimed a title in 24 different states with 13 different partners.

Depression driven

The sport was given a boost in the United States by the Great Depression of the 1930s. Starved of cash, Americans flocked to the beaches in their hundreds to take part in what was virtually a no-cost pastime and a free source of entertainment. It was only a matter of time before the International Volleyball Federation had to recognise the sport and that breakthrough came in 1986.

No stroll across the sand

Beach Volleyball is one of the most spectacular of Olympic sports for spectators, with players throwing themselves around the court to keep the ball in play and the action live. The sand-covered court's dimensions– it must be at least 40 centimetres deep – are the same as the indoor version. Each two-person team, with no substittues permitted, is allowed three hits to return the ball and no player can hit the ball twice in a row.

When the kit fits...

Women Beach Volleyball players have the option of playing in a one-piece uniform, but most prefer bikinis, which are more comfortable and allow for a greater range of motion. At the 2006 Asian Games, only one Muslim country fielded a team in the Beach Volleyball series, amid concerns that the uniform was inappropriate. Men Beach Volleyball players wear loose-fitting vests and shorts that hit mid-thigh.

Fans flock to the beach

Eighteen teams competed in the first women's Beach Volleyball tournament at the 1996 Games in Atlanta, an event attended by more than 107,000 spectators. Brazil dominated, with Jackie Silva and Sandra Pires beating fellow Brazilians Monica Rodrigues and Adriana Samuel for the gold medal. Australians Natalie Cook and Kerri-Ann Pottharst won bronze.

⬇ *Brazil's Sandra Pires (left) and Jackie Silva (right) won the first women's Beach Volleyball event in 1996.*

London 2012

⬆ *Kerri Walsh, left, blocks a spike from Jennifer Kessy during the London 2012 Games women's Beach Volleyball final at Horse Guards Parade.*

No changing guard

Two huge Olympic Flags hung incongruously over Whitehall as Beach Volleyball was played out, through the famous archways, on Horse Guards Parade in a 15,000 stadium alive with packed seats, music and live commentary. The Mayor of London, Boris Johnson, had described the 'semi-naked women' playing Beach Volleyball as 'glistening like wet otters' but the competition was deadly serious and women's competition saw the United States' women's pair win a third successive Olympic title. Misty May-Treanor and Kerri Walsh won the final to earn the accolade of 'the greatest Beach Volleyball team of all time' from beaten fellow Americans April Ross and Jennifer Kessy.

European breakthrough

The United States' domination of the women's Beach Volleyball was not matched by the men at the London 2012 Games. Both USA men's pairs were knocked out in early competition, one by Italians and the other by Latvians Martins Plavins and Janis Smedins who went on to win bronze medals. Germans Julius Brink and Jonas Reckermann won the men's Beach Volleyball gold medal, a breakthrough that reflected the increasing strength of European teams challenging the American–Brazilian duopoly. This was the first victory for Europe since the sport was added to the Olympic Games at Atlanta 1996. Reckerman said: 'I hope this will encourage everyone in the sport in Europe. It's great to be the ones who did it for the first time.'

Chapter Five
Cycling

Cycling's pride in its place among the foundation sports of the modern Olympic Games is justified by a glance at an oil painting in the Olympic Museum in Lausanne.

Painted by Charles de Coubertin – father of Pierre – it links the ancient Games with the modern. The goddess Athena is represented placing a laurel wreath on the head of a victorious modern athlete while cycling is among a handful of sports represented in the background.

Initially, Cycling at the Olympic Games was split between the Track contests and the Road Races. Mountain Bike competition 'arrived' only in 1996 in Atlanta – the same year professionals were formally allowed to compete for the first time. The 2008 Games in Beijing saw BMX Racing make its debut, a product of the need to enhance interest in the Games among young people worldwide.

Beijing 2008 also saw Great Britain's Cycling team enjoy unprecedented success. The 25-strong squad collected 14 medals (eight gold, four silver and two bronze) to top the Cycling medal table.

Chris Hoy was the first Briton to win three golds at a single Olympic Games in 100 years, while Rebecca Romero became the first British woman to win a medal in two different sports at the Games, Rowing at Athens 2004 and Cycling at Beijing 2008. At London 2012, the Track Cycling team won medals (seven gold) in nine of the ten events, while in Road Racing, Bradley Wiggins (gold) and Lizzie Armitstead (silver) both medalled.

Bradley Wiggins rides in splendid isolation on his way to the gold medal in the Time Trial, thus completing the unique double of Olympic Games gold medal and Tour de France yellow jersey in the same year.

Cycling – BMX

BMX Racing has been gaining in global prominence since the 1960s, with the International BMX Federation founded in 1981 and the first World Championships were staged 19 years later. Yet the landmark moment came when the International Olympic Committee approved its status as a full-medal sport in 2003 and it made its first appearance at Beijing 2008.

Dangerous name

With its sharp bends, challenging bumps and breakneck pace, BMX Racing is not for the faint-hearted. Australian cyclist Jamie Hildebrandt has played up the potential dangers more than most, by officially changing his name to Kamakazi. This might have been the most memorable thing about his performance at the 2008 Games, however, as he finished sixth out of eight in his men's semi-final.

Speed King Artur

In the 2008 men's BMX Racing event both the gold medal and the fastest lap time were claimed by Latvia – but by different cyclists. While Maris Strombergs came out on top, Artur Matisons achieved a best time of 35.903 seconds in his quarter-final but was eliminated after finishing seventh out of eight in his semi-final, not even completing his final circuit of the track.

Golden 'Oldie'

French cyclist Anne-Caroline Chausson received the first ever gold medal for women's BMX Racing when she won the event at the 2008 Games in Beijing, at the Laoshan BMX Field. The women's Final was held 10 minutes before the men's. Thirty-year-old Chausson went into the event as the oldest woman taking part – and also as someone who had only just returned to BMX Racing after 14 years away. Chausson gave up the sport in 1993 to concentrate on downhill mountain bike racing, in which she won nine world titles. But she made a comeback in 2007, lured by BMX's imminent Games debut. Chausson not only performed faster than all the other women competing, but also almost all the men – her quickest 350-metre lap was timed at 35.976 seconds, in the final.

France's Anne-Caroline Chausson surged to women's BMX Racing gold at the 2008 Games in Beijing.

↑ Colombia's Mariana Pajon wins the women's BMX gold medal.

Keep on riding

Shanaze Reade of Great Britain insisted it would be third time lucky at Rio 2016 after a second Olympic upset. The 23-year-old from Crewe missed out on a BMX Olympic Games medal for a second time. A world champion at both junior and senior levels, she was clear favourite at Beijing 2008 but crashed out of the final when trying to turn a certain silver into gold. Favourite again in London, she qualified easily for the final with 6,000 noisy fans including David Beckham cheering her on. Slow at the start, Reade was left behind by Colombia's Mariana Pajon, New Zealand's Sarah Walker and Dutch teenager Laura Smulders. Undaunted, she said later: 'Definitely I will keep training to be Olympic champion. I have the attributes, it is just about putting it together on the day.'

Tears of joy

Maris Strombergs, who cried from fear the first time he saw a BMX race, won gold again at London 2012 to follow up his success at Beijing 2008 when the sport was introduced to the Olympic Games. Strombergs led from first bend to finish line ahead of world champion and favourite Sam Willoughby. Colombian Carlos Mario Oquendo Zabala claimed bronze. Later Strombergs recalled being intimidated by his first sight of the sport when he was only five. Liam Phillips, Great Britain's medal hope, lost control on the penultimate bend while in apparent contention to challenge for a place. France's Joris Daudet, one of the pre-Games favourites, did not even make the final run after an earlier crash.

Mountain Bike

Mountain Bike Racing is a relative newcomer to the sporting world – the Union Cycliste Internationale (UCI) recognised it as a sport as late as 1990 (when it sanctioned the world championship). It did not take long to achieve full-medal status at the Games, however: it made its first appearance at Atlanta 1996 and has been on the programme ever since.

Blazing Gunn-Rita

Gunn-Rita Dahle, who claimed the 2004 women's Olympic title at the Athens 2004 Games, was another champion who stumbled into the sport. The Norwegian was encouraged to give a mountain bike a whirl, two months later was crowned national champion and six months after first sitting on an 'mtb' she signed a professional contract. A four-time world champion, Dahle took the race by the scruff of the neck at Athens 2004, storming into the lead on the first of the five 6km circuits and never relinquished it.

Absalon supremacy

The superstar of Mountain Biking has been double Olympic champion Julien Absalon. The Frenchman successfully defended his title at the Beijing 2008 Games thanks to his commitment, skill, stamina and determination to search out any and every advantage he could gain from his equipment. His bike weighed less than 10kg, thanks to its aerodynamic design and minimum number of gears. It wasn't for show, Absalon sought the lightest vehicle he could muster to help him when he was forced to carry it on the toughest parts of a course. Absalon's compatriot Jean-Christophe Peraud improved from 11th at Athens 2004 to silver medallist at Beijing 2008, with Nino Schurter winning a photo finish for bronze against fellow Swiss Christoph Sauser ... two minutes after Absalon.

Julien Absalon of France hurtles around the Cross-country course on his way to gold in the men's Mountain Bike event at the Beijing 2008 Games.

London 2012

Jaroslav Kulhavy completed the full set of championships by winning the men's Cross-country gold medal at the London 2012 Olympic Games.

Absalon out of luck

The Hadleigh Farm course was one of the venues outside London which made a powerful impression on competitors and spectators alike but will not be remembered with fondness by Beijing 2008 champion Julien Absalon. The Frenchman suffered an early puncture when leading in the final. That left him one minute down after the first lap and resigned to defeat. He said: 'After having been an Olympic champion, there was no point in fighting for a 10th place finish.' Instead, a decisive late push earned gold for the Czech Republic's Jaroslav Kulhavy, ahead of Switzerland's world No.1 Nino Schurter and Italian Marco Aurelio Fontana. Kulhavy could not have been happier, saying: 'I gave everything and now I've won everything: the World Cup, the world championship and the Olympic title. This is the most special day in the sport for me.'

Through the pain barrier

Julie Bresset recovered from a crash in training, two days earlier, to land France's only Cycling gold medal at the London 2012 Games with a solo victory in the women's Cross-country on 11 August. The 2011 World Cup winner led almost all the way to deny defending champion Sabine Spitz by a decisive 62 seconds. Bresset grabbed a French flag just before the finish line, waved it in celebration, then lifted her bike over her head in delight. Recalling her injury scare, she said: 'I was practising my start when my front wheel slipped. I cut an arm and a knee and was not good at all. I needed seven stitches.' Her triumph against the odds was France's fourth gold in Mountain Bike racing since the event was introduced at Sydney 2000.

Cycling — Road

Road Cycling, for men, was first contested at the Athens 1896 Games. The women's Individual Road Race has been contested since Los Angeles 1984. Two Road Races were contested at London 2012: a 250km race for men, and a 140km equivalent for women. Time Trials on the road were also held, with riders setting off 90 seconds apart. Team races were contested from 1912 to 1956, with each country's best performers' average counted, while Road Team Trials were held from 1960 to 1992.

A borrower be

Cycling featured at the inaugural Games in 1896 – a full seven years before the introduction of the Tour de France – with home country hero Aristidis Konstantinidis winning the men's Road Race through Athens. Yet Cycling would not return to the Games until 1912. In 1896, Konstantinidis completed his gruelling 87-kilometre (54-mile) ride from Athens to Marathon and back again in a winning time of 3:22.31 seconds despite falling off his bicycle at one point and reportedly having to borrow a replacement bike when his own broke. His luck ran out on the track in the 10km and 100km races, though – he finished fifth in the 10km after a collision with compatriot Georgios Kolettis and he was among the seven out of nine racers who failed to complete the 100km contest.

Krol's starring roles

Monique Krol of the Netherlands, winner of the women's Road Race in 1988, missed out on retaining her title when she could only finish third at Barcelona 1992. Yet her bronze medal there, four years after taking gold in Seoul, made her the first cyclist to win medals in the same individual Cycling event two Olympic Games in a row.

Leader of the pack

Not many races could be closer run than the 194-kilometre (121-mile) men's Road Race at Tokyo 1964, won by Italy's Mario Zanin. He finished in a time of 4:39:51.63 – only 0.2 seconds ahead of Denmark's Kjell Rodian. In fact, only 0.16 seconds divided the first 51 finishers, 26 of whom were all recorded at the third-best time of 4:39:51.74, though it was Belgium's Walter Godefroot who was awarded bronze.

Long-serving Longo

France's Jeannie Longo has competed in more Olympic Games than any other cyclist. The 2008 Games in Beijing were her seventh, Longo having first competed at Los Angeles 1984. She ended her career with four medals – one gold (from the Road Race in 1996), two silvers (the Road Race in 1992 and the Time Trial in 1996), and one bronze (from the Time Trial in 2000). Her final Games appearance saw her finish fourth in the 2008 Road Time Trial, just two seconds away from another bronze.

Cycle of victory

As expected given the sport's popularity in the country, France hold the record for the most gold medals in the men's Team Road Race (an event which ran from 1912 until 1992) with four wins – in 1920, 1924, 1936 and 1956. The USSR (with three successive wins between 1972 and 1980) lie second on the all-time winners list alongside Italy (1932, 1960 and 1984).

What goes on tour

Spain's Miguel Indurain became the first Tour de France champion to add an Olympic Games gold, when he won the first men's Road Time Trial at the 1996 Games in Atlanta. That triumph completed a stunning winning run, after he claimed five consecutive Tour de France championships between 1991 and 1995. He was helped, though, by the fact that Atlanta 1996 was the first to admit professional cyclists – the only people, before then, allowed to enter the Tour de France.

← *Five-time Tour de France winner Miguel Indurain added a gold medal to his trophy haul at Atlanta 1996.*

Hughes better, Hughes best

Canada's Clara Hughes really was a woman for all seasons. At the 1996 and 2000 Summer Games in Atlanta and Sydney she competed as a cyclist – securing two bronzes, in the women's Road Race and the women's Time Trial. She was also an accomplished speed skater, winning women's 5km bronze at the 2002 Winter Olympics and then women's 5km gold and women's Team Pursuit silver four years later. Hughes was the first person to win more than one medal at both the Summer and Winter Games.

➜ *Canada's Clara Hughes won two Cycling bronze medals in the Summer Games and a bronze and gold medal in the Winter Games – a unique feat.*

London 2012

Cavendish left behind

Alexandr Vinokurov upset British dreams when he, and not Mark Cavendish, sprinted away with Olympic gold in the men's Road Race. The euphoria fired by Bradley Wiggins's historic victory in the Tour de France had raised hopes of the British team bringing Mark Cavendish through to gold on the first formal day of competition and to maintain the momentum fired by the Opening Ceremony hours earlier. However, when Kazakh veteran Vinokurov and Colombia's Rigoberto Uran attacked out of a 26-rider breakaway with 8km left, the British team – who had appeared in command of the pace – were unable to raise an effective response. World champion Cavendish finished only 29th and massively disappointed at the manner in which the opportunity had escaped him.

➜ *Marianne Vos outlasted Lizzie Armistead to win the gold medal in the women's Cycling Road Race at London 2012. The last Dutch Cycling – Road medallist had been Leontien van Moorsel (née Zijlaard), who won gold in both the women's Road Race and the Time Trial at Sydney 2000 and the Time Trial again at Athens 2004.*

Lizzie the first

Lizzie Armistead confessed to feeling 'a bit shocked' after winning Great Britain's first medal of the London 2012 Olympic Games, silver in the women's Road Race on Day 2 of the Games. Marianne Vos of the Netherlands claimed gold with Russian Olga Zabelinskaya third after a thrilling, rain-soaked race ended with the trio leading a sprint finish on The Mall in front of Buckingham Palace. Armitstead, 23, from Otley in Yorkshire, had won five track cycling world championship medals in 2009 and 2011 before switching to road racing. She was the first of many British medallists to acknowledge home crowd support as 'the most special thing I've experienced, amazing.'

Cycling – Men's Track

Track Cycling has become more refined since the 1896 Games, when the Cycling events culminated in a gruelling 12-hour race. London 2012 featured only five men's Track events: Individual Sprint, Team Sprint, Team Pursuit, the Keirin and the Omnium, which involves six different races including sprints and time trials.

Sir Chris the greatest

At London 2012, Sir Chris Hoy strengthened an already valid claim to being the greatest male cyclist in the history of the Games. He retired from Olympic competition after winning six gold medals and a silver across the 2004, 2008 and 2012 Games. Hoy won his first gold medal at Athens 2004 – in the 1km Time Trial – and he set an Olympic record of 1:00.711, a mark which will not be beaten since it was the last time the event was contested.

Hoy responded by training in new disciplines. This paid off admirably at the Beijing 2008 Games, where his triumphs in the individual Sprint, Team Sprint and Keirin made him the first British athlete to win three gold medals at one Games since swimmer Henry Taylor at London 1908. He also set another Olympic Games record with a time of 9.815 in the individual Sprint.

A few months after his Beijing glory, Edinburgh-born Hoy was voted BBC Sports Personality of the Year and received a knighthood in the Queen's New Year Honours List.

Hurley's early glory

The record for most cycling gold medals in one Olympic Games was set more than a century before Chris Hoy's treble feat at the Beijing 2008 Games. At the 1904 Games in St Louis, the United States' Marcus Hurley, was victorious in the quarter-mile, third-mile, half-mile and one-mile races, as well as claiming bronze in the two-mile contest.

The feats of Flameng

France's Leon Flameng was rewarded for his sportsmanship when Cycling first appeared at the modern Games in Athens in 1896. He took gold in the 100-kilometre track race, despite stopping during his 300 laps, getting off his bike and waiting to be caught up by a Greek opponent who had been delayed by mechanical difficulties. Flameng fell from his own bike close to the finish, but still ended in first place – and with a French flag tied to his leg. Also on the Athens track that summer, he added silver in the 10km race and bronze in the 2km Sprint.

⬆ *France's Leon Flameng (left) took the gold medal in the 100km race at the inaugural Modern Games in Athens in 1896.*

Doubling up, twice over

Cheered on by his home crowd at the 1960 Games in Rome, Italy's Sante Gaiardoni became the first person to win gold in the 1km Sprint and 1km Time Trial events. He had gone into the Games as the reigning amateur world champion, but decided to turn professional before defending his Olympic crown. Gaiardoni was just as good in the paid ranks as he added the professional world title to his curriculum vitae in 1964.

⬅ *Chris Hoy was Great Britain's star performer at the Beijing 2008 Olympic Games, winning gold in the Individual Sprint, Team Sprint and Keirin.*

Back in the saddle

Britain's Bradley Wiggins became the first cyclist to make a successful defence of a Pursuit title at the Games, winning the Individual Pursuit gold at the 2004 Games in Athens and again in Beijing four years later. In Athens he also won silver for the Team Pursuit and bronze for the Madison, making him the first Briton to win three medals in one Games since track and field athlete Mary Rand at Tokyo in 1964.

← *Bradley Wiggins (left) leads Great Britain's Team Pursuit team to gold at the 2008 Games in Beijing. Wiggins changed disciplines after 2008, to go on the road and became, in 2012, the first British rider to win the Tour de France.*

London 2012

Britannia rules the track

Great Britain maintained their domination of men's Olympic Track Cycling, winning four of the five gold medals on offer, and bronze in the other event, the Omnium. This feat was more remarkable because a rule-change for London 2012 limited each nation to only one competitor in each event. Both Jason Kenny and Chris Hoy added two more golds to their personal hauls while Great Britain shattered world records in both the Team Pursuit and the Team Sprint. Kenny, a specialist sprinter, won gold at London 2012 in both Team Sprint and individual Sprint – in which he broke the world record – to add to his Team Sprint gold and Individual Sprint silver at Beijing 2008.

Hoy leads from the start

Sir Chris Hoy returned to London early from the cycling team's training camp so that he could be Great Britain's flag bearer at the London 2012 Olympic Games Opening Ceremony. Two weeks later he had ensured his place in British sporting folklore with his fifth and sixth gold medals, winning in both the Keirin and the Team Sprint events. This haul put him a little ahead of Bradley Wiggins – his seven medals comprise six and a silver, while Wiggins' seven are made up of four gold, a silver and two bronze. A former track cyclist who earned greater fame in Cycling Road events, Wiggins, like Hoy passed rower Steve Redgrave's previous record British of six medals (Redgrave won a previous Great Britain record of five golds). Hoy's struggle to hold back tears at the medals presentation was one of the iconic images of the Games.

↗ *Sir Chris Hoy waves to the crowd after winning one of his two gold medals at the London 2012 Games. The Scotsman, who announced his retirement from Olympic competition, won his fifth and sixth golds, added to the silver he won at Sydney 2000.*

World Record

Event	Name	Country	Record	Date
Men's Team Sprint	Great Britain	GBR	42.600	2 August
Men's Team Pursuit	Great Britain	GBR	3:51.659	3 August

Olympic Record

Event	Name	Country	Record	Date
Men's Team	Jason Kenny	GBR	9.713	4 August

Cycling – Women's Track

Women did not contest Road Racing until Los Angeles 1984 and Track Racing had to wait four years for the first Individual Sprint (at Seoul 1988) and eight for the first Individual Pursuit (at Barcelona 1992). Concerns about an imbalance between male and female races (the men had seven races compared to the women's three in 2008) were addressed at London 2012 – with five contests each.

Romero's conquests

Rebecca Romero became only the second woman to win medals in two different sports at a Summer Games when she clinched Cycling gold for the Individual Pursuit at Beijing 2008. She had earlier won a silver medal for Rowing at the 2004 Games in Athens, in the Quadruple Sculls event. But she switched to track cycling after a back injury forced her to give up rowing. Romero went to Beijing as the first Brit even to compete in two different sports at Summer Games. She hoped to defend her Cycling title at the 2012 Games in London – especially since she grew up in the south London borough of Sutton – but was disappointed when the Individual Pursuit was dropped from the programme.

Lion-hearted Leontien

Leontien van Moorsel's Cycling feats are more amazing when one takes into account her health struggles away from racing. She won four medals – including three golds – at the Sydney 2000 Games: gold in both women's individual races, and in the 3km Individual Pursuit, as well as silver in the track points race and was one of only six triple gold-winners at Sydney 2000. At Athens 2004 she retained her women's Road Time Trial title and added bronze in the 3km Pursuit. Before such successes, however, she fought against depression and anorexia that saw her lose 20kg in weight. She is the only woman cyclist to have to have won six medals at the Olympic Games, though Great Britain's Bradley Wiggins and Chris Hoy raised the bar for the men to seven at London 2012.

→ *The Netherlands' six-time Cycling medallist Leontien van Moorsel.*

So near, so far for Ferris

Australia's Michelle Ferris broke the Games record in the women's Sprint in Atlanta in 1996, completing a qualifier in 11.21 seconds. That time has not been beaten in any Games since – yet she still missed out on gold, finishing second behind Felicia Bellanger in the final. Ferris also finished a place behind Bellanger four years later in the women's 500m Time Trial – an event only staged at the 2000 and 2004 Games.

↑ *An Olympic record but no gold medal for Michelle Ferris at Atlanta 1996.*

Flying the flag

Two different countries – but the same athlete – won the first two sprint Cycling events contested by women at any Olympic Games. The race was introduced in Seoul in 1988, when Erika Salumae claimed gold for the USSR. Following the break-up of the Soviet Union, she competed for her native Estonia four years later when successfully defending her title in Barcelona. Salumae hardly put a foot wrong in becoming Estonia's first female gold medallist, as well as the country's first medallist since 1936 and the first gold medallist from any country formally separating from the Soviet Union. Alas, her Victory Ceremony was somewhat marred when organisers raised her country's flag the wrong way up – prompting Salumae to shake her head in amazement while standing on the podium, though she later insisted she minded the mistake 'only a little bit'.

↓ *Erika Salumae (centre) took Individual Sprint gold (for the USSR) at Seoul 1988 and defended her title (for Estonia) at Barcelona 1992.*

Ice Christa

Like Clara Hughes and Connie Carpenter-Phinney, East Germany's Christa Rothenburger won Olympic Games medals in both Speed Skating and Cycling – yet she is the only athlete to have claimed Summer and Winter Games medals in the same year. At Calgary 1988, she won silver in the 500km Sprint and gold in the 1000m. Seven months later, at the Summer Games in Seoul, she added a silver medal in the women's Sprint – having been persuaded in 1980 to take up Cycling by her coach and later husband Ernst Ludwig. She ended her career with two other Winter Olympics Speed Skating medals – gold in the 500m Sprint in Sarajevo in 1984 and bronze in the same event in Albertville eight years later.

← *Christina Rothenburger (right) was on a roll in 1988.*

London 2012

Trott at a gallop

Great Britain's Laura Trott exploded as the next Track Cycling superstar by claiming two golds at her first Olympic Games, in the Team Pursuit and the six-event Omnium. At the age of 20 she became the youngest woman to win gold at any Olympic Games Track Cycling event (Sir Chris Hoy won his first Olympic gold at 28) and joined a select band of British women – including Victoria Pendleton, Rebecca Adlington and Dame Kelly Holmes – to have won two Olympic gold medals. Trott's precocious talent had been recognised when she was drafted into the British team for the team pursuit at the 2011 World Championships. Team GB Cycling's performance director David Brailsford described Trott's London 2012 Games feats as 'phenomenal'.

Queen Victoria bows out

Victoria Pendleton, golden girl of British cycling after winning two medals at Beijing 2008, retired after London 2012 having added further lustre to her career with another gold and silver. It didn't start well for her when she and Jess Varnish were excluded from the Team Sprint for a technical fault, but she then won Keirin gold, before defending her Beijing 2008 Individual Sprint title against old Australian rival Anna Meares. Pendleton appeared to win race one of the three-leg final by 0.001sec but was again disqualified, this time for riding outside of her sprinting lane. Meares won the second race and Pendleton sportingly held her rival's arm aloft on their lap of honour.

↗ *Laura Trott burst on the women's track cycling scene at the age of 19 in 2011, but came of age in the London 2012 Olympic Games, winning two gold medals, including in the women's multi-discipline Omnium.*

World Record

Event	Name	Country	Record	Date
Women's Team Sprint	China	CHN	32.422	2 August
Women's Team Pursuit	Great Britain	GBR	3:14.051	4 August

Olympic Record

Event	Name	Country	Record	Date
Women's Sprint	Victoria Pendleton	GBR	10.724	5 August

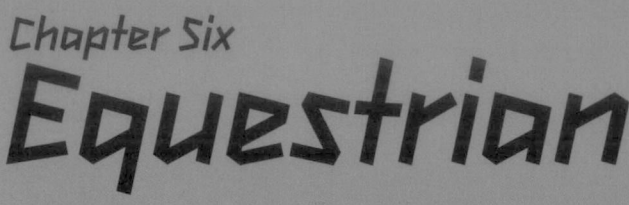

Chapter Six
Equestrian

The Equestrian competition has changed immensely since its debut at the 1900 Olympic Games in Paris. There, five nations competed in five different Equestrian events, with Belgium becoming the most successful country when they won Jumping and Long Jump gold.

After its inaugural appearance, there was a 12-year gap before horse and rider made a return to the Games, at Stockholm in 1912, in accordance with the wishes of Count Clarence von Rosen of Sweden, Master of the Horse to the King of Sweden.

By this time a more modern structure of events had been introduced, featuring a programme of Dressage, Eventing and Jumping, while events such as the Vault and Polo have long since disappeared from the Games agenda. There remained an elitist feel to the contest, however, and only military men were allowed to compete in Equestrian events until Helsinki 1952.

Nowadays Equestrian is regarded as a symbol of equality, with men and women competing on equal terms. It is also the only Games discipline in which humans and animals are permitted to compete together, the only stipulation being that all horses must be at least seven years old and the same nationality as their rider.

As we shall see, the Games have spawned a number of equine and human stars, and Equestrian events at the Olympic Games have featured competitors from all walks of life including royalty, prisoners of war and national heroes.

Such is the appeal of Equestrian competition that gold medallists have come from five continents, while scientific advances and changes in attitude have greatly improved safety for both horse and rider.

Zara Phillips (aboard High Kingdom), eldest granddaughter of Her Majesty Queen Elizabeth II, became the first member of the British Royal Family to win an Olympic Games medal, taking silver in the Eventing Team Competition at London 2012.

Dressage

Dressage competition at the Games remained an exclusive club open only to male cavalry officers until Helsinki 1952, when both male and female civilians finally gained admittance. Today, as a sport that is open to all, Dressage lays claim to being the fastest-growing Equestrian event at the Games.

King of the castle

Stockholm 1912 saw the debut of Dressage as a sport at the Olympic Games. The event was dominated by the host nation, with Carl Bonde and his white-faced steed Emperor leading a triumvirate of Swedish medallists. Such was Sweden's superiority that all six of its riders finished in the top eight of a truly international field of 21 competitors. Bonde later claimed further Games success, winning the silver medal at Amsterdam 1928, before he won the title of 'King of the Castle', when he inherited the spectacular Tudor castle of Tjolöholm in Fjärås, Sweden.

Out of sight but not mind

The Olympic Dressage competition at the 1956 Games did not take place in the Host City of Melbourne. Strict quarantine laws made taking horses to Melbourne in November impractical, and all of the Equestrian events took place in Stockholm the preceding June. As at Stockholm 1912, the Dressage events were won by Swedish riders, with Henri Saint Cyr and his mount Juli winning the Individual event as well as forming part of the triumphant gold medal-winning team. At the medal ceremony for the Individual event, Saint Cyr helped silver medallist Lis Hartel on to the medal podium.

Women's late start

Women were not allowed to compete in Dressage at the Olympic Games until Helsinki 1952. At those Games, Lis Hartel made the first mark for women when claiming a silver medal in the Individual event. Some 20 years later, at the 1972 Games in Munich, West Germany's Liselott Linsenhoff went one better, becoming the first woman to win an individual gold medal at the Games in any Equestrian event, when she captured the Individual Dressage crown. That particular competition featured 33 riders, of which 21 were women.

Beating adversity

Lis Hartel is arguably the highest profile competitor in the history of Dressage at the Olympic Games, and her legacy lives on. The Dane became the first woman in Equestrian history to win a medal at the Games when she won silver medals at the Individual Dressage in 1952 and 1956. What made her achievement all the more remarkable was that she competed despite having been paralysed below the knees as a result of contracting polio at the age of 23. Just eight years later, and walking on crutches, Hartel won her first silver in Helsinki. Her determination raised the profile of disabled sports and she played a major role in starting the movement for therapeutic riding schools.

⬇ *Denmark's Lis Hartel (left) – pictured with Henri Saint Cyr (centre) – defied disability to win two silver medals in Dressage (in 1952 and 1956).*

Kaiser Klimke

German Reiner Klimke holds the distinction of having been the most successful equestrian at the Olympic Games, as a member of West Germany's dominant Dressage team for three decades. In all Klimke won six gold and two bronze medals. He made his debut at Rome 1960, and four years later in Tokyo he secured his first team gold medal aboard Dux. He also featured in winning West German teams at Mexico City 1968 and at Montreal 1976, before claiming double gold at Los Angeles 1984. Riding Ahlerich, Klimke won the Individual Dressage competition and helped West Germany to team gold both at these Games and at Seoul four years later, his last appearance in an Olympic Games career that spanned 28 years.

London 2012

British breakthrough

Great Britain won the Dressage Team Competition for the first time since Amsterdam 1928. Charlotte Dujardin riding Valegro scored 83.286 in the final section. Carl Hester on Uthopia was third on 80.571 with Laura Bechtolsheimer on Mistral Hojris fifth with 77.794. Their combined team score of 79.979 saw them clinch the gold medal ahead of Germany in second on 78.216 and the Netherlands who finished third with 77.124. The extra significance was that the victory took Britain's gold medal tally past the 19 won at Beijing 2008. 'Valegro was unbelievable,' said Hester, its joint owner. 'He's the best horse in the world.'

Dujardin's winning tune

A mesmeric performance by Charlotte Dujardin, going last on Valegro, will live long in the memories of all at Greenwich Park as she claimed a first-ever British gold in the Dressage Individual Competition. Dujardin set an Olympic record score of 90.089 points. GB team-mate Laura Bechtolsheimer, leading at one point, finished with the bronze and fifth place went to Carl Hester, Dujardin's mentor and tutor. Silver went to Dutch rider Adelinde Cornelissen. Holst's 'Jupiter' from *The Planets* suite and Elgar's *Pomp and Circumstance* were appropriate choices amid the accompanying score.

⬇ *Charlotte Dujardin and Valegro 'danced' to double gold in Greenwich Park.*

German gold

The Team Dressage event at the Games was dominated by West Germany and Germany over a 24-year period. The German run of gold medals started with West Germany's victory at Montreal 1976 but was interrupted when the country boycotted the Moscow 1980 Games. West Germany returned to clinch gold at Los Angeles 1984, the first of five consecutive victories in the event – as the unified Germany from Barcelona 1992 – that climaxed with another win at Sydney 2000. This meant that the Germans had won the six successive Team Dressage events they had competed in. The 2008 team was led by Isabell Werth, who won her fourth Olympic Games Team gold medal to go with Individual gold at Atlanta 1996 and three Individual silvers.

⬆ *Germany's Isabell Werth won a total of five gold medals in Dressage.*

Writing on the wall...

Mystery shrouds the origins of the letters that adorn the 20 x 60 metre Dressage arena, which first appeared during the Olympic Games in the 1920s. Certain movements have to take place in the vicinity of specific letters and serve to guide the judges on just how much control the rider has of the horse. Although their debut came at the Olympic Games, two of the more plausible explanations for the letters pre-date the modern Games: one is that they were the initials of the first cities that the Romans conquered; while another theory is that the letters come from the time of the Old German Imperial Court, when courtiers representing the various dignitaries would be positioned around the stable yard in a strict order with the horses ready to ride.

Eventing

Eventing made its debut at Stockholm 1912. The competition has been through many format changes down the years, one of which saw Dressage completely dropped from the Eventing programme at the Antwerp 1920 Games, only to return in Paris four years later.

Clocking out

The Eventing competition at Athens 2004 was marred by confusion and controversy. During the Jumping phase, German rider Bettina Hoy twice passed between the start flags, first during her warm-up and then in the competition, blissfully unaware of the impact this had on the clock, which needed to be restarted. The ground jury realised the mistake and gave Hoy the 14 time penalties she would have received had her time started with the first, premature pass between the start flags. This dropped both Hoy and her German team out of the medals, when they had looked poised for Individual and Team gold respectively. The German team lodged an initially successful objection to the technical appeal committee and the gold medals were reinstated. However, the French team, backed by the British and Americans, argued to the Court of Arbitration of Sport that the technical committee should not have revoked the time penalties for Hoy's score and the original decision was upheld, resulting in France claiming the gold medal.

↑ *Bettina Hoy's error at the start of her stadium-jumping round cost Germany the Team Eventing gold medal at the 2004 Games in Athens.*

Welfare state

The Eventing competition at the Olympic Games has proven a breeding ground for innovations in horse welfare. The 1936 Games in Berlin saw new rules introduced to help protect horses from the use of performance-altering drugs, especially stimulants and sedatives. The same event brought in a new elimination rule for horses that were deemed exhausted or lame following the endurance test.

Cool riders

The Olympic Games have often introduced scientific advances to sport and the 1996 Games in Atlanta were no exception. They provided the setting for a new experiment to cool the horses down after the cross-country phase, including the deployment of misting fans, and added an additional hold during Phase C to ensure the horses were cooling properly. The competition also featured an extensive study of the effects on the horses of heat and of different methods of cooling. This was the first instance of an extensive veterinary study being conducted in conjunction with the Games.

Golden Australia

Few Olympians can match the determination of Bill Roycroft in the Team Competition at the 1960 Games in Rome. One of only five Australians to have competed at five separate Games, Roycroft's performance in Rome laid the foundations for a golden era for the Australian Equestrian team at the Games. During the cross-country phase, Roycroft took a heavy fall from his mount Our Solo. Reports vary as to the extent of his injuries – some suggested that he broke his neck – but they appeared to have cost his country the gold medal. However, Roycroft had other ideas and, after discharging himself from hospital the following day, rode a faultless round in the Jumping, which helped Australia to win its first Eventing gold medal.

Royalty reigns

Although women were allowed to compete in the Eventing competitions from Helsinki 1952, it was not until Tokyo 1964 that American Helena du Pont became the first female participant. Subsequent Games have enjoyed a royal seal of approval, with HRH Princess Anne, the daughter of Her Majesty Queen Elizabeth II, competing as part of the Great Britain Eventing team at Montreal 1976. She was the first member of the British Royal Family to compete at an Olympic Games, while her daughter, Zara Phillips, competed at the London 2012 Games and, riding High Kingdom, became the first British royal medallist, taking silver in the Team Eventing.

Singing for their...

Competing in Eventing at the Games has given riders varying degrees of gravitas. Great Britain's Mary King has bankrolled her Games successes – she won medals at Athens 2004, Beijing 2008 and London 2012 – with a wide variety of jobs, including working in a butcher's shop, in a kitchen and as a gardener. Team-mate William Fox-Pitt teaches the rich and famous how to ride, with pop star Madonna among his clientele.

→ *Mary King and Call Again Cavalier in Cross Country action during the Team Event at the 2008 Games.*

Kiwi inspiration

One of the most successful of all Three-Day Eventing riders at the Olympic Games is New Zealand's Mark Todd. He made his Games debut at Los Angeles 1984, winning the Individual gold medal riding Charisma. The pair were possibly the most formidable partnership in the history of Eventing at the Games, retaining their gold medal four years later, before Charisma was retired. Todd followed up with bronze in the Individual competition at Sydney 2000, and then announced his retirement. However, the lure of the Games proved irresistible and Todd returned to competition at Beijing 2008.

More than a sport

For triple Olympic Games gold medallist Adolph Dirk Coenraad van der Voort van Zijp, taking part in the Eventing competition at Paris 1924 was hardly the most difficult period of his life. A lieutenant in the Second Regiment of the Hussars in 1924, he was eligible – as a military man – to compete in Paris, where he won Individual and Team gold medals, and he went on to help the Dutch team to retain gold in Amsterdam in 1928. When the Second World War broke out, the Netherlands were invaded by the Nazis, Van der Voort van Zijp was captured and detained as a prisoner of war in Germany.

London 2012

German double for Jung

Germany repeated their double success from Beijing 2008 by collecting Eventing Team Competition gold while Michael Jung marked his 30th birthday by adding the Eventing Individual Olympic crown to his world and European titles. Although Great Britain were the only team to bring home three riders inside the endurance time – Zara Phillips on High Kingdom, Tina Cook (Miners Frolic) and Nicola Wilson (Opposition Buzz), the Germans maintained their advantage in the Jumping to claim gold with clear rounds from Jung on Sam, Dirk Schrade (King Artus) and Sandra Auffarth (Opgun Louvo). Great Britain took silver and New Zealand bronze. Jung progressed to Eventing Individual Competition glory after having been 11th at one stage. Sweden's Sara Algotsson Ostholt (Wega) took silver, ahead of Auffarth.

King the queen

Mary King of Great Britain was the oldest member of the entire Team GB squad in action at London 2012. At 51 she was representing her country in a sixth Games stretching back to Barcelona 1992. Her reward now totals two silver and one bronze medal in the Eventing Team Competition. Incredibly, she has maintained her career despite breaking her neck in a fall while exercising horses at her home in 2001. Less than a year later she was finishing third at the testing Burghley Horse Trials. King had been British champion a record four times and her other honours included two gold and one silver medal in the World Equestrian Games team eventing and four team gold medals at the European Eventing Championships along with one bronze and one silver medal in the individual event.

← *Michael Jung and Sam clear a gate in the jumping section of the Eventing competition on their way to gold.*

Jumping

Although an Individual Jumping event was contested at the 1900 Games in Paris, the current programme (of both Team and Individual events) did not take place until Stockholm in 1912, although it has featured at every Games since. Germany lead the way in both the Individual event (with five gold medals) and in the Team event (with eight successes).

Mighty Foxhunter

Great Britain's solitary gold medal at Helsinki 1952 came courtesy of its Jumping team, captained by the inimitable Harry Llewellyn and his mount Foxhunter. Llewellyn had previously been a successful jump jockey, finishing second in the 1936 Grand National on Ego. At the Games, a disastrous final morning had seen the British team slip to sixth position, with Llewellyn claiming that lack of sleep was partly to blame for his abject performance. An hour's sleep at lunchtime brought redemption, and the final afternoon phase saw the pair record the clear round that secured gold. The press treated Llewellyn as though he had single-handedly saved the honour of British sport, while both Winston Churchill and the new Queen, Her Majesty Elizabeth II, sent telegrams of congratulation. Foxhunter was retired in 1953, but his name lives on in the form of the Foxhunter Trophy, awarded to the most promising horses and riders of each new generation.

⬆ *Colonel Harry Llewellyn guides Foxhunter to a clear round at Helsinki 1952 to guide Great Britain to a memorable Team Jumping gold medal.*

Stamp of fame

The giant chestnut Big Ben holds a special place in Canadian hearts. Born in Belgium and later sold to Canadian equestrian Ian Millar, he won 40 showjumping Grand Prix events and two consecutive World Cups. He competed at two Olympic Games as part of the fourth-placed teams at Los Angeles 1984 and Seoul 1988. Few Olympians can have been more acclaimed: Big Ben has been honoured with his own stamp by Canada Post; was inducted into the Ontario Sports Legends Hall of Fame; had a statue erected and a book written about him; and is one of only two horses, along with the legendary racehorse Northern Dancer, inducted into the Canadian Sports Hall of Fame.

Double clears

It took a genuine Touch of Class for an equine competitor to transcend human endeavour at the Olympic Games. That was the name of the former racehorse that entered showjumping legend in 1984. The bay mare, with rider Joseph Fargis, won the Individual Jumping gold medal and was part of the victorious US team at Los Angeles 1984, posting the first double clear rounds in Games history into the bargain. Her golden exploits resulted in Touch of Class becoming the first non-human USOC Female Equestrian Athlete of the Year and she was inducted into the Show Jumping Hall of Fame in 2000.

Wall games

The life and times of Humberto Mariles Cortés could fill an entire book alone. The Mexican became his nation's first-ever gold medallist when, riding his home-bred horse Arete, he won the Individual competition at London 1948. Doubling up as a member of the jubilant Mexican team, Cortés deployed a bold approach: in the final round his horse jumped into the water obstacle, incurring faults, in what appeared to be a deliberate move. The tactic duly gave Arete the balance he needed to clear the following large wall – the only horse to do so. Cortés met a tragic end: he was imprisoned in Paris in 1972, having been caught drug-trafficking, and died in his cell later that year.

Nishi Memorial

An Olympian whose exploits came to be exploited in the movies was Japanese rider Takeichi Nishi, an aristocratic cavalry officer who won the gold medal in the Individual Competition at the Los Angeles 1932 Games. Riding Uranus, 'Baron Nishi' became – and remains to this day – the only equestrian from his country to strike gold. During the Second World War he took part in the defence of Iwo Jima with a tank regiment and died there in 1945, possibly during a mass suicide. His life was recorded for posterity in the Clint Eastwood film *Letters from Iwo Jima*.

Saudi success

The dawn of a new century also marked the rise of a new power in Jumping at the Games, with Khaled Al-Eid recording a rare medal for Saudi Arabia at Sydney 2000. The country had first entered the Jumping competition four years before, and by Sydney the team had improved under the guidance of Brazilian equestrian legend Nelson Pessoa, whose own son Rodrigo won an Olympic Games gold medal. In winning bronze, Al-Eid defied the label 'rank outsider' that had been bestowed by one news bulletin, attributing his success to patient training and the savvy accuracy of his mount Khashm al-'Aan.

⬆ *Khaled Al-Eid (on Khashm Al-'Aan) secured Saudi Arabia's first-ever equestrian medal when he took Individual Jumping bronze at Sydney 2000.*

Here comes the cavalry

William C. Steinkraus is a six-time Olympian who in 1968 became the first American to win an Olympic Games individual gold medal in Equestrian sport, by triumphing in the Jumping in Mexico City. Educated at Yale, Steinkraus served with the US Cavalry during the Second World War before embarking on a career in equestrian, first competing at the Helsinki 1952 Games as a member of the US bronze medal-winning team. He remained on the US team at every subsequent Olympic Games through to Munich 1972 and is perhaps best remembered for his association with the former unsound racehorse called Snowbound, his willing partner at the Mexico City 1968 Games.

London 2012

Skelton and Co in the clear

Great Britain captured their first team Jumping Team Competition gold in 60 years – since Helsinki 1952 – after a dramatic tie-breaking jump-off with the Netherlands. The jump-off demanded that all team members jump a shortened course, one country alternating with the other. Three clear rounds in the jump-off assured victory for the British team. One clear was achieved by veteran Nick Shelton, who had missed out on a medal at five previous Olympic Games. Dutch rider Jur Vrieling had a clean round but the Netherlands dropped to silver with two rails down for Maikel van der Vleuten and one for Marc Houtzager. A clear for Peter Charles (Vindicat) was vindication indeed.

London pride is silver

Appropriately, a horse named London – with 2012 in mind – was a medallist in the Jumping Individual Competition, but he was under the control of Dutch rider Gerco Schroder rather than a British competitor. They won silver behind Switzerland's Steve Guerdat (riding Nino Des Buissonnets) Ireland's Cian O'Connor (aboard Blue Loyd 12) taking the bronze medal. Guerdat had been a member of the Swiss team which won the Team Competition bronze medal at Beijing 2008. He was the only rider not to collect any jumping or time faults in both rounds A and B. British veteran Nick Skelton (on Big Star) had been in contention for gold until he took a rail out of an upright inspired by the Cutty Sark, a historic tea clipper berthed close to Greenwich Park. He and team-mate Scott Brash (with Hello Sanctos) finished in joint fifth place.

⬆ *Steve Guerdat urges Nino Des Buissoneets over a rail during one of his two clear rounds in the Jumping Individual Competition at Greenwich Park.*

Chapter Seven
Gymnastics

Gymnastics at the Games consists of three separate disciplines: Artistic, Rhythmic and Trampoline. In Artistic Gymnastics events, a gymnast is judged on performances on a series of apparatus. The Rhythmic Gymnastics discipline is solely for female competitors and requires graceful and athletic movements to music using different hand-held implements. Trampolinists are graded on skills exhibited in their routines on the sprung surface.

The Artistic Gymnastics side of the sport is recognised as one of the mainstays of the Games programme, with the likes of Olga Korbut and Nadia Comaneci having become worldwide celebrities after their stunning performances at Munich 1972 and Montreal 1976 respectively. The combination of grace, power, agility and nerve makes Artistic Gymnastics one of the hottest tickets at any Games and ensures the sport has a massive global audience.

Gymnastics in some form has been a part of every celebration of the modern era. The first gold medal was claimed by the German men's Parallel Bars team at Athens 1896, when the first individual champion was Carl Schuhmann in the Vault. Those first Games saw only men involved in five individual Artistic apparatus contests, team events on the Parallel Bars and Horizontal Bars, plus an idiosyncratic Rope Climbing discipline. Women made their Gymnastics debut at Amsterdam 1928, Rhythmic Gymnastics came on to the scene at Los Angeles 1984 and Trampoline was first staged at Sydney 2000.

Because individuals are able to claim multiple medals at each Games from the various Team, All-Around and apparatus finals, the top Artistic gymnasts have been among the most decorated of all participants at the Olympic Games.

Kristian Thomas performs his routine on the rings during the Team Competition at London 2012. Great Britain won its first men's Team Competition medal since Stockholm 1912, claiming the bronze behind China and Japan.

Men's Artistic Gymnastics

Men's Artistic Gymnastics is one of the few sports to have been contested at every Olympic Games since Athens 1896. Gymnasts from the Russian Federation (in all its guises – as the Soviet Union and as the Unified Team in 1992) have been the most successful over the years, capturing almost 25 per cent of the total medals available.

Ever present

The men's Individual All-Around competition is the only Gymnastics event to have been staged at every Olympic Games since Paris 1900. The leading performers from the Team Competition qualify for the All-Around Final. The gymnasts perform a routine in each of the six disciplines – Floor, Horizontal Bar, Parallel Bars, Pommel Horse, Rings and Vault. Formerly the marks gained were added to their scores from the team round. Now the champion is the man with the highest overall tally in the pressure-cooker atmosphere of the final.

↑ The Unified Team's Vitaly Scherbo dominated the men's Gymnastics competition at Barcelona 1992, winning six of eight available gold medals.

Super Scherbo

Vitaly Scherbo won an unprecedented six of the eight possible Gymnastics gold medals at Barcelona 1992. Owing to the fall of the Soviet Union, Belarussian Scherbo was part of the 'Unified Team' made up of the individual republics that had yet to achieve formal recognition by the IOC. He won four of the individual apparatus finals – Rings, Horizontal Bar, Parallel Bars and Vault – to add to his All-Around and Team honours. Only swimmers Mark Spitz and Michael Phelps have ever won more gold medals in a single Games.

Stukelj finds secret to long life

Leopon Stukelj lived most of his life as one of the elder statesmen of gymnastics. Born in what is now Slovenia in 1898, the All-Around champion at the 1924 Games lived to within four days of his 101st birthday and nearly saw in his third century. He attended the 1996 Games in Atlanta and was presented to the crowd at the Opening Ceremony as the oldest living gold medallist. At the age of 97 he walked jauntily to the presentation platform to join the likes of Carl Lewis, Bob Beamon, Nadia Comaneci and Vitaly Scherbo.

↘ Aleksandr Dityatin in action at the Moscow 1980 Games.

Aleksandr the great

In 1980, at the height of Soviet bloc domination of Gymnastics at the Games, Aleksandr Dityatin delighted the Moscow crowd with an awesome series of displays to claim Individual All-Around gold. Dityatin also made history by becoming the first male gymnast to claim medals in each of the eight competitions open to him at one Games. He went on to win three gold medals at the 1981 World Championships, but then retired through injury.

Close shave

At Los Angeles 1984, Japan's Koji Gushiken held off the challenge of home favourite Peter Vidmar to claim Individual All-Around gold by the slenderest of margins: 0.025 points. Remarkably, Gushiken was a lowly fifth going into the final. Even Gushiken's obvious competitive spirit could not prevent China from romping away with the Team title at Beijing 2008 when, as coach, he guided Athens 2004 winners Japan to silver. However, the indefatigable old warrior vowed that he would learn from the heavy defeat and 'be up for the next challenge'.

Handy Andrianov

The most prolific medal winner in the history of men's Gymnastics at the Games is the 1976 Individual All-Around champion, Nikolay Andrianov. The Soviet superstar won 15 medals across three Games from 1972 to 1980, a tally that included seven gold, five silver and three bronze medals. However, it could all have been so different, as Andrianov only established himself in the powerful USSR team after being called up as a late substitute for the 1971 European Championships. He won six medals there and never looked back.

⬆ *The Soviet Union's Nikolay Andrianov won an unprecedented 15 medals – seven of them gold – in three appearances at the Games.*

Champion Chukarin

Viktor Chukarin was the star turn at Helsinki 1952, having overcome great suffering to compete. Chukarin was a prisoner of the Nazis during the Second World War, but after his release made up for lost time by dedicating himself to gymnastics. He went on to defend the title in Melbourne four years later and was rewarded by the Soviet Union with the post of head of gymnastics at the renowned Institute of Physical Culture in Lvov.

⬇ *Viktor Chukarin heads to gold in the Parallel Bars at Melbourne 1956.*

Roll up! Roll up!

Italian Alberto Braglia was the first man to win successive Individual All-Around golds when he followed up his title at London 1908 with a similar success in Stockholm four years later. Braglia opted to join a circus as an acrobat as his next challenge, but he returned to the Olympic Games as his country's chief coach at Los Angeles 1932. Braglia led his charges to second in the medal table, still the best showing by the Azzurri at a Games.

Flipping Brilliant

Rowland Wolfe of the United States was just 17 years and 307 days old when, at the Los Angeles 1932 Games, he won the only Tumbling competition ever held at the Games. Wolfe's ability to go head over heels earned him the unimaginative nickname of 'Flip'.

⬆ *Sawao Kato (centre, with Michail Voronin, left, and Akinori Nak) wave to the crowd at the Mexico 1968 men's All-Around Individual Gymnastics medal ceremony.*

Tiny Kato a big star

Sawao Kato, the 1968 and 1972 Individual All-Around champion, was a diminutive 5ft 3in, but made up for his lack of stature with absolute composure and stunning skill. In 1968 he had a stirring battle for the gold medal with the Soviet Union's Michail Voronin, but at the troubled Munich Games four years later no one could match him. Kato won 12 medals at the Games, including eight golds, and is Japan's most successful Olympian. He was head judge in the Gymnastics competition at the Athens 2004 Games.

Team champions

The first medals to be decided in Gymnastics competitions at the Games are those for Team Competition honours. During qualifying, five of a team's six gymnasts perform on all six items of apparatus, with the highest four marks counting. The scores determine which teams advance to the final and which individual gymnasts reach the All-Around Competition and apparatus finals. In the final, three of each team compete on each apparatus with all scores counting. The team with the most points wins.

China – the new power

At Beijing 2008, on home soil, China won Team Competition gold for the second time in three Games, to add to seven of the previous world titles in the event. Coach Yubin Huang described the display at Beijing 2008 as 'perfect'. The Chinese won their first-ever men's Team Competition gold at Sydney 2000 but failed to build on the achievement at Athens 2004, losing to arch-rivals Japan and only finishing fifth. At Beijing 2008 the pressure was intense in the National Indoor Arena, but Kai Zou, Wei Yang, Qin Xiao, Xiaopeng Li, Xu Huang and Yibing Chen were all triumphant. And China then made it three golds in four Games at London 2012.

↑ Considered the best Gymnastics team in history, the Soviet Union eased to Team All-Around gold at the Seoul 1988 Games.

Soviet strongmen

The 1988 Soviet Union men's squad is widely recognised as the greatest Gymnastics team in the Games' history. They recorded six perfect 'ten' scores, including three by Dmitri Bilozertchev, who three years earlier had broken his left leg in 42 places in a road accident. Valeri Lyukin achieved the highest possible score on the Pommel Horse and Parallel Bars, while Vladimir Artemov was awarded ten for his work on the Horizontal Bar. Both Lyukin and Artemov subsequently emigrated to the United States. The margin of the Soviet's victory in Seoul was all the more impressive as East German Holger Behrendt and Japanese duo Daisuke Nishikava and Koichi Mizushima also achieved the ultimate score, each on the Rings. 'It is the best display of team gymnastics I have ever seen,' said Peter Vidmar, a member of the United States team that won the gold medal four years earlier in Los Angeles.

↑ China's men's team delighted the home crowd when it stormed to Team All-Around gold at the Beijing 2008 Games.

The ultimate team player

Japan was the powerhouse of men's gymnastics in the 1960s and 1970s. At the Montreal 1976 Games, 'the land of the rising sun' was going for a fifth straight Team Competition title. However, disaster struck when Shun Fujimoto injured himself on the floor, sustaining a broken kneecap. Showing incredible team spirit and will to win, Fujimoto hid the extent of his injury and completed his final two events. On the rings he scored 9.7, executing a dismount despite his ailment. His score helped the Japanese earn yet another gold.

Child star

The first modern Olympic Games in 1896 saw team events held for each individual apparatus rather than across multiple disciplines. Unlike today, there was no age restriction on competitors. Dimitrios Loundras was 10 years and 218 days old when he won a silver medal in the team Parallel Bars.

← Shun Fujimoto produced one of the most courageous performances in sporting history at Montreal 1976 when he defied a broken kneecap to compete in the final two rounds to help Japan to men's Team All-Around gold.

Simply Fin-tastic

Finland were the foremost nation at London 1948, picking up the men's Team championship with a collection of six gold, two silver and two bronze medals. Among the Finnish team was the remarkable Heikki Savolainen, for whom this was the fifth out of six Olympic Games in a career stretching from Amsterdam 1928 (where he won a bronze medal in the Pommel Horse competition) to the Games Finland hosted – at Helsinki 1952 – in which he took the Olympic Oath on behalf of the competitors and claimed a Team Competition bronze. In the Pommel Horse competition at London 1948, Savolainen had the same score as team-mates Veikko Huhtanen and Paavo Aaltonen, and uniquely for Gymnastics at the Games each was awarded a gold medal. London 1948 was the heyday of Finnish gymnastics; they have only won five Gymnastics medals since, the last coming at Mexico 1968.

Old man Manilo

Italy's Manilo Pastorini is still the oldest Gymnastics gold medallist, more than 90 years after he was a member of the champion team at Antwerp 1920. Pastorini was 41 years and 117 days when he struck gold as part of the victorious Italian squad. Pastorini, though, was a relative pup compared to one of the bronze medallists in that competition, France's Lucien Demanet was 45 years and 266 days old. Demanet remains the oldest Gymnastics medallist at the Games and, like Pastorini, will surely hold on to the accolade in perpetuity.

Chinese fireworks

The Los Angeles 1984 Games saw the first appearance of a team from mainland China in the Summer Games for 32 years. Its star performer was male gymnast Ning Li, who picked up six medals – three golds, two silvers and one bronze. Li's duel with Peter Vidmar for the Pommel Horse crown was one of the highlights of the action in the Pauley Pavilion. The astounded judges could not split them.

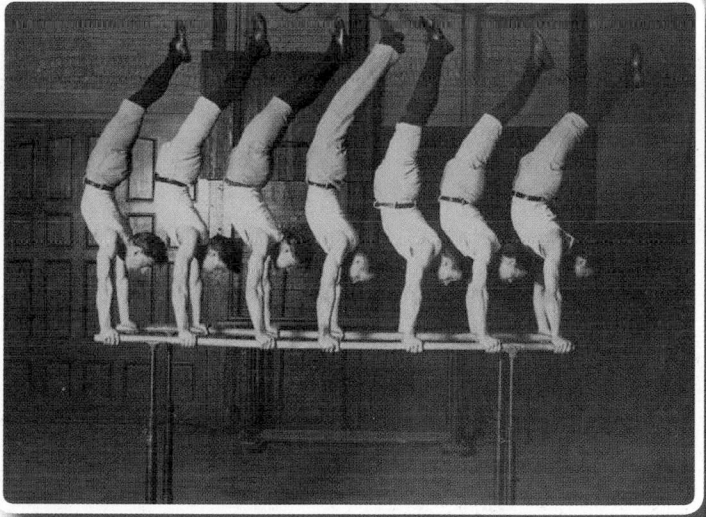

↑ *A wooden leg proved no handicap for George Eyser (centre): the United States' athlete picked up three gold medals at St Louis 1904.*

Eyser overcomes handicap

At the St Louis 1904 Games, United States won the first men's Team Competition. George Eyser was a leading member of that squad, also winning gold in the Parallel Bars and Vault competitions. Eyser's achievements were all the more remarkable ... because he had a wooden leg.

Glory for Greece

Despite being the birthplace of Gymnastics, Greece has had a less than glowing history in the sport in the modern Olympic Games. When World Championship silver medallist Dimosthenis Tampakos prepared to mount the Rings in the final of that discipline at Athens 2004, it was in the knowledge that only one Olympic gold medal had been won by the Hellenic nation in almost 100 years. Tampakos held his nerve and completed a near-faultless routine to win gold and bring the crowd in the Maroussi Indoor Hall to its feet.

Selariu's costly slip

At the Athens 2004 Games, Romania, who had never won men's Team Competition gold at the Games, were leading going into the final piece of apparatus. The narrow margins of victory and defeat in this technical sport were then summed up by the luckless Razvan Selariu falling off the horizontal bar, which allowed Japan to snatch the title, their first in the event for 28 years.

← *Romania's mission to take Team Competition gold for the first time at Athens 2004 failed when they slipped from first to third in the final round.*

Individual apparatus champions

There are six apparatus disciplines. The Floor exhibits tumbling and strength skills. The Horizontal Bar, 2.5 metres above the ground, sees swings, releases and twists. The Parallel Bars involves swings, balances and releases performed on two bars 42 centimetres apart. The Pommel Horse sees gymnasts perform on top of a gym 'horse' with two rings attached. The Rings (suspended at 5m) tests strength, power and flexibility. The Vault sees gymnasts sprinting down a runway and leaping from a springboard to perform twists, somersaults and a landing.

↑ *Nobody could touch Japan's Sawao Kato on the Parallel Bars at Munich 1972 and Montreal 1976.*

Fantastic Finns

The Pommel Horse Competition at the 1948 Games in London produced the only three-way tie for a gold medal in the history of Gymnastics at the Games. All three men hailed from Finland.

Kato first bar none

Japan's Sawao Kato won a record eight Gymnastics gold medals across three Games from 1968 to 1976. He remains the only man to have successfully defended the Parallel Bars title.

Blanik breaks the mould

Only one non-Chinese male gymnast claimed a title at Beijing 2008. Leszek Blanik secured Poland's first-ever Gymnastics gold medal at the Games with a supreme display of vaulting beyond even the impressive hosts. The only gymnast who was able to match Blanik was Thomas Bouhail of France. He equalled Blanik's score, but was awarded only the silver medal on a tie-break analysis of the judges' marks.

→ *Polish vaulter Leszek Blanik was the surprise winner of the gold medal at Beijing 2008.*

Japan's Tsukahara makes his mark

Innovation is celebrated in gymnastics, with new techniques and moves named after their instigators. Perhaps the most famous example is the legendary Japanese Misuo Tsukahara, who claimed back-to-back Horizontal Bar titles at the 1972 and 1976 Games and is still the only man to have retained that crown. Tsukahara appeared to be fearless and both his somersault dismount from the high bar and his complex cartwheel vault were added to the Gymnastics skills manual in his honour.

→ *Misuo Tsukahara performs his legendary dismount from the Horizontal Bar at Munich 1972.*

London 2012

Brits end long wait

Great Britain won their first men's Olympic Gymnastics Team Competition medal in a century when they claimed bronze. Louis Smith, Max Whitlock, Daniel Purvis, Sam Oldham and Kristian Thomas totalled 271.711 points in front of a royal audience which included Prince William, Duke of Cambridge, and Prince Harry of Wales. Britain had initially been awarded silver but an inquiry into the score of Kohei Uchimura's pommel horse routine saw Japan claim silver and Britain downgraded to bronze. This was Britain's first Olympic Gymnastics Team Competition medal since winning bronze at the Stockholm 1912 Games. China retained their gold medal with Beijing 2008, with silver medallists Japan leapfrogging Britain with an upgraded total of 271.952.

Uchimura rocks for Japan

Kohei Uchimura added Olympic gold in the men's Individual All-Around to the world titles he had claimed in the previous three years. His domination was enveloping with gold all but his at the halfway point. Uchimura's score of 92.690 was more than 1.5 points ahead of silver medallist Marcel Nguyen of Germany. Yet the Japanese star had been off-colour in qualifying where he finished ninth after falling off both high bar and pommel horse. 'He's been a rock the last four years and really deserved that gold medal,' said Britain's Kristian Thomas. 'I had no doubt he'd bring his A game. That's the sign of a true champion.'

Kohei Uchimura continued Japan's long run of success in men's Gymnastics with a gold medal in the Individual All-Around Competition.

↑ *Epke Zonderland of the Netherlands lived up to his dreams when he won the gold medal in the men's Horizontal Bar Competition at London 2012.*

'Flying Dutchman' surprises himself

Epke Zonderland turned up a real-life 'Flying Dutchman' performance to win the Horizontal Bar Competition and bring the Netherlands the country's first-ever Gymnastics gold medal. To achieve this, Zonderland outdid Beijing 2008 Olympic champion Kai Zou, who had been the favourite, especially as China had won every Olympic Games and world title on the apparatus since 2008. Zou was surpassed with ease by Zonderland's breathtaking routine and was even pushed down to bronze medal position by Germany's Fabian Hambuechen. Zonderland said: 'I dreamed about this for so long. It's unique to be in a Olympic final if you're a Dutch gymnast, but winning the gold is bizarre.'

Smith ever closer

Britain's Louis Smith transformed his Beijing 2008 bronze medal into silver in the men's Pommel Horse Competition final at the North Greenwich Arena, while team-mate Max Whitlock took bronze. Two Britons thus stepped up on to the podium in an individual Gymnastics event for the first time in Games' history. The 23-year-old Smith was captain of the men's team. On being told that the Duchess of Cambridge had been watching, he said that 'if I'd have seen her, I'd have probably blown her a kiss.' Hungary's Krisztian Berki, who beat Smith into silver in both the world and European championships, took gold again. Smith matched Berki's 16.066 but Berki had a fractionally better execution score.

Women's Artistic Gymnastics

From Olga Korbut to Nadia Comaneci, women's Gymnastics has produced some of the most legendary names in the history of the Olympic Games. Team competitions were contested for the first time at Amsterdam 1928, with individual competitions introduced at Helsinki 1952. The Soviet Union were the dominant force over the years, winning 33 gold medals.

Ten-up Nadia

Nadia Comaneci of Romania became the Games' youngest women's All-Around Gymnastics champion in 1976 when she astounded the world with her skill at the tender age of 14 in Montreal. She followed up with first places in the Balance Beam and Uneven Bars apparatus finals, achieving an unprecedented seven perfect 'ten' scores. No gymnast had previously been awarded a single ten in the Gymnastics Competition at the Games. Comaneci raised standards to a new level and her prowess led to revisions of the judging criteria.

← *Nadia Comaneci's performance on the balance beam at the Montreal 1976 Games sent massive shockwaves around the sporting world.*

Latynina on cloud nine

Larisa Latynina of the Soviet Union, the 1956 and 1960 Individual All-Around champion, won nine Gymnastics gold medals in her Olympic Games career, a record for a female competitor in any sport. Latynina travelled to the London 2012 Games, where she watched her total of 18 medals eclipsed by legendary swimmer Michael Phelps. The American also owns the record for most golds with 18. The grace and artistry displayed by Latynina evolved from her training as a ballet dancer from the age of 11.

All-around champions

The women's Individual All-Around title is awarded to the gymnast with the highest score across all four women's disciplines – Floor, Balance Beam, Uneven Bars and Vault. The leading performers from the Team event, up to a maximum of two per nation, qualify for the Individual All-Around Final, in which they perform the four routines. The marks gained used to be added to their scores from the Team round, but in recent years the champion has been decided solely on performances in the final. The champion is the competitor with the most points.

Caslavska triumphs

Vera Caslavska was the first Gymnastics superstar. Representing Czechoslovakia at Mexico City 1968, just two months after her country had been invaded by the Soviet Union, the charismatic Caslavska defeated all the mighty Soviet squad in her successful defence of the Individual All-Around title she had won at Tokyo 1964. Her amazing career over those two Games brought 11 medals. Caslavska was forced into hiding when Soviet tanks rolled into Prague, but at the Games she gained inspiration from the strife back home. Afterwards she presented the four gold medals she had won in Mexico to her country's ousted leaders.

Retton's dramatic victory

The 1984 Olympic Games at Los Angeles were boycotted by most of the Eastern European nations, including the awesome Soviet team. Their absence allowed the United States to claim the women's Individual title through the charismatic Mary Lou Retton – but only just. In an incredible finish, Retton needed to score a perfect 'ten' in her exercise to deny Romania's Ecaterina Szabo. She achieved it and became a national hero.

↑ *Mary Lou Retton produced a perfect final routine at the Los Angeles 1984 Games to edge out Romania's Ecaterina Szabo for the gold medal.*

Height matters

Half-way through the women's All-Around competition at the 2000 Games in Sydney, Australian gymnast Allana Slater questioned whether the vaulting horse was the correct height. She was right: the apparatus was 5 centimetres below the prescribed height of 125cm. The horse was raised and all of the gymnasts who had already vaulted the horse when it was at the wrong height were offered the opportunity to retake their vault. It was too late for many, though, as the likes of Svetlana Khorkina had done badly on the incorrectly set horse and subsequently produced poor scores in their later disciplines because they had been under the extra pressure of knowing that a further mistake would ruin their chances of victory.

Keeping it in the family

Nastia Liukin, the 2008 Individual All-Around champion, was following in a proud family tradition that crossed not only eras but also political history when she came first in Beijing. Both her parents were champion gymnasts. Liukin's father, Valery, was a member of the 1988 Soviet Union team in Seoul and won gold medals in the Team and Individual Horizontal Bar events. Her mother is former world rhythmic champion Anna Kotchneva. Liukin emigrated to the United States in 1992 aged two and was coached to success by her father at his gymnastics academy in Texas.

⬆ *Nastia Liukin emulated her father's success with gold at Beijing 2008.*

Patterson peaks to deny Khorkina

At Athens 2004, American Carly Patterson ensured that Svetlana Khorkina would be remembered as arguably the greatest gymnast never to have won the Individual All-Around title at the Games. Khorkina had won the World Championship on three occasions, but in 1996 and 2000 had failed to achieve the ultimate prize in the sport. This was her last chance. Khorkina led at the half-way stage, but slipped back to second after the Balance Beam, allowing 16-year-old Patterson to swoop.

⬇ *Russia's Svetlana Khorkina was a three-time world champion who was never able to manage to hit the same golden heights at the Olympic Games.*

Kim proves a point

Nellie Kim defied the opinion of Soviet gymnastics legend Larisa Latynina (who, when Kim was a child, said she had no future in the sport) to become one of the most celebrated gymnasts of all time. In her much-storied battle with Nadia Comaneci at Montreal 1976, she took three gold medals (in the Team All-Around, the Vault and the Floor – in the latter, recording a perfect ten). She also took silver in the Individual All-Around event, despite becoming the first gymnast to record a perfect ten on the vault. Four years later, at Moscow 1980, she shared gold with Comaneci in the Floor and won the fifth gold of her Olympic career in the Team All-Around.

⬅ *The elegant Nellie Kim won three gold medals at the Montreal 1976 Games.*

Team champions

Team honours in women's Gymnastics at the Olympic Games are decided on a similar basis to the men's equivalent. During qualifying, five of the six gymnasts on each team perform on each apparatus, with the highest four marks counting. The scores determine which teams advance to the final and which individual gymnasts reach the Individual All-Around and apparatus finals. In the final, three of each team compete on each apparatus, with all three scores counted. The team with the highest overall tally wins the gold medal.

⬇ *The Netherlands' gymnasts delighted the home crowd by taking the inaugural team title at the Amsterdam 1928 Olympic Games.*

Soviet might

For 40 years teams from the Soviet Union dominated women's Gymnastics at the Olympic Games. From 1952 through to 1988 the line-up of gymnastic talent drawn from the 15 republics won the women's Team title every time they turned up. In 1992, the Unified Team (the coming together of the majority of the 15 while each was not formally recognised by the IOC) continued the tradition, but then the break-up of the old superpower meant that none of its constituents, now independent nations, had the resources to lift the title. The Russian Federation, Ukraine and Belarus are all very competitive, but none has the strength of the Soviets. A good illustration is the extraordinary 1976 Soviet team, which even the inspired Romanian Nadia Comaneci could not prevent from retaining the Team title. Its three biggest stars were Lyudmila Turishcheva (born in Grozny, now Russian Federation), Olga Korbut (Grodno, Belarus) and Nelli Kim (Leninabad, Tajikistan). In recent years that awesome trio would have been competing in different teams, which just goes to show that sometimes there is no escaping the fact that politics and sport are inextricably linked.

➔ *A sign of their power: at the Montreal 1976 Games, Soviet gymnasts Ludmila Tourischeva (left) with a silver medal and Nelli Kim (right) with gold pushed the legendary Nadia Comaneci into bronze in the Floor Competition.*

Comaneci the spark

Nadia Comaneci was the catalyst behind Romania's challenge to the Soviet dominance. The gymnast, famed for her string of perfect scores at Montreal 1976, led the Romanians to their first Team silver medal that year, and her legacy led to them lifting the title in 1984, when the Soviets were absent – ironically beating a United States team led by Comaneci's former coach Bela Karolyi. Romania's time came again in 2000 and 2004. In Sydney it was Andreea Raducan (who was allowed to keep her team gold despite being disqualified from the Individual event after failing a drugs test) and Simona Amanar who were the main contributors, and four years later in Athens Catalina Ponor and Monica Rosu took up the mantle.

Tragic first champions

The Team title was the first of the women's events to be accorded medal status, at the 1928 Games in Amsterdam. There was delight for the hosts as the Dutch became the first-ever women's Gymnastics Team champions. However, within 15 years four of the 12-strong line-up were dead – Ans Polak, Jud Simons, Helena Nordheim and Estella Agsteribbe all perished during the Second World War in Nazi concentration camps. Elka de Levie was the only Jewish member of the team to survive the Holocaust.

Really youthful

Gymnastics was notorious for making stars out of children, but in recent years a minimum age limit of 15 has been in force. There was no such rule at Amsterdam 1928, when 11-year-old Luigina Giavotti helped Italy to the silver medal in the women's Team Competition. Giavotti is the youngest women's Gymnastics medallist at the Games.

Ageless Seymour

Ethel Seymour was 46 years and 222 days old when she won a bronze medal as part of the Great Britain team at the 1928 Games in Amsterdam. Old enough then to have been silver-medal winner Luigina Giavotti's grandmother, she remains the oldest medallist in the history of women's Gymnastics at the Olympic Games.

⬇ *Great Britain's Gymnastics team perform their bronze medal-winning routine at the Amsterdam 1928 Olympic Games.*

⬆ *The United States team take the plaudits after winning Team Competition gold at Atlanta 1996. It remains the country's last taste of victory in the event.*

US steps up

The United States were second-raters in the women's Gymnastics Team Competition during the years of Soviet domination. A bronze medal at the 1992 World Championships provided a hint of change, and then, on home soil at Atlanta 1996, the US won its first women's Team title, with Shannon Miller and Kerri Strug leading the way. Despite individual success for Carly Patterson and Shawn Johnson in 2004 and 2008 respectively, there has been no team gold since, as the Romanians and then the Chinese showed just a little more strength in depth.

Individuals carry teams

Czechoslovakia and Hungary owe their success in the Team Competition to the inspiration provided by two incredible individuals. The Czechs won three successive Team silvers in the 1960s with the peerless Vera Caslavska as their leader. Hungary had been a force in the 1950s thanks to the example set by quadruple gold-medal winner Agnes Keleti. Neither country has been on the women's Team podium since 1972.

Chinese resent age slur

China's women gymnasts were slower than the men to challenge at world level, but are now one of the leading powers. The world team title in 2006 was a forerunner to their landing a first Team title at the Games at Beijing 2008. The success was called into question by media reports that some of the team were under 15, the minimum age for participation in the Games. In particular, the slight Kexin He was said to be only 14 years old at the time, but the Chinese authorities produced documentation that they said proved she was 16.

⬆ *It may have taken a technicality to separate them, but China's Kexin He edged out Nastia Liukin of the USA to take gold in the Uneven Bars at Beijing 2008.*

He just makes it...

Chinese gymnast Kexin He was adjudged to be the winner of the 2008 women's Uneven Bars Competition thanks to the sport's complex rules. He and American Nastia Liukin were locked together after both recording scores of 16.725 and, incredibly, identical tallies of 7.700 and 9.025 from the two judging panels. Rather than letting them share the gold, however, the International Federation invoked their analysis of 'lowest variance', which showed that the Chinese gymnast had a slightly more even spread of scores from the various judges.

Individual apparatus champions

Women compete in four disciplines: the 10-centimetre-wide Balance Beam, which tests the gymnast's acrobatic and dancing skills; the Floor, a combination of tumbling and moves to music; the Uneven Bars, in which gymnasts perform a routine on bars set at heights of 241cm and 161cm and 130–150cm apart; and the Vault, where gymnasts run, twist and turn in the air and perform a landing.

Super Szabo

In the Soviet Union's absence, the 1984 women's Gymnastics competition developed into a match between the United States and Romania. Home favourite Mary-Lou Retton took the All-Around title, but Romania won the Team title and Ekaterina Szabo stole the show in the apparatus finals, winning the Floor and Vault Competitions, plus sharing the Balance Beam crown with team-mate Simona Pauca. Szabo's four golds equalled the record for a woman gymnast at one Games.

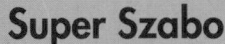

← *Although she missed out on the All-Around title to Mary Lou Retton, Ekaterina Szabo struck gold a record four times at Los Angeles 1984.*

Captivating Korbut

Arguably the first gymnast to earn worldwide stardom was Olga Korbut. At just 17, Korbut stole the show at the 1972 Games in Munich. Her impish displays on the Floor earned her a gold medal to add to that for her virtuoso Balance Beam routines, which were rated the best on show. Korbut was edged out into silver by East German Karin Janz in the Uneven Bars, but her standing back flip to catch on the apparatus was considered a move before its time. The Soviet star's nerve, coupled with a flashing smile, brought a brief thaw to the Cold War.

↑ *Olga Korbut won three gold medals at the Munich 1972 Games: on the Balance Beam, on the Floor and as part of the victorious Soviet team.*

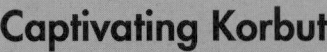

→ *Larissa Latynina of the Soviet Union embarked on her epic Olympic Games journey at Melbourne 1956.*

Just perfect

Before 1976, no male or female gymnast had ever achieved Gymnastics perfection at the Olympic Games. At Montreal 1976, Nadia Comaneci scored seven perfect tens, including two on the Uneven Bars. It was on this apparatus that she made history by being awarded her first maximum on 18 July 1976. Her feat was replicated by fellow Romanian Daniela Silivas in 1988.

Share of the glory

Women's Gymnastics at the 1956 Games was dominated by the Warsaw Pact countries and by two performers in particular. Only one medal went outside the Soviet bloc as Hungary's Agnes Keleti and the USSR's Larissa Latynina annexed the five individual gongs. All-Around champion Latynina, who was also part of the victorious Soviet team, won the Vault, with Keleti claiming Balance Beam and Uneven Bars honours. On the Floor the judges could not split them, so the gold was shared and Keleti, aged 35, became the Games' oldest women's Gymnastics champion.

London 2012

Bronze and farewell

Beth Tweddle won a medal at last in the final Olympic Games appearance of her Artistic Gymnastics career. The British 27-year old's score of 15.916 took bronze in the Uneven Bars Competition. She had won four world titles and was the most decorated British gymnast ever but an Olympic medal had eluded her. The Russian Federation's Aliya Mustafina won gold ahead of Beijing 2008 champion Kexin He of China. Tweddle might have finished in silver medal place herself but for a step back on landing. She said later: 'Everyone kept saying to me: "You're a great champ, it doesn't matter what happens today."' I kept trying to tell myself that but I knew if I walked out of here without a medal, I'd have been really disappointed because this is definitely my last Olympic Games.'

Order re-established

The United States women put on a dominant display as they won Team Competition gold ahead of China, Romania and Russian Federation – the latter taking silver. Romania and China fought it out for the bronze medal, Romania winning it on the vault in the last rotation. The USA success was built on consistency, starting with McKayla Maroney's 16.23 vault score, the highest of the day. Gabby Douglas, Jordyn Wieber and Alexandra Raisman all scored 15.0 or above in their climactic floor exercises. This was only the second time the US women had won a Team Competition gold in Artistic Gymnastics. The last time they took the gold, at Atlanta 1996, the same three countries – the USA, Russian Federation and Romania – medalled in the same order.

⬇ Gabby Douglas of the United States produced an outstanding display to win the Individual All-Around Competition gold medal.

⬆ Beth Tweddle, Great Britain's most successful gymnast ever, had won four world championships but no Olympic Games medals until she earned a bronze in the Uneven Bars Competition at London 2012.

Squirrel's golden horde

Gabrielle 'Gabby' Douglas – also known as the 'Flying Squirrel' – became the first African-American to win the women's Individual All-Around Competition gold. Her display was rated as the most striking for an United States woman since Mary Lou Retton at Los Angeles 1984. At the start of the year Douglas ranked third in the United States, behind world champion Jordyn Wieber and team captain Alexandra Raisman. But Wieber failed to qualify and Raisman slipped out of contention. Douglas then stepped up to head two contestants from the Russian Federation and win the United States' third successive gold in the event. Praise for Douglas could come no higher than that which came from Olympic Games Gymnastics icon Nadia Comaneci. She described Douglas's performance as 'exceptional, unbelievable'.

China at the double

China's women's team captain Linlin Deng won the gold medal in the Beam competition, ahead of team-mate Lu Sui who won silver. This was the only one-two finish in Artistic Gymnastics at the London 2012 Games and represented Deng's second Olympic gold medal, having been part of China's Team success at Beijing 2008. The 20-year-old, who finished on 15.600 points, led the event from start to finish after pre-Olympic favourite Gabby Douglas fell, finishing last. World champion Sui won silver with a score of 15.500 while Alexandra Raisman of the United States was awarded bronze. Romania's Catalina Ponor matched Raisman's total of 15.066 points, but she lost out on a medal as the American scored better in the tie-breaking countback of execution.

Rhythmic Gymnastics

Only women compete in Rhythmic Gymnastics, with individual competitors executing choreographed movements to music using five types of apparatus: rope, hoop, ball, clubs and ribbon. In the Group Competition teams of six gymnasts complete one routine with five ribbons and another with three hoops and two balls. Two panels of judges award points for each performance.

Russian Federation on top

The Russia Federation dominates Rhythmic Gymnastics, with its gymnasts taking gold at the last four Olympic Games. Evgeniya Kanaeva was the third successive Russian winner at Beijing 2008, when identical scores of 18.850 with the rope and hoop and a superb club routine earned her the highest rating of any display in the final – 18.950. It was a performance to make the inhabitants of Kanaeva's home city of Omsk in Western Siberia very proud, coming four years after another woman from Omsk won the silver in the Individual competition – Irina Tchachina. Inna Zhukova of Belarus won the silver this time round, and Ukraine's Anna Bessonova claimed the bronze to ensure that all the Individual All-Around Competition medallists came from former Soviet Union nations.

The apparatus

Rope: Made of hemp or a synthetic material, the rope must be proportional to the gymnast's height. It can be swung and circled during the routine, which requires jumping and explosive movements.

Hoop: Made of plastic or wood, the hoop has an interior diameter of 80–90 centimetres and must weigh at least 300 grams. Favoured movements include rolls over the body or on the floor, rotations around the hand, throws and catches and passing over or through the hoop. It offers the greatest variety of movements and technical skills. Any vibration of the hoop in the air is penalised.

Ball: Made of rubber or a synthetic material, the ball is 18–20cm in diameter and weighs 400g. It is thrown, caught, bounced and rolled over the body or on the floor, but no grip is allowed as the movement should be 'flowing and sensuous'.

Clubs: Made of wood or a synthetic material, the clubs are 40–50cm long, weigh 150g each and are circled, thrown, caught and tapped.

Ribbon: Made of satin and at least 6m long, the ribbon is held by a stick to enable the gymnast to circle, spiral, throw and catch. Any knots in the ribbon are penalised.

Fung the first

In Rhythmic Gymnastics more than most sports the rare absence of Eastern Europeans has a devastating effect on the pecking order. Such a phenomenon happened in 1984, when the withdrawal from the Olympic Games of the Soviet Union and most of the Warsaw Pact countries drastically lowered the quality of the Rhythmic field. Thus the fact that the first Rhythmic Gymnastics gold was won by a Canadian remains an anomaly. Lori Fung from Vancouver edged to the top of the podium ahead of Romania's Doina Stainculescu. In the World Championships the following year, Fung could only finish ninth.

← Canada's Lori Fung, champion at Los Angeles 1984, remains the only non-Eastern European Rhythmic All-Around gold-medal winner.

Little Miss Perfect

Perfection is always sought in sport, but rarely achieved. According to the judges at the 1988 Games in Seoul, Rhythmic gymnast Marina Lobach achieved it. The Belarussian (competing under the Soviet flag) received a perfect 'ten' for all of her routines during the qualifying and the final rounds of the All-Around Competition. Others were also given the ultimate score during the finals, but none could match Lobach over both phases of the event. Her score of 60.000 is her sport's equivalent of a hole-in-one at golf or a 147 in snooker. Silver medallist Adriana Dunavska came so close to glory (59.950), but you just can't beat perfection. Lobach was a phenomenon – the youngest Rhythmic Gymnastics champion at the Games, she retired the following year at the grand old age of 19.

Late developer

Rhythmic Gymnastics began in the former Soviet Union in the 1940s before being officially recognised as a competitive event in 1961. It became part of the Games programme in Los Angeles in 1984, and the Group Competition was introduced 12 years later at the Atlanta 1996 Games.

↑ *A slip-up for Russia's Yanina Batyrchina – she dropped the ribbon – cost her a chance of a Rhythmic Gymnastics All-Around gold medal at the Atlanta 1996 Games.*

Ribbon ruins it

Just as one punch in Boxing or a throw in Judo can mean instant heartbreak for a potential gold medallist, so a dropped ribbon can do the same in Rhythmic Gymnastics. At Atlanta 1996, Russia's Yanina Batyrchina was duelling for the title with Ekaterina Serebryanskaya of Ukraine going into the final discipline. Alas for Batyrchina, the stick tied to the satin slipped through her fingers and her chance had gone. Serebryanskaya was not faultless herself with the ribbon, but her errors were not as cataclysmic as Batyrchina effectively 'dropped the baton'. Serebryanskaya became the first Rhythmic gymnast to hold the European, World and Olympic Games All-Around gold medals at the same time, a feat equalled by Russia's Alina Kabayeva eight years later.

Old at 22

The sheer flexibility required to compete at the highest level in Rhythmic Gymnastics means that athletes are considered already too old at an age when they would be nowhere near their peak in most other sports at the Olympic Games. At Sydney 2000, aged 21, Yulia Barsakova became Rhythmic Gymnastics oldest gold medallist in the sport. Her big moment came at the expense of Alina Kabaeva, who would succeed her at Athens 2004. The age record fell at London 2012, to 22-year-old Evgeniya Kanaeva.

➔ *Yulia Barsakova (centre) is the oldest All-Around champion – aged 21.*

London 2012

Kanaeva the dancing queen

Evgeniya Kanaeva made history in becoming the first rhythmic gymnast to defend her Olympic Individual All-Around Competition title. The 22-year-old was in a class of her own. Her score of 116.900 left silver for fellow Russian Federation team member Daria Dmitrieva with Liubou Charkashyna of Belarus taking bronze. The three-time world champion took an instant lead after the opening hoop and then followed up with grace and style illuminating her routines with the ball, clubs and ribbon. The secret of her success is nothing more than dedication and hard work. Kanaeva said: 'Gymnastics has been part of my life since I was six. Since that time I have practised every day, eight hours a day.'

↑ *The Russian Federation continued to dominate the Rhythmic Gymnastics Group Competition, winning a fourth consecutive gold at London 2012.*

Team GB make a start

Great Britain's success at London 2012 in the Rhythmic Gymnastics Group Competition was merely in being there. They made their competition debut after winning an appeal against their own federation and then funding their preparation through raffles and sponsored skips. Britain finished 12th and last in the qualifying stage but close enough behind Germany and Canada to feel their efforts had been justified. Lynne Hutchison said: 'We definitely deserved to be here and we proved that by coming that close to Canada. We weren't expected to beat anyone here but to come that close shows we can compete with Olympic countries.' The Sarajevo 1984 Olympic Winter Games ice dance champions Jayne Torvill and Christopher Dean had mentored the team originally and had some input in their choreography.

Trampoline

The trampoline was invented in 1935 by Americans George Nilsen and Larry Griswold. They bolted together an iron frame and attached a piece of canvas to it using springs. The name comes from the Spanish word 'trampolin', meaning springboard. Trampoline became a mainstream competitive activity when the International Trampoline Federation merged with the International Gymnastics Federation in 1999.

Karavaeva kicks it off

One of the trampoline's inventors, George Nilsen, then 86 years old, was there to see Russia's Irina Karavaeva enter the record books as the inaugural women's Individual gold medallist in the sport, thanks to her success at Sydney in 2000. Ukraine's Oxana Tsyhuleva took silver and Canada's Karen Cockburn bronze before admitting to an unusual phobia for a trampolinist: 'It's an adrenaline rush. I'm actually afraid of heights... But it's a different feeling on the trampoline.' Germany's Anna Dogonadze led after the qualification round, but bounced off the trampoline during her final routine.

He makes Chinese breakthrough

He Wenna won China's first-ever gold medal in Trampoline at the conclusion of the 2008 women's competition in Beijing. She finished ahead of Canadian Karen Cockburn by 0.80 points. Ekaterina Khilko struck a blow for Uzbekistan by claiming the bronze, the country's first medal in Trampoline. Germany's Anna Dogonadze, the 2004 gold medallist, fell mid-way through her routine and finished fourth, while Sydney 2000 winner, Russia's Irina Karavaeva, came fifth.

At Beijing 2008, Wenna He became China's first-ever Trampoline champion at the Games.

⬆ *Alexander Moskalenko took home a men's Trampoline silver medal from Athens 2004 to add to the gold he had won at Sydney 2000.*

Magnificent Moskalenko

The foremost competitor in the history of trampoline has been Alexander Moskalenko. The Russian 'king of spring' dominated the sport in the 1990s and early 2000s, winning five world titles and the first men's Olympic Games title at Sydney 2000. He won the 1990 and 1992 World Championships and then, at the age of 22, decided to retire, unable to find 'the right motivation'. His absence did not last long, as he came back to secure the 1994 global crown before once again leaving the scene. The news that Trampoline would make its Olympic Games debut in 2000 was too much of a lure for Moskalenko, and he prepared by claiming a fourth world title in 1999. Sydney was then the stage for the greatest display in the sport's history as Moskalenko utterly outclassed the opposition in the final, winning by the enormous margin of 2.40 points in a sport where often fractions of a point make the difference. He concluded a career that compares to any of the all-time greats in other sports by claiming the 2001 World Championship and the 2002 European title, after which he was only denied the 2003 world crown on a tie-break and also narrowly lost in the final at the Athens 2004 Games.

New kids on the block

Trampolinists are judged by a panel on the technical difficulty and execution of their moves. There are two phases to each competition, qualification and final. The qualification round has two routines. The first must include special requirements, the second is voluntary. The top eight from these two routines qualify for the Final. Scores from the qualification round do not carry over to the final, which has one voluntary routine, with the highest scorer declared the winner. Synchronised Trampoline, a feature of the World Games, has yet to make its Olympic Games debut.

Nikitin nicks it

At the Athens 2004 Games, Ukraine's Yuri Nikitin claimed the men's title by the narrowest of margins. Nikitin finished just 0.3 points ahead of five-time world champion Alexander Moskalenko from Russia.

Greek tragedy for Karavaeva

Reigning women's Individual champion Irina Karavaeva endured a disastrous defence of her title at the 2004 Games in Athens. The Russian finished in 15th place, second last, at the end of the qualifying routines to miss out on the chance to progress to the final. Germany's Anna Dogonadze claimed gold, with the then world champion Karen Cockburn from Canada having to settle for silver and China's Shanshan Huang taking bronze. Dogonadze became the first non-Russian to win Trampoline gold at the Olympic Games, although her heritage ties her to the former Soviet Union. She was born in Mtskheta, the former capital of Georgia, and represented that country from 1992 to 1997. Prior to Georgia's independence, she had competed under the Soviet banner, but on marrying her former coach she became a German citizen.

↑*Irina Karavaeva's defence of her women's Individual title ended abruptly when she finished 15th out of 16 in qualifying at Athens 2004.*

China's Lu doubles up

The day after Wenna He's triumph, Chunlong Lu followed her example to become the first Chinese man to win the men's Individual Trampoline title. Lu, the top qualifier for the final, scored 41.00 to win gold, showing superior style while executing a slightly easier routine than Jason Burnett, who won the silver, the best result in the sport for a Canadian man. Lu's team-mate Dong Dong, at 19 the youngest competitor in the final, took bronze.

London 2012

MacLennan out on her own

Rosannagh MacLennan returned to Canada with the country's only gold medal at London 2012 in the women's Trampoline Individual Competition after Chinese favourite Wenna He fell on her last move. MacLennan's gold was also Canada's first in the women's Trampoline Individual Competition, which became an Olympic sport at Sydney 2000. The 23-year-old score of 57.305 had already edged her past another Chinese favourite in Shanshan Huang so when 2008 champion He stumbled, MacLennan knew she had won gold. MacLennan, seventh at Beijing 2008, had started fifth in the finals round but rose to the challenge to record the best marks of her career. She thought that winning gold might allow her a treat – 'maybe a little chocolate'.

➔ *Dong Dong, world champion in 2009, produced a superb final routine to take the men's Trampoline gold medal at the London 2012 Games.*

Dong bounces back

China's Dong Dong bounced past the Russia Federation's Dmitry Ushakov to upgrade his Beijing 2008 bronze to gold to reward his competitive consistency in the men's Trampoline Individual Competition. Dong, who defied injury fears, had been individual runner-up at the 2007 World Championships in Quebec. Bronze at Beijing 2008 was followed by individual victory in the 2009 World Championships in St Petersburg. Ushakov had thought he had a realistic prospect of gold after the qualification round. Dong had been third then but surprised the Russian by stepping up the level of difficulty of his routines.

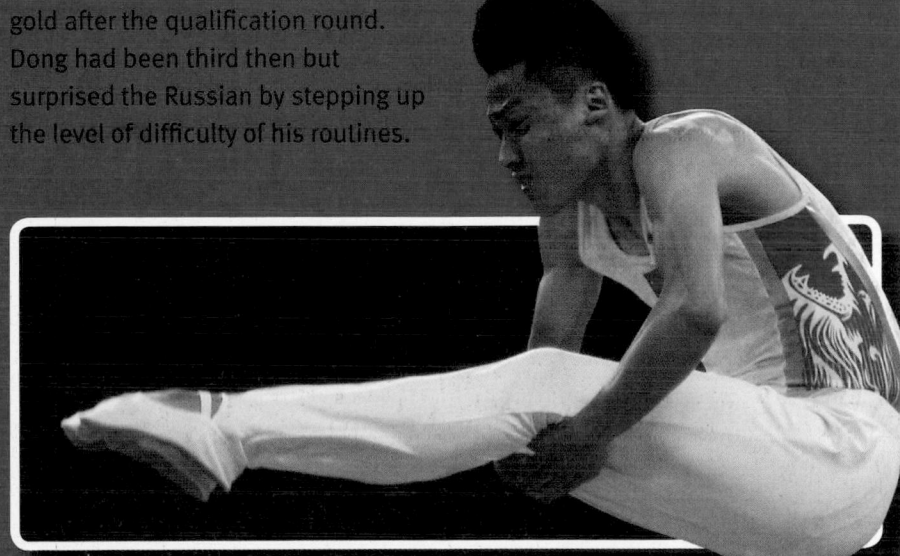

Chapter Eight
Martial arts
and combat sports

George Orwell once said that serious sport is 'war minus the shooting'. The author might have been describing the ferocity displayed at the Olympic Games inside the boxing ring, fencing sale or dojo, or on the wrestling mat, where some of the hardest-fought sporting contests are staged every four years.

Statues and paintings found in archaeological digs demonstrate that some form of wrestling has been known as a sport in Japan and China, Babylon and Egypt in antiquity. The ancient Greeks also practised it, as Homer has an account of a wrestling match in the *Iliad*.

Thus Wrestling was included in the first modern Olympic Games in 1896. The international Freestyle and Greco-Roman styles, as introduced at the Games, became the universally accepted version of the sport.

Boxing traces its history back to the ancient Greeks, to around 686 BC. Yet, despite professional pugilism's popularity in Victorian times, the amateur sport was omitted from the first two modern Games, the official attitude being that it was ungentlemanly and practised by the dregs of the population. That view was revised by 1904 and since 1920 Boxing has been one of the highlights of every Olympic Games. The London 2012 Games did, however, witness a significant change in the Boxing programme, as women's events were staged at the Games for the first time amid great success. There were three weight categories for them, Fly Weight (51kg), Light Weight (60kg) and Middle Weight (75kg), and 10 for the men.

Combat sports introduced to the Olympic Games have often reflected the culture of a particular Host City. Thus at Tokyo 1964 Judo made its bow and Taekwondo, the Korean martial art, was introduced at Seoul 1988.

Nicola Adams (left) made history at the London 2012 Games as the first woman to win an Olympic Boxing gold medal. The 29-year-old from Yorkshire was also the first of three British boxers to win gold.

Boxing

With the exception of 1912 (because Swedish law banned the sport at the time), Boxing has been contested at every Olympic Games since 1904. Several of the sport's all-time greats – including Muhammad Ali, Joe Frazier, George Foreman and Lennox Lewis – have used their gold-medal-winning exploits as a springboard to greatness on the professional circuit.

Patterson steps up

Floyd Patterson, who would later become the youngest-ever professional world heavy weight champion, won Middle Weight gold at the 1952 Games. During his pro career, he would twice encounter the silver medallist in the Heavy Weight division at those Games, Ingemar Johansson, winning once and losing once to the Swede for the world heavy weight title.

Ali's shining light

Muhammad Ali, the gold-medal winner at Light Heavy Weight at the 1960 Games in Rome, remains one of the all-time Games greats. Ali, then a brash 18-year-old boxing under his original name, Cassius Clay, was the outstanding boxer of those Games, and his subsequent career underlined that gold-medal success as an amateur can be a springboard to a professional career. Ali is such an iconic sporting figure (so much so that he is widely regarded as one of the most recognisable figures of the 20th century) that is was no surprise he was chosen to light the Cauldron at the Opening Ceremony of Atlanta 1996 and for a role in the flag presentations at London 2012.

↑ *Cassius Clay proves too strong for Australia's Tony Madigan in the semi-finals of the Light Heavy Weight event at the Rome 1960 Games.*

Savon the successor

Following his retirement, Teofilio Stevenson became Cuba's national boxing coach. His team's star performer was Felix Savon, who went on to match his hero by winning Super Heavy Weight gold in 1992, 1996 and 2000. Savon was formidable, standing 6ft 5in (1.96m) tall and with a reach of more than 2m. He dominated amateur boxing, and won six world amateur championships from 1986, before retiring after the Sydney 2000 Games. Felix's son, Erislandy, boxed at the London 2012 Games, but lost on points to eventual Super Heavy Weight (+91kg) champion Anthony Joshua.

Best of British

Born on 1 June 1892, London policeman Harry Mallin was the British ABA Middle Weight champion in 1919 and 1920 and had his first taste of the Olympic Games at Antwerp 1920. He cruised through to the final, in which he faced Art Preud'Homme – a French-Canadian soldier who had won all of his previous bouts by knockout. Mallin won on points to take gold. At Paris 1924, Mallin began the defence of his title at the Velodrome d'Hiver with two straightforward victories, won a controversial quarter-final fight against French hero Roger Brousse, out-pointed Belgium's Joseph Beecken in the semi-final, before beating compatriot John Elliot on points in the final. In doing so, Mallin had become the first boxer, at any weight, to defend a title at the Games and remains the only British boxer ever to have won two Boxing gold medals.

Lennox Lewis's springboard

The big boys who have won Boxing medals at the Olympic Games have regularly featured future professional world champions among their ranks. The 1988 Super Heavy Weight final was a gripping contest between two future heavy weight champions of the world, with Lennox Lewis, then representing Canada, defeating Riddick Bowe, of the USA. Other medallists who have gone on to win professional world titles include Joe Frazier and George Foreman, both of the USA, who won the Heavy Weight gold medal in 1964 and 1968 respectively, and Wladimir Klitschko, of Ukraine, who won Super Heavy Weight gold at Atlanta 1996. Ingemar Johansson, the only Swede ever to hold the professional world heavy weight title, won the silver medal at Helsinki 1952. He was probably glad of the opportunity to box at all: Sweden's national ban on boxing had seen the sport excluded altogether in 1912 when the Games were held in Stockholm.

➔ *Joe Frazier finds the target against Hans Huber en route to the Heavy Weight gold medal at Tokyo 1964.*

Stevenson's amateur ethos

Three-time gold medallist Teofilio Stevenson of Cuba consistently refused all entreaties to turn pro, famously declining one offer of US$2m. He said: 'Professional boxing treats a fighter like a commodity, to be bought and sold and discarded when no longer of use.' Such was Stevenson's domination of the Heavy Weight competition from 1972 that it was not until he met Hungary's Istvan Levai in the semi-final at Moscow 1980 that another boxer was able to last the full three rounds with him. Even then, Levai spent nine minutes back-pedalling away from the Cuban's punch. Denied the possibility of a fourth gold medal by Cuba's boycott of the Los Angeles 1984 Games, Stevenson won his last amateur world title in 1986, aged 34. He died in 2012.

➔ *Cuba's Teofilo Stevenson won three Heavy Weight gold medals between 1972 and 1980, but always resisted the lure of professional boxing.*

British hat-trick

The 1908 Olympic Games, the first time the event was staged in London, saw an achievement that cannot be repeated in 2012: all three Heavy Weight boxing medallists came from Great Britain. Albert Oldman won the final with a knockout in just two minutes, beating his compatriot Sydney Evans, while Fred Parks took the bronze medal by defeating the other losing semi-finalist. In order to participate in the Games, Oldman had to take time off from his day job, as a policeman in the City of London. It is understood that afterwards he never encountered much trouble while walking his beat. Today, nations are only allowed to enter one boxer in each weight division. Since 1952, bronze medals have been awarded to each of the losing semi-finalists.

Ali's medal journey

The story of Muhammad Ali's Olympic Games gold medal has, in just half a century, entered into folklore, and is seen by some as symbolising how sport in general, and the Olympic Games in particular, have helped to improve race relations. Ali loved his medal. On his return to Louisville, Kentucky, in the Deep South of the United States, he kept his medal with him at all times, even sleeping with it. But what he could not do with his medal was take it with him into a whites-only restaurant in the home town that had given him a hero's welcome on his jubilant return from Rome 1960. After a confrontation with the restaurant owner and a white gang, Ali was so disgusted with his treatment that he tossed the medal into the Ohio River. Nearly 50 years later, in recognition of Ali's stance for human rights, the International Olympic Committee presented its former champion, by now badly affected by Parkinson's disease, with a replacement gold medal in a special ceremony during the 1996 Games in Atlanta.

Weights and measures

The growing size and stature of the population in general has seen regular adjustments made to the weight categories in Boxing at the Games. For instance, in 1904, when Boxing was contested for the first time, the Heavy Weight division was open to anyone weighing 11 stone 4 pounds (72 kilograms) or more. By the time of the Athens 2004 Games a century later, Heavy Weights were boxers weighing between 81 and 91kg, with the biggest category by now Super Heavy Weights, for the giants of more than 14 stone (89 kg). There has been a Super Heavy Weight category since Los Angeles 1984. The Light Heavy Weight category has remained unchanged since Helsinki 1952, for boxers weighting between 75 and 81kg (a little more than 12½ stone).

↑ *The USA's Tyrell Biggs (left) and Yugloslavia's Salihu Aziz square off in the first-ever Super Heavy Weight competition at Los Angeles 1984.*

Style standard

The Middle Weight and Welter Weight boxers at the Olympic Games have consistently been seen as among the most stylish boxers in the tournament, possessing the swiftest of hands and providing the best examples of the sweet science. At every Games since 1936, a trophy named the Val Barker Cup – in honour of the first general secretary of the World Amateur Boxing Federation (AIBA) – has been awarded to a boxer chosen from the entire tournament who displays the best style and technique. The recipients of the Val Barker have usually been gold medallists in their division, and they regularly feature the winners of the Middle Weight or Welter Weight class.

All that glitters – but never gold

After turning professional, Roy Jones Junior went on to enjoy a fabulous 20-year career. Regularly named as the world's best 'pound-for-pound' boxer, he won world titles at every weight division from middle to heavy weight. Before that, the 19-year-old Jones had won the Val Barker Cup, as the most stylish boxer at Seoul 1988 – even though he did not win the gold medal. Boxing at Light Middle Weight, Jones met the Republic of Korea's Si-hun Park in the final and landed 86 punches to his opponent's 32. Park even apologised for the verdict which led to a change in the scoring system. Jones put the disappointment behind him to turn professional seven months later. Within a further four years he had seized the first of his world titles. In Washington DC, Jones defied the pain from a broken right hand to outpoint Bernard Hopkins and secure the IBF Middle Weight crown.

⬆ *The shock can be seen in their faces as Park Si-hun (right) is declared the winner against Roy Jones (left) in the Light Middle Weight Final at Seoul 1988.*

Tipping the scales

The weight limits in the Middle Weight division at the Olympic Games have been altered frequently over the past century. Since 2004, the Middle Weight division has been for boxers between 69 and 75 kilograms. The Light Middle Weight category was first contested at the 1952 Games in Helsinki, but was dropped after Sydney 2000. Since the 2004 Games, the Welter Weight division has been for boxers weighing between 64 and 69kg. The Light Welter Weight division, which from 1952 until 2008 was contested by boxers weighing between 60 and 64kg, has been dropped from the programme for 2012. With three new weight divisions for women being introduced, the IOC is still maintaining a strict limit on the total number of competitors at the Games.

Sweet Sugar

One of the most renowned champions in Boxing history at the Olympic Games is Sugar Ray Leonard, winner of the Light Welter Weight gold medal at Montreal 1976. Leonard turned professional just months after his golden moment, and went on to become the first professional boxer ever to earn more than US$100 million in his career. Leonard's bouts with Roberto Duran, Tommy Hearns and Marvin Hagler have become the stuff of sporting legend, and helped install the American as 'The Boxer of the Decade' for the 1980s.

➔ *Sugar Ray Leonard won Light Welter Weight gold at Montreal 1976.*

Endurance test

Winning medals in Boxing is among the most gruelling and demanding of all the challenges offered by the Olympic Games. The competition lasts almost the entire duration of the Games and culminates in two days of finals, completed not long before the Olympic Flame is extinguished in the stadium at the Closing Ceremony. In some cases, boxers have had to get through three bouts before reaching the semi-finals, giving them sometimes less than 48 hours for recovery and the repair of any cuts or injuries sustained along the way.

Stretching the limit

Amateur boxing was always used to be contested over three rounds, each of three minutes. Recently, in the tournaments at the 2000, 2004 and 2008 Games, the contests lasted four rounds, each of two minutes, as the sport sought to minimise damage to boxers through exhaustion and blows to the head. Boxing experts, however, felt that the traditional format of three-minute rounds demanded more stamina from the contestants, and in London the Boxing tournament reverted to that format for men. Women continued to box over four two-minute rounds.

Simple in St Louis

The International Olympic Committee continues to recognise St Louis 1904 as the Games at which Boxing made its debut. In the Boxing tournament staged at St Louis, many of the contests were simply one-off, straight finals. This helped Oliver Kirk to claim a unique place in history as the only boxer to win in two weight divisions at a single Games. Kirk, of the United States, beat another American, Frank Haller, for the Feather Weight title, and at Bantam Weight, he stopped George Finnegan in the third round.

Marvellous McTaggart

Dick McTaggart, one of 18 children from a family in Dundee, is widely regarded as Britain's finest ever boxer at the Olympic Games. The 21-year-old Scot won the Light Weight gold medal at Melbourne 1956, where he also received the Val Barker Cup as the tournament's most stylish boxer. McTaggart boxed again at the 1960 Games in Rome, winning the bronze medal, and at Tokyo in 1964, where he was eliminated in his second bout. In both 1960 and 1964, McTaggart was beaten by Polish boxers, first Kazimierz Pazdzior and later Jerzy Kulej, who both went on to win gold medals. McTaggart's career achievements included five ABA titles, a Commonwealth Games gold medal and the European Championship, and he won 610 of his 634 bouts. He never turned professional.

⬆ *Scotland's Dick McTaggart picked up two medals (one gold, the other bronze) at three appearances at the Games between 1956 and 1964.*

Wrong target

Spanish Featherweight Valentin Loren has gone down in infamy for his performance in the Boxing tournament at the 1964 Games. The referee, Hungarian Guorgy Sermer, stepped in and disqualified Loren in round two of his first-round bout for repeated holding and punching with an open glove. The Spaniard was so furious with the decision that, according to some ringside observers, he landed his first punch with a proper fist on the referee's nose. Loren duly received a lifetime ban from international boxing.

← *Spain's Valentin Loren flattens referee Guorgy Sermer at the Tokyo 1964 Games – it was his last action in an international boxing ring.*

➜ *Oscar De La Hoya (USA), still a teenager, celebrates winning Light Weight gold at the 1992 Olympic Games in Barcelona.*

Safety features

All modern amateur boxers now wear headguards, while their large, padded gloves have white areas in the scoring area, with the aim of scoring a point with each punch they land successfully on their opponent's head or upper body. Other safety measures in amateur boxing include an age limit: senior boxers can be no younger than 17 and no older than 34. Boxers are also banned from wearing beards.

Great Gunn

Amateur boxing's age rule makes it impossible for Richard Gunn, the Feather Weight champion when the Games were first held in London in 1908, to lose his record as the oldest ever Boxing champion in history. Gunn was 37 in 1908. He had been British amateur champion from 1894 to 1896, but had retired because of a lack of competition and only came out of retirement for the 1908 Games. With the gold medal duly won, Gunn retired once more, this time for good, having lost one bout in 15 years.

Ultimate Oscar winner

One of the greatest boxers of all time, amateur or professional, was Oscar De La Hoya, the Los Angelino who, as a teenager, won the Light Weight gold medal at the 1992 Olympic Games in Barcelona. A year beforehand, De La Hoya had pledged to his mother, who was dying from cancer, that he would win the Boxing gold medal. At the Games, duly inspired, De La Hoya would drop to his knees after each of his victories and point to the sky. De La Hoya won the Light Weight Final by beating Marco Rudolph, the German who had beaten him in the World Championship final a year before. The triumph at the Games set up De La Hoya for a professional career in which he dominated the lighter weight divisions for the rest of the decade.

Papp perfection

The Boxing tournament at Melbourne 1956 will always be remembered for the feat of the Hungarian Laszlo Papp. Having won the Middle Weight title at London 1948, Papp won the new Light Middle Weight title in 1952 and retained it at Melbourne 1956. That made him the first boxer ever to win three gold medals at the Games, a feat that was unique until Teofilio Stevenson matched it in the 1970s. In his amateur career, Papp scored 55 first-round knockouts. In the 1956 Light Middle Weight Final, Papp defeated José Torres, the Puerto Rican fighting under the flag of the United States, who would go on to become light heavy weight world champion as a professional.

➘ *James DeGale ended Great Britain's 40-year wait for Middle Weight gold at the Beijing 2008 Games.*

←*Hungary's Laszlo Papp won three successive gold medals between 1948 and 1956 – the first of two boxers to achieve the feat.*

DeGale's breakthrough

Middle Weight British boxers have struggled to make their mark at the Olympic Games. James DeGale, the Middle Weight champion at Beijing 2008, was the first British boxer to win Middle Weight gold for 40 years. The last British Middle Weight champion before him was Chris Finnegan, who struck gold at the 1968 Games in Mexico City, despite being knocked down in his first bout, against Titus Simba of Tanzania. In his semi-final, Finnegan, a hod-carrier by trade, was given two standing counts of eight in his contest with Al Jones of the United States, but battled his way through to the final, where he won a majority points decision over the Soviet Union's Aleksei Kiselov.

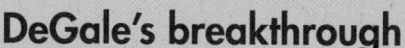

London 2012

Joshua's London pride

Great Britain's Anthony Joshua staged a remarkable last-round revival to take the Super Heavy Weight (+91kg) gold medal after poor defence had left him three points behind Italian policeman Roberto Cammarelle. A rousing climax saw Joshua land powerful shots of his own on the reigning Olympic champion and the judges gave him the victory on countback. The Italian team appealed the decision, but Joshua was eventually confirmed as the gold medal winner 10 minutes later. Joshua, who lost by a single point in the World Amateur Championship final at Baku in 2011, said: 'I gave it my all in the third round. My legs and everything were killing me, sometimes I wanted to stop but my mind was working and my arms were just flying around.'

⬆ Reigning Super Heavy Weight (+91kg) champion Roberto Cammarelle (right) was beaten on countback by Great Britain's Anthony Joshua in a thrilling London 2012 Olympic Games final.

⬆ Katie Taylor tries to land a left to the head of Sofya Ochigava during the final of the women's Light Weight (60kg) final. Taylor prevailed 10-8 to win Ireland's only gold medal of the London 2012 Games.

Carrazana one to watch

Robeisy Ramirez Carrazana, an 18-year-old Cuban in a great national boxing tradition, left London with the world at his feet after winning the men's Fly Weight (52kg) gold against Mongolian Tugstsogt Nyambayar. Cuba's boxing golds make up almost half of their Olympic Games medal total, and Carrazana laid immediate claim to No. 34 in taking a close first round. Carrazana maintained his lead in the second round and started to land damaging shots of his own in the third. He fell to his knees when the final score of 17-14 was announced and then rose to take a lap of honour with the Cuban flag. He said: 'It's overwhelming. I am 18 and I becoming part of my country's history.'

Irish eyes are smiling

ExCeL was turned all-green as Irish fans took over the venue to cheer 26-year-old Katie Taylor to a thrilling victory in the first women's Light Weight (60kg) final. After hugging her Russian Federation opponent Sofya Ochigava at the end of the bout, Taylor embraced her father and trainer Peter and then saluted her supporters before draping an Irish flag around her shoulders. Taylor was without doubt one of the personalities of the London 2012 Boxing tournament. She received messages of congratulations from personalities as diverse as boxer Mike Tyson, film star Sylvester Stallone and golfer Rory McIlroy, before heading home for civic and government receptions back in Dublin.

Nicola makes history

Women's Boxing made its debut at London 2012 and Nicola Adams made history by winning women's Boxing's first ever gold medal in at the Olympic Games. Adams grew up in Yorkshire, but moved to Haringey, North-East London, just a few miles from the Olympic Park and ExCeL, to train in advance of London 2012. She won gold in the women's Fly Weight (51kg) by a decisive 16-7 points margin against China's Cancan Ren. It was sweet revenge for Adams, who had been beaten by Ren in the world amateur final three months earlier. 'I can't believe I've actually done it,' said Adams, whose mile-wide smile lit up television screens during London 2012. 'I've been dreaming about this moment since I was 12. It's a fairytale ending.' Her interest in boxing had been sparked on seeing, 20 years earlier, a video film of Muhammad Ali's victory over George Foreman in the Rumble in the Jungle.

Fencing

Fencing is one of just five sports – with Athletics, Cycling, Gymnastics and Swimming – to have been an ever-present in every modern Games since 1896. Fencing also has a unique place in Games history, because, at the first two Games of the modern era, in Athens 1896 and Paris 1900, amateurs and professionals were allowed to compete. There are three forms of Fencing at the Games: Epée, Foil and Sabre.

Setting the rules

Fencing's international governing body was not formed until 1913, and at the early Games, as with so many sports, the competition rules set by the International Olympic Committee and the local organisers often had a formative influence on many facets of the event. Since it was commonplace at the turn of the 20th century for fencing masters and their pupils to enter parallel competitions, it seemed almost natural to allow both to compete in the first two Games, in Athens and Paris. Contests had no time limits until the 1930s, when one match lasted seven hours. In modern fencing, the bout lasts for three rounds, each of three minutes.

Judges wired in

In the days before automatic electronic scoring revolutionised fencing, matches depended on the sharp eyes and quick wits of a set of expert judges. Two side judges stood behind and beside each fencer, watching for hits made by that fencer. A 'director' observed from several feet away. He would end each action by calling 'Halt!' and then poll the judges. If the judges differed, or abstained, the director could overrule. Judges began to be replaced in Fencing at the 1936 Olympic Games in Berlin, when an electrical scoring system was used for the Epée, with a buzzer and lights indicating if a competitor had made a touch. The foil was scored electronically from the time of the 1956 Games in Melbourne, but the sabre, with its cut and thrust style, had to wait until the 1988 Games in Seoul before it, too, had automated scoring. As well as reducing the possibility of judges being open to any accusations of bias, the introduction of electronic scoring (and with it the possibility of more accurate scoring with faster actions previously unseen by the human eye) allowed fencers to perform subtler, lighter touches, and more touches to the back and flank than had been the case beforehand. A touch of a mere 15 milliseconds is now enough for a fencer to register a score.

Magical Magyars

In Team Sabre competition at the Games, Hungary's men went unbeaten between 1928 and 1960 – one of the longest winning streaks in Olympic Games history. In all, the Hungarian Sabre teams won 46 matches at the Games and seven gold medals. After losing the title in 1964, Hungary did not win the Team Sabre gold medal again until 1988.

A question of honour settled by a duel

When the French and Italian Foil teams competed at the 1924 Games in Paris, a disputed call by a judge led to an extraordinary incident: a real duel, and possibly one of the last to be fought in the 20th century. After the Games, the Italian team issued a statement that accused the Italian-born Hungarian fencing master, Italo Santelli, of supporting a competition judge's decision in favour of one of the Hungarians. When he heard of the insult, Santelli, although 60 years old, issued a challenge to the captain of the Italian team, Adolfo Cotronei. Government permission was required before the duel could be fought, and Santelli's son, Giorgio, stepped in for his ageing father. Using sabres, but not electronic scoring equipment, Santelli jnr was declared the winner after three minutes of duelling and honour was satisfied.

→ *Hungary's Aladar Gerevich (right) registers a point against Italy's Gastone Darè in the men's Individual Sabre at London 1948. The Hungarian went on to collect Individual and Team gold.*

Six-hit Gerevich

Aladar Gerevich, the Individual Sabre gold medallist the last time that the Olympic Games were staged in London, in 1948, won a total of seven golds, one silver and two bronze in a Games career that began at Los Angeles in 1932. All but one of Gerevich's golds came in the Team Sabre competition, from 1932 through to his final Games, in Rome in 1960, when the Hungarian was 50 years old. It makes Gerevich the Olympian who has recorded the most consecutive victories – six.

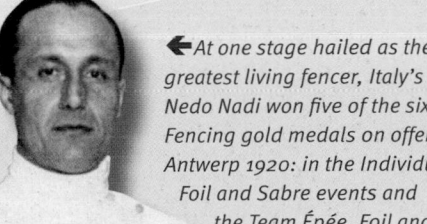

← *At one stage hailed as the greatest living fencer, Italy's Nedo Nadi won five of the six Fencing gold medals on offer at Antwerp 1920: in the Individual Foil and Sabre events and the Team Épée, Foil and Sabre events.*

Fencing equality

Since the 1992 Olympic Games in Barcelona, there have been ten Fencing events contested, and at London 2012 there will again be five events for men and five for women fencers. The Fencing events (for both men and women) at the 2012 Games will be: Individual and Team Foil, Individual Epée (the team event being dropped from the programme), and Individual and Team Sabre.

Nadi spans the war

In the early part of the last century, Nedo Nadi did much to establish Italy's precedence in the salle. As an 18-year-old in 1912, Nadi won his first title in the Individual Foil in Stockholm. War then intervened, but Nadi emerged from it a stronger fencer; at Antwerp in 1920, in the absence of several European teams, including the Hungarians, he not only retained his foil title but also won five of the six available gold medals, three of those with his team-mates. His victory in the Individual Sabre left his brother Aldo nursing the silver medal.

Pals' progress

Fencing has always been a rich source of medals for the Hungarians at the Olympic Games. Aladar Gerevich's team-mate Pal Kovacs, who beat him to the Individual Sabre gold medal in 1952, had a similarly long and illustrious career, winning six gold medals and a bronze at five Games between 1936 and 1960. Pal Schmitt, a Team Epée gold medalist for Hungary at both Mexico City 1968 and Munich 1972, and was elected as his country's President in August 2010.

Zhdanovich breaks in

Given that the sport drew heavily upon its traditions in the French school, and its strong Italian influence, perhaps it shouldn't have come as a surprise that the men's Foil events at the early Games were dominated by French and Italian fencers. It wasn't until the 1960 Games, staged in Rome, that the Franco-Italian duopoly of the event finally came to an end, with Viktor Zhdanovich of the Soviet Union winning gold (to become the first Soviet fencer to win an Olympic Games gold medal), his compatriot Yuri Sisikin taking silver and American Albert Axelrod claiming bronze.

Fencing for the Fatherland

Women fencers have competed at the Olympic Games since Paris 1924, when 33-year-old Ellen Osiier, of Denmark, became the Games' first woman Fencing champion. Osiier beat Great Britain's Gladys Davies to the gold medal in the Individual Foil after winning all 16 of her bouts in Paris. At the next Olympic Games, in Amsterdam in 1928, the Individual Foil was won by Helene Mayer, of Germany, at the age of 17. Eight years later, and by now living in the United States, Mayer was included in the German Fencing team again for the 1936 Games staged in Hitler's Germany, despite her being Jewish. This time Mayer, who had placed fifth in the 1932 competition in Los Angeles, picked up a silver medal.

→ *Denmark's Ellen Osiier became the Games' first-ever women's Fencing champion when she beat Great Britain's Gladys Davies to win the Individual Foil event at Paris 1924.*

Silver linings

Before Gillian Sheen won her gold medal at the 1956 Games, British fencers had won six silvers. Three of those had come in the men's Team Epée event. Great Britain's individual medals had all been won by women: Gladys Davies (1924), Muriel Freeman (1928) and Judy Guinness Penn-Hughes (1932) – and all the medals were won in the Individual Foil.

Latin links

Given that the two countries are often credited as being the birthplace of modern fencing (national fencing schools abounded in the two countries in the late 19th and early 20th centuries), it comes as little surprise that France and Italy dominate Fencing's all-time medal table. Since 1896, the two countries' have won 86 gold medals between them – with Italy leading the way with 45 to France's 41. France lead the way on the overall medals count, however, with 115 (41 gold, 40 silver, 34 bronze) to Italy's 114 (45 gold, 38 silver, 31 bronze). Both countries took home two gold medals at the 2008 Games in Beijing: France in the Team Épée and the Team Sabre; and Italy in the men's Individual Épee (Matteo Tagliariol) and the women's Individual Foil (Valentina Vezzali).

The French have a word for it...

Fencing has a vocabulary all of its own, much of it derived from ancient French. Thus a contest is termed a 'bout', with a specific number of hits as the target for victory; a 'barrage' is a fight-off to determine a result, or qualifier, in the event of a tie. Given the sport's deadly origins, it may be reassuring to know that in fencing there is an offence called 'brutality', when a fencer performs with an unacceptable level of force or violence. A fencing sword has a forte and a foible. The foible is the flexible part of the blade furthest away from the hilt, while the forte is the wider, stiffer part of the blade closer to the hilt.

Excellence at ExCel

The Fencing events at the 2012 Olympic Games in London were staged at ExCel, in the heart of Docklands. The arena, a home for numerous trade fairs and other events, has also staged major sporting events, including world championship boxing and the annual London Triathlon. ExCel was also the home to other sports at London 2012, including Boxing, Judo, Table Tennis and Taekwondo.

Sheen's gold

In the history of the modern Olympic Games, Britain has won but a solitary Fencing gold, won by Gillian Sheen, a 28-year-old dental surgeon from London, who took the Individual Foil title in Melbourne in 1956. Sheen managed to edge into the final by defeating the world champion, Lídia Dömölky-Sákovics, of Hungary, in a barrage to decide the fourth place in her semi-final pool. In the final, Sheen lost her first bout to Olga Orban-Szabo, of Romania, but won her other six bouts to finish equal first with the Romanian. The gold medal was decided on a barrage between these two and, despite having already lost to Orban earlier, Sheen managed to win by four touches to two at the second attempt. Sheen would compete again at the 1960 Games in Rome, before marrying and moving with her husband to live and work in New York.

⬈ Hungary's Erna Bogen (right) finished behind Great Britain's Heather 'Judy' Guinness (left, silver) and Austria's Ellen Preis (centre, gold) to claim women's Individual Foil bronze at the Los Angeles 1932 Games.

Family business

There is often a strong family aspect to Fencing events at the Games. Albert Bogen is proof of this. He competed for Austria at the 1912 Games in Stockholm (picking up a medal in the Team Sabre) and for Hungary at the 1928 Games in Amsterdam (a Jew, he had moved to Hungary). His daughter, Erne Bogen, won bronze for Hungary in the women's Individual Foil at the 1932 Games in Los Angeles. She later married one of Hungary's greatest Olympians, seven-time Sabre gold medallist Aladar Gerevich. And Erna and Aladar's son, Pal, won bronze medals in the Team Sabre in 1972 and 1980 – a third generation of the Bogen family to win an Olympic Games medal.

London 2012

Hungarian revival

Aron Szilagyi revived Hungarian Fencing honour by winning gold in the men's Individual Sabre after his brilliant display outclassed Italian Diego Occhiuzzi 15–8. The victory saw Szilagyi become the first Hungarian Olympic Games Individual Sabre champion in 20 years. Szilagyi led 8–1 at the first break after a series of lightning attacks to wrist and arm, parry-ripostes and attacks on preparation. Occhiuzzi matched Szilagyi hit for hit in the second period but that was all he could manage. The Hungarian ranked sixth in the world, had been the highest seed to reach the semi-finals. In the bronze medal match, the Russian Federation's Nikolay Kovalev overcame Rares Dumitrescu of Romania 15–10.

Three out of three

Italy's Elisa Di Francisca beat her Italian compatriot Arianna Errigo 12-11 in extra time to win the women's Individual Foil London 2012 Olympic Games gold medal. An Italian clean sweep was secured when three-times former champion Valentina Vezzali won bronze the bronze medal match. Luckless Errigo was 11-8 up with just 45 seconds left but Di Francisca scored three times in quick succession to equalise. In the one minute of extra time, Di Francisca had priority and launched a surprise attack followed by an immediate remise to score the winning hit. Three of the last four fights went to the last hit but even more dramatic was the bronze medal match in which world No.1 Vezzali came back from apparent defeat to beat the Republic of Korea's Hyun Hee Nam 13–12 in extra time. This was Vezzali's unprecedented fifth individual medal at her fifth Games, having won silver at Atlanta 1996 and gold at Sydney 2000, Athens 2004 and Beijing 2008.

⬆ *Aron Szilagyi (right) parries a lunge from Diego Occhiuzzi in the final of the men's Individual Sabre at the London 2012 Games. He ended Hungary's 20-year wait for another Fencing gold medallist.*

Forza Italia!

Italy beat Japan to win the men's Team Foil gold and thus resisted pressure from the Republic of Korea for the status of being the world's leading Olympic Fencing nation. A 45-39 victory over Japan in the final gave the Italians their seventh medal of the Olympic Games, one more than the Koreans. The final touch came from the blade of anchor Andrea Baldini who had missed Beijing 2008. The bronze medal match saw a decisive victory for Germany over the United States.

Consolation for Shin

Ukrainian Yana Shemyakina won the women's Individual Epée gold but her thunder was stolen by the Republic of Korea's A Lam Shin who forced a lengthy delay to competition after breaking down in tears after her semi-final loss to German Britta Heidemann. Shin appeared to have Heidemann beaten in sudden death, only for the clock to be reset with one second remaining. Heidemann then managed a decisive hit for a 6–5 win. Shin broke down in tears and sat, inconsolable, on the piste while team officials launched an objection. After lengthy discussions Heidemann's win stood and Shin subsequently lost her bronze medal match to China's Yujie Sun. Shin was later offered a consolation medal to acknowledge her 'respect of the rules' by the International Fencing Federation.

⬅ *Elisa Di Francisca (right) defeated her Italian team-mate Arianna Errigo in a dramatic women's Individual Foil final at ExCeL.*

Judo

Judo is a modern martial art and combat sport that was invented in 1882 by Kano Jigoro in Japan; the object is to throw, or take down, one's opponent to the ground with one of a number of possible moves. It was contested for the first time at Tokyo 1964 and (with the exception of Mexico City 1968) has been ever-present at the Games since then. A women's event has been running since Barcelona 1992.

Geesink puts an end to Japan's monopoly

In 1961, for the first time since the event started in 1956, the Dutchman Anton Geesink became the first judo fighter to defeat a Japanese fighter at the World Championships, winning the open (unlimited weight) category. Three years later, when Tokyo staged the Olympic Games, the Japanese won three weight divisions and were desperate to add a fourth in the Open category. In the final, Geesink, 1.98 metres tall and weighing more than 120 kilograms, towered over Akio Kaminaga, only 1.70m although weighing 102kg. Geesink, who had defeated Kaminaga in the preliminaries, managed to hold down the Japanese fighter to take gold. It was a pivotal moment in the sport: the landscape of international judo had changed for ever.

⬆ *Anton Geesink (Netherlands) denied Japan a whitewash of Judo gold medals when he won the Open category at the 1964 Tokyo Games.*

Sadness to happiness

Spain's Miriam Blasco was the favourite to win the -57kg class at the Barcelona 1992 Games. She was the 1991 world and European champion, but a few weeks before the Games, her coach, Sergio Cardell, was killed in a car crash. She wore his black belt for the final against Great Britain's Nicola Fairbrother. It was a very close contest, with Blasco securing victory and the gold medal, but the rivals became close friends, later entering into business together running a judo centre in Spain.

Parisi wins for Europe

Born in the Frosinone province in central Italy, Angelo Parisi was brought up in London and had to have a change of nationality rushed through government departments in 1970 so he could represent Britain at the European Junior Championships, which he won. After taking a bronze medal at the 1972 Games in Munich, he married a French girl and switched nationalities again. Parisi's fluent throwing style could uproot the most stubborn of opponents and he won the Heavyweight title for France at the 1980 Games in Moscow, as well getting as a silver medal in the Open classes in 1980 and 1984.

⬆ *Italian-born Angelo Parisi won a bronze medal for Great Britain at Munich 1972 and gold for France at Moscow 1980.*

Gold on one leg

Built, as one opponent remarked, 'like a refrigerator with a head on top', Yasuhiro Yamashita was the outstanding heavyweight in the world from 1977 until his retirement in 1985, being unbeaten in 203 consecutive bouts, including four world titles. However, Japan boycotted the 1980 Games in Moscow and he had to wait four years, until 1984, for the supreme title, the Olympic Games gold medal. Yamashita was expected to cruise to victory in Los Angeles, but he tore a right calf muscle early on and had to limp for the rest of the tournament. In the final, Egyptian Mohammed Ali Rashwan lasted barely a minute before being held down. A fully fit Yamashita would have made the contest even shorter.

Adams felled at the last

Neil Adams – coached at the same London club, the Budokwai, as Angelo Parisi – was possibly the finest-ever stylist apart from the Japanese. Although European champion four times and world champion in 1981, he only managed to collect two silver medals at the Olympic Games, losing in the Moscow 1980 -71kg final to Ezio Gamba and the Los Angeles 1984 -78kg final to Frank Wieneke of West Germany. In the latter, Wieneke cleverly made a half-hearted attack and, as Adams pulled his shoulder back, the Briton left himself open to a superb left seionage (shoulder throw) and was hurled to the mat.

No short cut

At the 2000 Games in Sydney, Debbie Allan was among the favourites for the Featherweight title. On the morning of the event, the Briton weighed in under the 52-kilogram limit on the practice scales, but it was discovered that paper had been inserted in the mechanism. After the scales were recalibrated, she was found to be overweight. In a desperate attempt to make the weight before the time limit expired, she began vigorously exercising, stripped naked and even had her hair cut off. But she was still 50 grams overweight and was barred from competition.

A real-life comic-book character

No female Japanese judo fighter has ever inspired as much fascination in her country as Ryoko Tani, whose resemblance to the comic-book character 'Yawara-chan' made her a celebrity. A bronze medallist at the age of 16 in 1992, she was favourite for the -48kg in 1996, having been unbeaten for four years, but she lost to a wild-card entry from the People's Republic of Korea, Sun-hui Kye, in the biggest upset in the history of the sport. Four years later in Sydney, with Japanese cameramen surrounding the mat, she took the coveted title at last – and went on to retain it at Athens 2004.

⬇ Japan's Ryoko Tani won the women's -48kg events at Sydney 2000 and Athens 2004.

London 2012

⬆ Gemma Gibbons was one of the bravest British medallists, her silver in the women's Half-Heavyweight (70-78kg) class came with a broken thumb.

Gibbons beats the pain

Gemma Gibbons became Great Britain's first Olympic Judo medallist for 12 years by taking a surprise silver in defeat to American Kayla Harrison in the women's Half-Heavyweight (70-78kg) final. Gibbons's coach, Kate Howey, had been Britain's last women's Judo medallist, securing silver at Sydney 2000. Earlier, Gibbons, ranked a lowly No.42 in the world, had touched the hearts of the nation by mouthing: 'I love you Mum,' after a victory move in the semi-final. Jeannette Gibbons, Gemma's mother, had encouraged and supported her daughter's career before dying of leukaemia when Gemma was 17. Early in the competition Gibbons suffered a broken thumb but the medical team, assessing that it could not be damaged further, allowed her to fight on – and told her about the fracture only after she won her medal.

Riner on a roll

Popular Frenchman Teddy Riner won the men's Heavy Weight (over 100kg) title, comfortably beating the Russian Federation's Alexander Mikhaylin, supported by a large, highly vocal French supporting contingent. Riner was a class better than his rivals throughout the competition. Born in Guadeloupe but raised in Paris, Riner won a bronze medal at Beijing 2008, as well as an unprecedented five individual world titles. His golden progression began in the European and world championships in 2007 in Belgrade and Rio de Janeiro, respectively. 'For the people of France he is the king of the Games,' said Marie-Jose Perec, the one-time 400m runner who, like Riner, was born in Guadeloupe. 'Really, he's just like a big bear.'

Taekwondo

A relative newcomer to the Games programme, Taekwondo appeared twice as a demonstration sport (at Seoul 1988 and Barcelona 1992) before becoming a full-medal sport at the Sydney 2000 Games. The Republic of Korea has been the dominant force in the event, winning 10 of the 32 gold medals contested. At London 2012 men and women each competed in four categories – -58kg, -68kg, -80kg and +80kg and -49kg, -57kg, -67kg and +67kg, respectively.

↑ *Iran's Hadi Saei Bonehkohal launches an attack on Chinese Taipei's Chih Hsiung Huang on his way to gold in the Lightweight Final at Athens 2004.*

Controversial start for Steve

Steve Lopez was the first person to win a Taekwondo title at the Olympic Games. This was at the Sydney 2000 Games in the Featherweight division, when Lopez met the Republic of Korea's Joon-Sik Sin. The Korean was ahead until Lopez scored with a back kick. At the scheduled end of the bout, the referee awarded the bout to the American stating the Korean had been penalised for two half-points during the contest. In fact, the rules stated that the bout should have continued until one fighter had scored. The referee was suspended for a year, but Lopez kept what proved merely the first of two Olympic and five world titles. His world title success in 2005 was notable because both his brother Mark and sister Diana also collected gold medals at the same championships in Madrid.

Vietnamese join in

Vietnam finally joined the long list of countries to have won Olympic Games medals when Tran Hieu Ngan took silver in Taekwondo at the 2000 Games in Sydney. Two years earlier, Ngan had taken a bronze medal in the Southeast Asian Games and a gold medal in the Asian Championships, but her performance in Sydney made her a national celebrity. The 26-year-old Ngan, whose father, the owner of a confectionery shop, had died a week before the Games opened, lost 2–0 in the Featherweight (Under 57kg) Final to Jung Jae-Eun, the reigning world champion.

Bronze medal for Afghanistan

Afghanistan won their first ever Olympic medal when Rohullah Nikpai took bronze in the men's 58kg event at the Beijing 2008 Games. Nikpai beat world champion flyweight Juan Antonio Ramos of Spain in the repechage. Afghanistan president Hamid Karzai immediately called to congratulate Nikpai and gave him a house at the government's expense.

Iranian auction

Iranian Hadi Saei Bonehkohal, a triple world champion, was one of the favourites for the Featherweight (Under 68kg) title in Sydney but he lost to the Republic of Korea's Joon-Sik Sin in the semi-final. Three years later an earthquake flattened his home town of Bam, and the competitor, a former national sportsman of the year in Iran, auctioned his medal collection to help the victims. He was, therefore, without any trophies when he arrived in Athens for the 2004 Games – but he soon had the best trophy of all. In the final, he defeated Huang Chich Hsiung of Chinese Taipei to take the gold medal.

Champion Chu

Mu-Yen Chu won the gold medal in the Flyweight (Under 58kg) category at Athens 2004, Chinese Taipei's first-ever gold in the Olympic Games. He went into the Athens 2004 Games as the World Champion, having claimed that title at Garmisch–Partenkirchen in 2003, and the World Student Games (Universiade) at Daegu in the same year. A student at the University of Pittsburgh in the United States, he earned an MSc, masters degree, in Occupational Therapy in December 2008, four months after claiming bronze at the Beijing 2008 Games. Chu's girlfriend, Shun-chun Yan lost in the semi-final of the Under 49kg category to gold medallist Jingyu Wu of China and then in the bronze medal match to Daynellis Montejo of Cuba.

First for Taiwanese

Chen Shih-Hsien became a celebrity in Chinese Taipei when she beat Cuba's Yanelis Labrada to win the Flyweight (Under 49kg) gold medal in Athens in 2004. In doing so, she became the first competitor in any sport from her country to win an Olympic Games title, although she was followed a few minutes later by her compatriot Chu Mu-Yen, also in Taekwondo. At the Victory Ceremony, the Chinese Taipei Olympic Flag was flown rather than the country's national flag because of an original ruling by the International Olympic Committee at the behest of the Chinese government. She said afterwards: 'I am a single girl who has wandered around for ten years. My parents now want me to settle down.'

➡ *Shih-Hsien Chen (right) of the Chinese Taipei made history when she won the women's Fly Weight Taekwondo event at Athens 2004.*

London 2012

Even better for Tazegul

Turkey's Servet Tazegul won Taekwondo gold by defeating Iran's Mohammad Baghrei Motamed 6–5 in the men's Under 68kg competition to underline his status as the world No.1 and improve on the bronze medal he won at Beijing 2008. Top seed Tazegul, who defeated Britain's Martin Stamper to reach the final, dedicated the gold medal – Turkey's first of the Games – to his mother, who had died in June. Stamper missed out on a medal after losing 6–5 to Rohullah Nikpah of Afghanistan. Nikpah had won his country's first-ever Olympic Games medal with a bronze at Beijing 2008.

Jones' sweet revenge

Jade Jones claimed Great Britain's first Olympic Games Taekwondo gold medal when she beat Yuzhuo Hou of China 6–4 in the women's Under 57kg competition. It was sweet revenge for the 19-year-old, who had been beaten by the Chinese fighter, in sudden-death, at the 2011 World Championships. Thrilled, Jones – from Bodelwyddan, near Prestatyn in North Wales, said afterwards: 'I sang the national anthem and it was the best moment of my whole life. Amazing. I've seen this medal on pictures and seen other people get them. To finally have one round my own neck, I still don't believe it. It's just crazy.' Britain's previous best result had been Sarah Stevenson's bronze medal, which she won at the Beijing 2008 Games.

⬅ *Jade Jones (right) avenged her loss in the World Championships to Yuzhuo Hou by beating her in the Olympic Games final.*

Freestyle Wrestling

Freestyle Wrestling, which unlike Greco-Roman Wrestling allows the use of legs in both offence and defence, has been contested at every Games since St Louis 1904 by men and since Athens 2004 by women. The United States have been the sport's most successful country, winning 112 medals, 48 of them gold.

⬆ *Nigeria-born Daniel Igali won Freestyle Wrestling gold for Canada in the 69kg category at Sydney 2000.*

Unbeaten champion

No other international wrestler has had a record as perfect as that enjoyed by Osamu Watanabe who, in a brief but glorious career, won the featherweight title at the 1962 and 1963 World Championships, finished first in the 1962 Asian Games and then competed at the 1964 Games in Tokyo amid huge expectation. The 24-year-old from Hokkaido, the island renowned for producing fighters, captured gold without conceding a point. He had won 186 consecutive bouts and retired after the Games.

Banging the gong

British heavyweight Ken Richmond got a bronze medal at the 1952 Games in Helsinki and finished fourth equal in Melbourne four years later. Richmond, who was also picked, although never fought, for Great Britain in Judo, was desperately unlucky in Helsinki, losing on a split decision to the Georgian Arsen Mekokishvili, the eventual gold medallist. Yet Richmond's face and physique would become better known than those of any of his contemporaries: he was the man who was seen banging the gong at the start of the J. Arthur Rank films.

⬇ *A bronze medallist at the Helsinki 1952 Games, Great Britain's Kenneth Richmond achieved greater fame on the silver screen.*

The family man

Daniel Igali was born in Nigeria and captained the national Wrestling team. After competing at the 1994 Commonwealth Games at Victoria, Canada, he stayed in the country, being accepted as a refugee because of political unrest in Nigeria at the time. Igali continued to wrestle and was supported in his career by his 'surrogate' mother, Maureen Matheny, even though she was battling cancer. At the 1999 World Championships, he won gold and was able to show her the medal before she died. A year later Igali won gold at Sydney 2000.

Ultimate American winner

Dan Gable was not only one of history's outstanding freestyle wrestlers, but was also a stunningly successful coach. The Iowa-born-and-raised American lost only six of his 308 bouts in a career climaxed by his victory in the Lightweight division at the 1972 Games in Munich, despite a ravaged left knee and a deep cut over his left eye. Gable's ferocious training routine included taking a pack of cards, turning each one over and doing the number of press-ups equivalent to the figures on the card – he would see how often he could go through the pack. Gable then moved into coaching, leading Iowa University to 15 victories in the National Collegiate Championships. In 1984, he coached the US Olympic team to seven gold and two silver medals in Los Angeles.

Making amends

When women's Freestyle Wrestling was introduced to the Games' programme in 2004, the Japanese, with their background in Judo, were expected to win most of the titles. It wasn't to be. Heavyweight Kyoko Hamaguchi was controversially beaten in a preliminary bout before bouncing back to take bronze and, in the Flyweights, Chiharu Icho picked up a silver. Thirty minutes later, however, Chiharu's younger sister, Kaori, won Middleweight gold, Saori Yoshida won the Lightweights, and Japan ended up capturing half the titles.

The greatest pin?

When Werner Dietrich, the 120-kilogram super-heavyweight German competed at Munich 1972, he wanted to be the first wrestler to win medals in five successive Games, having won a record total of five competing in both Freestyle and Greco-Roman. His first bout in was against Chris Taylor, who weighed a huge 195kg. After 13 seconds, Dietrich produced a suplex, bending backwards as the American lent on his chest and then turning the airborne Taylor on to his back for a pin – an extraordinary feat. However, Dietrich's Games ended with him finishing fifth.

Medved the magnificent

Between 1962 and 1972, Ukraine's Alexander Medved missed out on the Olympic Games or world title only once, when he drew a bout with Turkey's Ahmet Ayik in the 1965 World Championships and forfeited the gold medal through having more bad marks. Otherwise he was supreme, moving up from Light Heavyweight to Heavyweight and finally to Super Heavyweight, and winning three consecutive gold medals. He was described by British contemporary Ron Grinstead as 'the Muhammad Ali of the sport – like Ali he has terrific strength but is very skilful as well'. His final triumph in the Super Heavyweights, weighing only 108 kilograms and outweighed by most of his rivals, was at Munich 1972. He announced his retirement by kissing the mat.

Bobby dazzler

In 1964, the Japanese were confident that they would dominate both Judo and Wrestling when Tokyo hosted the Olympic Games. Dutchman Anton Geesink ended their hopes of a clean sweep in Judo and, in Wrestling, Denis McNamara, a 38-year-old London policeman, pinned Japanese heavyweight Masanori Saito after 1:23.00, silencing a huge crowd which included Emperor Hirohito. Saito had to cut off his pigtail in penance for bringing disgrace on his country. McNamara did not win a medal, finishing fifth overall.

Golden brothers

The United States' Dave Schultz won Welterweight gold at the Los Angeles 1984 Games while brother Mark took the Middleweight title. Displaying immense ability, Dave overwhelmed the opposition, and although most communist countries were not present, he was the 1983 world champion and probably would have triumphed anyway. He retired three years later, but in 1993, inspired by the prospect of competing at Atlanta 1996, started wrestling again. Sadly, however, the man who was top-ranked American at the time, was shot dead in January 1996 by squad sponsor John Du Pont.

London 2012

Joy for Japanese

Japan's Tatsuhiro Yonemitsu won his country's first men's Olympic Games Wrestling gold medal since Mitsuru Sato at Seoul 1988. He recorded a 3–1 win over India's Sushil Kumar in the final of the 74kg category. Yonemitsu was always in control against the railway worker from Delhi who had hoped to become India's first-ever Olympic Wrestling champion. The Japanese wrestler was 1–0 up after a tight first period but pulled clear in the second. Kumar, however, blamed a stomach virus for upsetting his gold-medal pursuit. Livan Lopez of Cuba and Kazakhstan's Akzhurek Tanatarov took the bronze medals. This was Japan's fourth Freestyle Wrestling gold of the London 2012 Games and their best medal tally since 1968.

↑ *Tatsuhiro Yonemitsu (right) grabs the leg of Sushil Kumar during the men's 74kg Freestyle Wrestling final at the London 2012 Games. The Indian silver medallist was also battling a stomach complaint.*

Hat-trick heroines

Japan's women took three of the four Freestyle Wrestling gold medals, with extra-special celebrations being set off by Saori Yoshida (63kg) and Kaori Icho (72kg). Both women won their third consecutive golds, Yoshida lifting her total of Olympic and world titles to 12, thus matching the legendary Aleksandr Karelin. Yoshida and Icho both said it was too soon to say if they would attempt to defend their titles at the Rio 2016 Games. If they do, they may confront changes as the sport's governing body is lobbying for the number of women's Freestyle Wrestling weight classes to be raised from four to seven – the same number as the men – to promote and popularise the sport in the Gulf region.

Greco-Roman Wrestling

Greco-Roman Wrestling, despite its name, has its origins in 19th century France. It was contested at the inaugural Modern Games in 1896 and has been a constant presence at the Olympic Games (as a men-only sport) since London 1908. Unlike Freestyle Wrestling, competitors cannot make any holds below the waist.

All for nothing

There must be huge sympathy for the winner of the longest Wrestling bout in Olympic Games history. Estonia's Martin Klein fought Finland's Alfred Asikainen for 11 hours in the fierce sun of the outdoor arena in the Middleweight semi-final at Stockholm 1912. Klein was actually representing Russia, because Estonia was then part of the Czarist Empire, as was Finland, his opponent's country. Although there were regular breaks, the continuous struggle was an enormous strain on both competitors. Eventually, Klein pinned the Finn to end the bout and earn himself a place in the final against Sweden's Claes Johanson. However, Klein was too exhausted to fight another bout, so the Swede was declared the winner.

⬇ *Russia's Martin Klein (left) and Finland's Alfred Asikainen in their epic 11-hour battle in the Middleweight semi-final at the Stockholm 1912 Games.*

Pole with an eye for the ladies

Poland's Kazimierz Lipiern had a series of ferocious Featherweight battles with Ukraine's Nelson Davydyan during the 1970s and, after losing to him in the 1975 World Championships, gained revenge by taking the gold medal in Montreal ahead of Davydyan the following year. Afterwards, Lipiern advised wrestlers not to drink alcohol or smoke. To this the Hungarian bronze medallist Lazlo Reczi added: 'And no women.' Lipiern responded: 'That is taking sacrifices too far. Women are good to wrestle with too.'

⬆ *Jeff Blatnick battled his way to a memorable and popular victory in the Super Heavyweight category at the 1984 Los Angeles Games.*

A brother's inspiration

Few gold-medal winners were more emotional at the 1984 Games in Los Angeles than Jeff Blatnick, a 110-kilogram American. In 1977, he had lost his brother Dave in a motorcycle accident and, in 1982, Jeff himself was diagnosed with Hodgkin's lymphoma, a form of cancer. He had his spleen and appendix removed and underwent radiation therapy – three weeks later he was wrestling again. In the Super Heavyweight final, he defeated Sweden's Thomas Johannson. After his victory, watched by his parents, Blatnick sank to his kees, made the sign of a cross and told reporters: 'Thinking about Dave helped me keep my mind in perspective.'

The rolling Swede

Carl 'Calle' Westergren is a unique figure in Greco-Roman Wrestling at the Games. The Swede won three gold medals between 1920 and 1932, all at different weights, this despite losing to Finland's Onni Penninen in the first round in 1928. He won his first gold medal, at the age of 24, at Middleweight in 1920, leaving Artur Lindfors of Finland with the silver medal, moved up to Light Heavyweight four years later, where he beatcompatriot Rudolf Svensson, and finally to Heavyweight for his last gold medal in Los Angeles, defeating Josef Urban of Czechoslovakia. Westergren once recalled that when he stood on the edge of the mat, he used to put his thumbs inside his suit and say to himself: 'Considering how strong I feel today, no one can beat me.' His speciality move was the 'Westergren Roll', with which he used to tip opponents over.

The power of faith

When Yury Melnichenko, a Jew living in the Ukraine, visited Jerusalem in 1991, he placed a paper in the 'Wailing Wall' stating that his ambition was to become champion at the Olympic Games. Five years later, having transferred his allegiance to Kazakhstan because of the superior training environment there, he stormed through the early rounds of the Bantamweight division in Atlanta. Then, in the decisive bout with American Dennis Hall, who had upset him in the World Championships in Prague in 1995, Melnichenko scored three points for a lift and throw just 90 seconds into the contest, quickly stretched his lead to four points and then hung on to win a memorable gold medal.

Karelin – the real fridge magnet

Russian Aleksandr Karelin is the greatest Greco-Roman wrestler in history. He won three successive Super Heavyweight titles and was unbeaten in international competition for 13 years until, at the 2000 Games in Sydney, while still recovering from an injury, he was beaten in the final by American Rulon Gardner. At Atlanta 1996, when he won his third title at the Games, he was called 'the bouncer in the meanest bar in Hell'.

At 1.93 metres tall and weighing 125 kilograms, he was so robust that once, when the lift broke down at his block of flats in Siberia, he carried a fridge up eight flights of stairs. An exponent of the reverse body lift, he locked hands under an opponent's prone body, lifted him to waist height and hurled him to the mat.

➜ *Russia's Alexandr Karelin in action at Atlanta 1996.*

London 2012

Lopez out on his own

Cuba's Mijain Lopez successfully defended the men's 120kg Greco-Roman Wresting title he had won at Beijing 2008, and he was the only man to retain his crown. Lopez, 29 and four times a world champion, was his country's flag-bearer at both Games and the event favourite. He duly overpowered Turkey's Riza Kayaalp in the semi-finals and then Estonia's Heiki Nabi 3–0 on points in the gold medal match. The Islamic Republic of Iran topped the Greco-Roman Wrestling medal table with three golds, their best return since they first competed in the sport at the London 1948 Games. Cuba and the Republic of Korea each claimed one gold while the Russian Federation won two.

Power in the land

World champion Roman Vlasov of the Russian Federation displayed a level of style and skill which belied his 21 years as he won the (84kg) Greco-Roman Wrestling gold medal by beating Armenia's Arsen Julfalakyan in the final. Arsen almost emulated his father, Levon, who won gold (representing the Soviet Union) in the 68kg division at Seoul 1988. Vlasov had beaten the long-time world No.1 Selcuk Cebi in his rival's home town of Istanbul to win the 2011 World Championship and had followed it up in early 2012 with European title success. Cebi lost to Sweden's Robert Rosengren in the last 16. A significant height advantage helped Vlasov secure command of the final and win the gold medal. The two bronzes in the (84kg) division were awarded to Aleksandr Kazakevic of Lithuania and Emin Ahmadov of Azerbaijan.

⬅ *Mijain Lopez (red) of Cuba attempts to drive Heiki Nabi of Estonia onto the mat during their men's (120kg) Greco-Roman Wrestling final. The Cuban took the decision on points, winning 3–0.*

Chapter Nine
Multi-event sports

Modern Pentathlon was created by the founder of the modern Olympic Games, Baron Pierre de Coubertin. He wanted an event that echoed the classic pentathlon event held at the ancient Greek games. His 'modern' pentathlon drew on the story of a soldier delivering a message. In order to make sure that the message got through, he had to fence, swim, ride, and run and shoot.

It was introduced at the Stockholm 1912 Games and celebrated 100 years as a sport at the London 2012 Games. A women's competition has been part of the programme since Sydney 2000. At London 2012, the Modern Pentathlon was effectively made up of four events because, after the fencing, swimming and riding, the competition concluded with the combined event (shooting and running).

Triathlon is in every way the new kid on the block at the Olympic Games. Although there had been attempts at something similar in the early 20th century, the first triathlon as it is known now was held only in the mid-1970s. Its popularity grew so rapidly that it was accepted as a full medal sport less than 30 years later and it made its debut at the Sydney 2000 Games.

The brutal combination of swim-bike-run has persuaded many to make the switch from other sports. Distances vary from competition to competition, with the gruelling 'iron man' among the most testing. The Olympic Games Triathlon features a 1.5-kilometre swim, a 40km cycle ride and a 10km run. All three elements happen sequentially, with no break in between.

Alistair Brownlee is already draped in a Union Flag as he approaches the finish line at the end of the London 2012 Triathlon with victory assured. His brother Jonathan joined him on the podium after winning bronze.

Modern Pentathlon

Invented by Baron Pierre du Coubertin, the father of the Modern Games, Modern Pentathlon – the word 'modern' distinguishes the event from the Ancient Games' original pentathlon – has been contested at every Games since Stockholm 1912 (and by women since Sydney 2000). Athletes contest fencing, swimming, riding and the combined event (shooting and running).

⬆ *Second World War hero George S. Patton finished fifth in the Modern Pentathlon at the Stockholm 1912 Games.*

Patton too accurate

The American pentathlete who finished fifth in the first competition at Stockholm 1912 was none other than George S. Patton junior. As General Patton, he commanded the 7th Army during the Second World War invasion of Sicily and later led the 3rd Army across France after the Normandy landings. Patton, a graduate of the West Point military academy, was a lieutenant at the time of his Games participation. It was shooting, strangely, that proved to be his weakest discipline. Patton always maintained he would have won gold had one of his shots not been ruled a miss. He insisted his shot had gone through an existing hole in the target.

Magnificent Magyars

A Team event was held in Modern Pentathlon from 1952 until 1992. This competition was run concurrently with the Individual event and the winners were calculated by adding the combined scores of three participating pentathletes from each nation. Hungary were the first Team champions and won the competition on four occasions. The Soviet Union also won four gold medals. Despite objections, each victorious team was only given one medal to be shared between the three members.

Courting trouble

American pentathlete Orben Greenwald, a World Championship Team silver medallist in 1975, faced a court martial for insubordination shortly before the 1976 Games in Montreal. Incredibly, the charge was brought by his team manager, one Colonel Donald Johnson. Although the matter was eventually dropped, Greenwald was not allowed to compete.

Onishenko out

In 1976, Soviet competitor Boris Onishenko was disqualified in the biggest scandal to hit the sport. Before the fencing phase of the competition, he had tampered with the handle of his épée so that it could register a hit when no contact had been made. This was discovered after he had recorded a hit during his bout with Great Britain's Jim Fox. Onishenko, a silver medallist at the 1972 Games, was thrown out of the competition. That opened the way for Poland's Janusz Peciak to take gold in the Individual event. It also put the Soviet team out of the running for the Team event, in which Great Britain took gold.

Hall's unique double

Swedish athletes enjoyed huge success in the Modern Pentathlon's early years. The competition was dominated by members of the military, and every gold medal from 1912 to 1956 was won by a Swedish competitor. The 1952 winner, Lars Hall, a carpenter from Gothenburg, was the first non-military winner. He enjoyed a stroke of good fortune on the way. He arrived late for the shooting phase, but was allowed to take part because a protest had delayed the competition. Hall was back in action at Melbourne 1956, when he won the gold medal once more and remains the only man to have won the event twice.

Seven-up Soviet

Pavel Lednev, with seven medals in a career spanning four Games between Mexico City 1968 and Moscow 1980, can stake a claim as the most successful competitor in Modern Pentathlon, even though he never won the Individual title. Lednev was a member of the gold medal-winning Soviet Union team in both 1972 and 1980, but, despite winning four Individual medals, his best performance in Individual competition came at the 1976 Games in Montreal, when he finished in the silver-medal position.

⬅ *Sweden's Lars Hall, a carpenter from Gothenburg, became the Modern Pentathlon's first non-military winner at the Helsinki 1952 Games.*

Double gold

Hungary's gold medal-winning team in the Rome 1960 Games featured two individual champions. Ferenc Nemeth won his prize at the same Games, but Andras Balczo had to wait a further 12 years for his personal moment of glory. He finally became Individual champion at the 1972 Games in Munich, aged 34.

Man with all the answers

Bjorn Ferm kept himself occupied during breaks in the long and exhausting fencing section of the Modern Pentathlon competition at the Mexico City 1968 Games by reading a detective novel. Ferm, an economics student from Jönköping in Sweden, eventually completed the cross-country course four seconds inside the target time to take the gold medal.

Doctor knows best

Great Britain's Stephanie Cook put her career as a doctor on hold to prepare for the inaugural women's Modern Pentathlon at the Sydney 2000 Games. This was held on the last day of the Games and Cook, an outstanding runner, made up 49 seconds on American Emily de Riel – a former team-mate at Oxford University – to win gold.

Grut the great

The 1948 champion was Swedish army captain Willie Grut, who won the riding, fencing and shooting disciplines. At the 1948 Winter Games in St Moritz, Grut was second in a demonstration Winter Pentathlon event, comprising alpine and cross-country skiing, shooting, fencing and equestrian sport. Not surprisingly, he was voted Sweden's sportsman of the year.

Arresting practice

At the 1932 Games in Los Angeles, Sweden's Johan Oxenstierna decided to fire some practice shots in some nearby woods just before the pistol shooting discipline begin. It was not a wise decision as a suspicious local police officer raced over and threatened to arrest him. After much persuasion, the policeman eventually realised that the Swede was a genuine competitor, and the officer stayed to watch the shooting competition. Despite the earlier alarm, Oxenstierna went on to take the gold medal.

London 2012

Murray ends it on a silver

The Modern Pentathlon's Samantha Murray says the passionate home crowd 'spurred me on' as she claimed a silver medal in the final strides of what was the very last event of the London 2012 Olympic Games. The 22-year-old was fourth at the start of the concluding run-shoot segment, the last part of the competition. Inconsistent initial shooting saw her slip to seventh at the end of the first of the three laps in the 3,000m cross-country course but she ran bravely until she had only Lithuania's Laura Asadauskaite and Brazil's Yane Marques in her sights. Murray overtook Marques coming out of the last shooting stop and the crowd, as she acknowledged, fired her on to silver. Remarkably, she had taken up the sport only four years earlier.

➤ *Samantha Murray turns to run away from the shooting section of the final segment in the Modern Pentathlon. Her accuracy in the last shooting stop helped her win a bronze medal at London 2012.*

Svoboda stands up for sport

London 2012 was a pressure point for Modern Pentathlon not only among the competitors but for a sport itself seeking to maintain its presence on the Olympic programme. David Svoboda of the Czech Republic did his best on behalf of the sport. He beat China's Zhongrong Cao to the gold medal only after a highly dramatic conclusion. Svoboda had claimed an early lead in the fencing but slipped behind Cao after the swimming, only to regain the advantage in the riding stage, before finishing six seconds clear following the combine event finale. The army officer thus claimed an Olympic record of 5,928 points. Hungarian Adam Marosi took bronze.

Triathlon

Although World Championships in the sport have been staged every year since 1989, Triathlon had to wait until Sydney 2000 before it made its first appearance at the Games. The events are contested over international distances (1.5km swim, 40km cycle and 10km run).

Parisian approval

The decision to introduce Triathlon as a full-medal sport at the Games was taken in Paris at the 103rd session of the International Olympic Committee held in 1994. The International Triathlon Union itself had only been formed five years before.

Gold Hawaii

Switzerland's Brigitte McMahon was the first triathlete to win an Olympic Games gold medal. Initially a Swiss swimming champion, she was bitten by the Triathlon bug while working in Hawaii as a teaching assistant at the university. At the 2000 Games in Sydney she left it late to make her surge to gold and her final victory margin was only two seconds ahead of home favourite and long-time race leader Michellie Jones of Australia.

Three in one...

Although the sport was not invented until the 1970s, all three elements were performed simultaneously during the 1908 Games in London. This was possible because the White City Stadium, where the Games were held, featured not only a running track (536 metres in length) but also a 600m cycle track and a 50m swimming pool. On certain days, events in all three sports were scheduled at the same time.

Taking to the water

The inaugural women's Triathlon at the Games was one of the first medals to be decided on the opening day of competition at Sydney 2000. Competition began with a swim in Sydney Harbour and the event helped introduce the landmarks of the Host City to millions of television viewers worldwide. The Sydney police estimated that nearly 500,000 spectators lined the streets to watch the cycling and running in the women's event on one day and the men the next.

⬇ *The 2000 Games got off to a spectacular start when the women's Triathlon got under way in Sydney Harbour.*

Switch in time

New Zealand's Hamish Carter was a rower at school who switched to triathlon when he realised he would never be tall enough to row at senior level. His main rival at the 2004 Games was compatriot and sometime training partner Bevan Docherty, then reigning world champion. Carter was only 33rd after the swim, but had an excellent cycle ride and dismounted to find himself among a small leading group with Docherty. With 1km to go, the Kiwis were out on their own, before Carter escaped to win by seven seconds.

Lucky 13 for Whitfield

Canada's Simon Whitfield was ranked only 13th in the world at the time of his men's Triathlon triumph at Sydney 2000. He had decamped to Australia for three years to train during the Canadian winter and actually held joint citizenship in both countries. After the swim and cycle ride he was in 28th place, but in the run he picked his way through the field and overtook the eventual silver medallist Stefan Vuckovic of Germany less than 100 metres from the finish. His victory helped him fulfil a childhood ambition that he had since he competed in his first triathlon aged 12. He had decided he wanted to do something that would merit inclusion in the *Encyclopaedia Britannica*. Whitfield also won men's Triathlon silver at Beijing 2008.

← *Canada's Simon Whitfield put a crash in the cycle ride behind him to win men's Triathlon gold at the Sydney 2000 Games.*

Paying the price

In the last 300 metres of the Beijing 2008 men's Triathlon, Sydney 2000 gold medallist Simon Whitfield and Athens 2004 silver medallist Bevan Docherty were in the lead group. Docherty made a break, only for German Jan Frodeno – who took up the sport while in South Africa and sold his bike to help fund his fare home – who was not noted for a sprint finish, to burst past everyone and win a surprise gold medal.

Married bliss

Katherine Allen, winner of the 2004 women's Triathlon, hailed from Geelong in Australia. On a backpacking holiday in Europe, she visited Austria, where she met and later married Austrian triathlete Marcel Dichtler. She became an Austrian citizen and qualified to represent them at Athens 2004. She was 44th after the swim in the Aegean, but rose to 28th (still some three minutes behind the leaders) after a good bike ride. Her performance in the run was superb. Allen finally took the lead from Australia's Loretta Harrop in the last 200 metres and went on to win by 6.72 seconds.

Snowsill beats the odds

Australia's Emma Snowsill overcame personal tragedy and serious injury to win gold at the 2008 Games in Beijing. Her boyfriend, fellow triathlete Luke Harrop, was killed by a car in a hit-and-run accident while training in 2002. The following year she became world champion, but suffered a stress fracture of the femur, which ruled her out of contention for the Australian team at the 2004 Games in Athens. She won the World Championships in 2005, took the 2006 Commonwealth title and then won the world title again to seal her place in Beijing. There she led as the field completed the bike ride, and she eventually had such a lead that she was able to pause to grab an Australian flag from a fan before crossing the line a minute ahead of her nearest rivals.

↑ *Great Britain's Marc Jenkins feels the heat during the men's Triathlon at Athens 2004.*

Carry on … in the heat

At the 2004 men's Triathlon in Athens, Great Britain's Marc Jenkins had his medal prospects ended by a crash mid-way through the cycling leg. With broken spokes his bike was impossible to ride. He refused to retire, but the wheel was so badly buckled that he was forced to carry the bike on his shoulders in blistering heat for nearly two kilometres to the next repair point. When he finally reached the finish line he received a standing ovation from the crowd, even though he was in last place, some 15 minutes behind the winner.

↑ *The Brownlee brothers were two of the leading contenders in the men's Triathlon and both finished on the podium.*

Brothers on the podium

Triathlon and Olympic officials had been concerned about how they should react if family loyalties prompted the Brownlee brothers – Alistair and Jonathan – to cross the gold-medal winning line together – as was a definite possibility if not even a probability. In the event both won medals but a joint finish was not an issue. Elder brother Alistair always looked in command of the competition. Jonny, however, collected a 15-second time penalty for an over-hasty transition along the way. This meant they were split at the finish by Spain's former world champion Javier Gomez. Alistair still had more than enough time to drape a Union Flag around his shoulders and walk over the line in one hour 46 minutes 25 seconds. He and Jonny, with gold and bronze, were the first siblings to feature together on the Olympic medals podium in an individual event in more than 50 years.

Spirig makes a splash – just

The battle for gold in the women's Triathlon competition was so tight that the result could not be confirmed until after the facts and statistics had been reviewed by the Court of Arbitration for Sport. Switzerland's Nicola Spirig and Lisa Norden of Sweden crossed the finish line in identical times of 1.59:48 and only a photo-finish gave the victory to Spirig. Swedish Olympic and Triathlon officials asked for the pair to be ranked as joint winners, but sport's supreme court ruled that it could not intervene in a 'field-of-play decision'. Judges decided that Spirig's torso had been a little less than 15 centimetres ahead of Norden when the two finished – an incredibly slender margin after almost two hours of swimming, cycling and running.

Chapter Ten
Racket sports

Tennis was one of the original sports at the first modern Olympic Games at Athens 1896. It was the first sport to embrace women participants and was a fixture in the early years of the Games. Indoor and outdoor events were both part of the programme, but the sport was removed from the roster in 1924.

There were moves to bring it back in the 1960s, but the advent of the open era in tennis created difficulties because the Olympic Movement insisted on a strict amateur code at this time. In the 1980s the situation changed when the International Olympic Committee decided to relax its rules on eligibility, effectively making the Games open to all. Tennis made a successful return as a demonstration event at the Los Angeles 1984 Olympic Games and was subsequently restored to the full Games agenda for Seoul 1988.

Table Tennis grew in popularity from the late 19th century, but although the first World Championships in the sport took place in the 1920s, it was not until 1988 that the sport finally entered the Olympic Games for the first time. It enjoys enormous popularity in China and other Asian countries and Chinese players have dominated at every tournament.

Badminton had to wait well over a century for a spot in the Olympic Games. It was not until Barcelona 1992 that it was included as a full-medal sport. Ever since, competitors from Asia have dominated both men's and women's competitions and only one champion has come from outside the continent.

Andy Murray returned to Wimbledon a few weeks after losing the grand slam tennis championship final, but made no mistake in the Olympic Games men's Singles final, beating top seed Roger Federer in three sets.

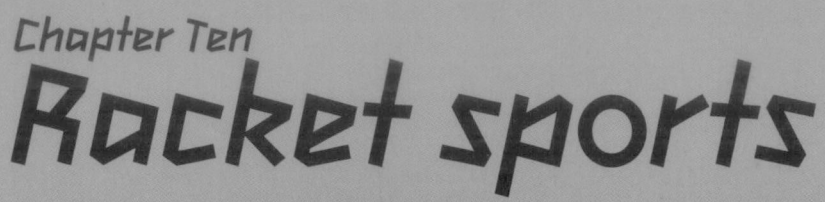

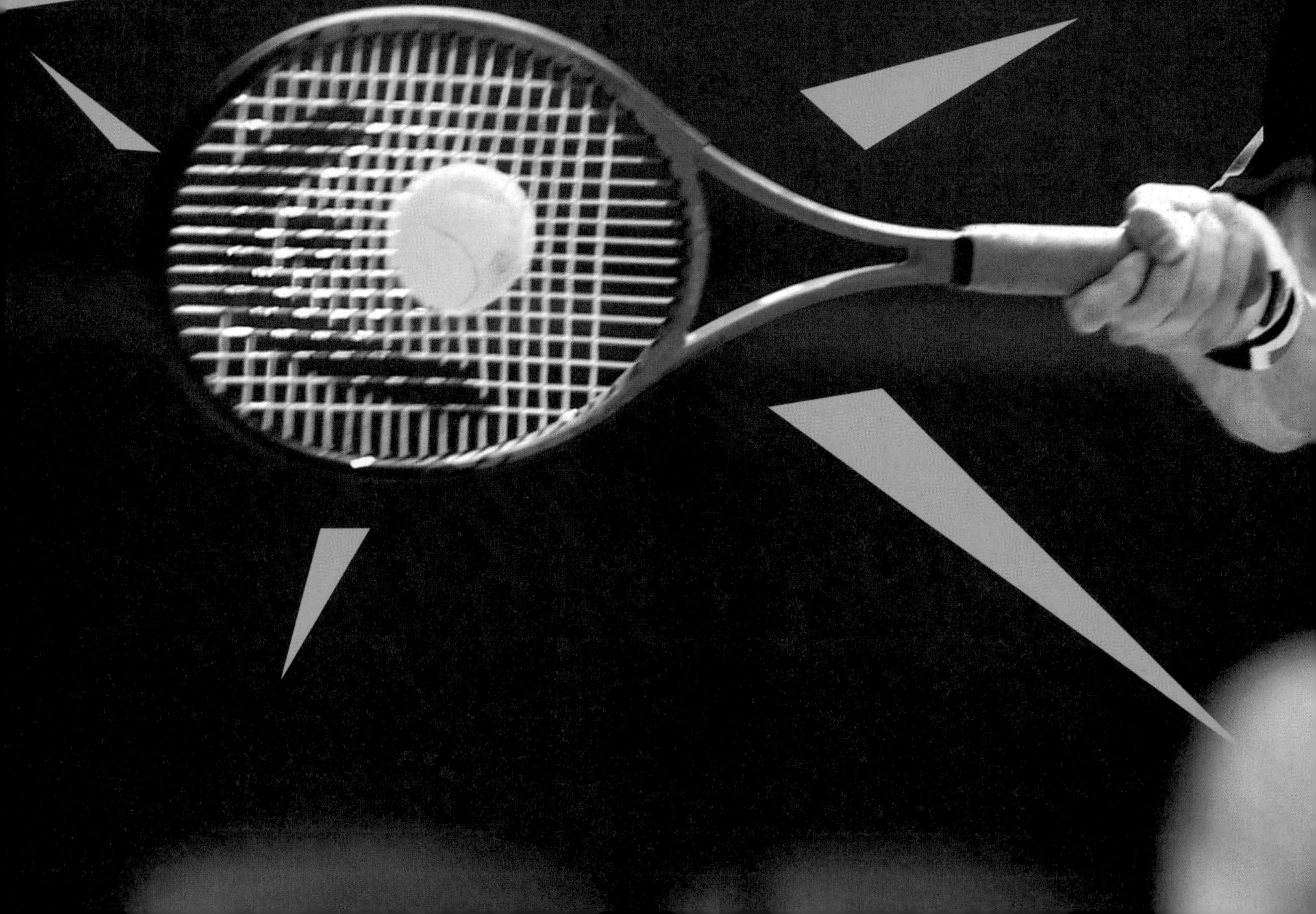

Badminton

Badminton was a demonstration sport at Munich 1972 but had to wait until Barcelona 1992 before making its first full-medal appearance at the Games. Competitors compete in Singles and Doubles events (for men and women) as well as Mixed Doubles. China leads the all-time medal count since Barcelona 1992 with 38, 16 of them gold.

Gao's history game

Ling Gao and her partner Jun Zhang won successive Mixed Doubles titles at the Sydney 2000 and Athens 2004 Games. Gao also won silver and bronze in the women's Doubles. She has won more Olympic Games medals in the sport (four) than any other player.

No joke for Koreans

Soo-hyun Bang, daughter of a popular Korean comedian, was deadly serious about Badminton and lost only one match in her entire Olympic Games career. That single defeat came in the final of the women's Singles in 1992, which she lost to Indonesia's Susi Susanti. Four years later, in Atlanta, she faced Susanti once more, this time at the semi-final stage, in which she avenged her Barcelona defeat. She played another Indonesian, Mia Audina, in the final and made her experience tell to win the gold medal.

↑ *Soo-hyun Bang took the women's Singles title at Atlanta 1996.*

Europe's best yet

For the only time in any Badminton event at the Games, three European pairs reached the last four of the Mixed Doubles in 2004. In the all-European semi-final, Nathan Robertson and Gail Emms from Great Britain beat Denmark's Jonas Rasmussen and Rikke Olsen to reach the final. They had to settle for the silver medal, though, losing to defending champions Jun Zhang and Ling Gao from China, but the British pair came within four points of the gold. The pair won the gold medal at the 2006 World Championships, but were knocked out in the quarter-final at the Beijing 2008 Games.

← *Nathan Robertson and Gail Emms celebrate their Mixed Doubles semi-final victory at Athens 2004.*

Susanti keeps it in the family

Indonesia's Susi Susanti had already become a national hero for winning back-to-back All England titles when she travelled to Barcelona for the 1992 Games. There she beat Korea's Soo-hyun Bang in the women's Singles Final to seal her place in her country's sporting hall of fame for ever. Hers was the first Olympic Games gold medal ever won by an Indonesian. That same day, her husband-to-be, Alan Budikusuma, overcame his fellow countryman Ardy Wiranata to win gold in the men's Singles. Their twin triumphs sparked tremendous scenes back in Jakarta when they returned home. There was a huge victory parade through the streets, led by a car carrying a giant shuttlecock. The couple each received a bonus of US$500,000 and they were married after the 1996 Games in Atlanta. Although neither had completed the fairytale with another gold medal, Susanti did win a Singles bronze.

Super star

At Beijing 2008, home favourite Dan Lin reached the men's Singles final in without dropping a set. A soldier in the Chinese People's Liberation Army, and No. 1 in the world that year, he was known as 'Super Dan'. He lived up to his nickname in the final, in which he swept aside the challenge of Malaysia's Chong Wei Lee to take the gold medal.

← *Dan Lin became China's second men's Singles champion at Beijing 2008.*

Peer Pressure

Badminton can trace its origins to early games played in India, China and Greece. Previously known as battledore or shuttlecock, the sport takes its name from one of the stately homes of England – Badminton in Gloucestershire, the ancestral home of the Duke of Beaufort. His Grace enthusiastically championed the sport in the 1870s, teaching visitors to his home how to play. A shuttlecock can be either synthetic or use goose or duck feathers.

Determined Danes

Denmark have been the most successful European nation in Badminton events at the Games. B. Thomas Stuer Lauridsen was the first player from outside Asia to win a medal when Badminton made its debut appearance at Barcelona 1992. He lost to the eventual winner Alan Budikusuma (Indonesia) in the semi-final. At the first tournament, both losing semi-finalists were awarded bronze medals. Subsequently a third-place play-off was introduced. At the Atlanta 1996 Games, Denmark's Poul Erik Hoyer Larsen beat defending champion Alan Budikusuma and world champion Heryanto Arbi on the way to the final, in which he beat Chinese world number one Jiong Dong to become the Games' first, and to date only, non-Asian Singles gold medallist.

Moving success

Mia Audina has won Olympic Games medals in Badminton for two different countries. Born in Jakarta, Indonesia, she was a child prodigy at the sport. She was chosen for the 1996 Games at the tender age of 16 years 338 days and, unsurprisingly, she was the youngest player ever to enter a Badminton tournament at the Games. Even so she reached the Final of the women's Singles in Atlanta, losing to Korean Soo-hyun Bang. Audina later married a Dutchman and moved to the Netherlands, where she became a Dutch citizen. She represented her new country at Sydney 2000 and at Athens 2004, where she again reached the final. By now a comparative veteran at 24, she was beaten this time by China's Zhang Ning.

Martin settles for silver

Denmark's Camilla Martin was the first European woman to win an individual Olympic Games medal for Badminton. Back home, she was considered the best female player of her generation and, in a land where standards are very high, she won 13 consecutive national titles. After victory at the 1999 World Championships, she travelled to Sydney 2000 as one of the favourites. She played superbly to reach the final, but was denied gold by China's Zhichao Gong.

↖ *1999 world champion Camilla Martin took the silver medal in the women's Singles event at the Sydney 2000 Games.*

London 2012

Zhao at the double

China's Yunlei Zhao made history when she and Qing Tian – their country's No.2 partnership – crushed Japan's Mizuki Fujii and Reika Kakiiwa to win gold in the women's Doubles in a exhilarating tournament. Zhao thus became the first player to win Badminton gold medals in two events at the same Games, having already won the all-China Mixed Doubles final with partner Nan Zhang. The stream of Chinese talent did not stop there. A 21-year-old comparative newcomer, Xuerui Li, cruised through the women's singles and secured gold by defeating top-seeded compatriot Yihan Wang in the final. Not so fortunate was Xin Wang. She retired hurt in the bronze medal match which left India celebrating a maiden Badminton medal for Saina Nehwal.

Super Dan's the man

'Super Dan' Dan Lin ranks as perhaps the finest player of all time after successfully repeating his gold medal success in the Badminton men's Singles competition. The London 2012 final was a superb repeat of the Beijing 2008 contest against Malaysia's Chong Wei Lee. This time, Lee came within two points of gold but ultimately was left facing the end of his career without ever having won an Olympic, world or Asian Games title. Lin is only male player to retain the Olympic men's Singles title – yet another feat to rank alongside his unique career achievement as the only man to have completed the 'Super Grand Slam' of all nine major titles in the sport. China took all five Badminton gold medals available at London 2012. Veterans Yun Cai and Haifeng Fu succeeding in the men's Doubles, beating beat Denmark's Mathias Boe and Carsten Mogensen, where they had come up short at Beijing 2008.

⬇ *Dan Lin salutes the crowd after retaining his Badminton men's Singles title at London 2012.*

Table Tennis

Singles and Doubles events (for men and women) in Table Tennis have been contested since the Seoul 1988 Games with Team events introduced for the first time at Beijing 2008 to replace the Doubles event. China dominate the sport's all-time medal table at the Games with 47 medals (24 of them gold).

Chinese Clean sweep

At Beijing 2008, host nation China won every Table Tennis medal available to them. China's men beat Germany in the final of the Team event, while the women won their final against Singapore to add a second gold. Lin Ma won the men's Singles title (with compatriots Hao Wang taking silver and Liqin Wang bronze); and Yining Zhang won the women's Singles event (with compatriots Nan Wang taking silver and Yue Guo bronze).

Little giant

China's Yaping Deng had always been considered too short to make the grade in international Table Tennis. A child prodigy, who won regional tournaments at the age of nine, she was originally ignored by the Chinese selectors because of her height. Eventually, though, they were forced to relent and she was picked for the national team aged only 16, by which time she had reached her adult height of 4ft ½in (1.49m). She partnered Hong Qiao to win the World Championships doubles and went on to win the singles title in 1991. Her persistence in never taking no for an answer was rewarded when she was selected for China's team for the 1992 Games in Barcelona and took gold in the women's Doubles with Qiao. Two days later, the pair faced one another in the women's Singles final and Deng won an epic encounter, 21-6, 21-8, 15-21, 23-21. She retained both her titles at the Atlanta 1996 Olympic Games, and in 2003 she was voted China's female athlete of the century and was also chosen for the IOC Athletes' Commission.

← *China's Yaping Deng silenced those who said she was too short to play the game when she won the women's Singles and women's Doubles Table Tennis events at Barcelona 1992.*

Out of date...

On the eve of the 2004 Olympic Games in Athens, China's Table Tennis squad was thrown into turmoil by what officials described as a 'dating scandal'. Reigning Mixed Doubles champion Lin Ma began a relationship with another member of the squad. His girlfriend was dropped from the group because Chinese officials felt as though her presence would have an unsettling effect on the both the squad and its training programme. Ma himself was only spared the axe because his world ranking at the time was so high. The selectors' decision was vindicated, however, when (in partnership with Qi Chen) he went on to take gold in the men's Doubles. Four years later, in Beijing, Ma won the men's Singles event, beating compatriot Hao Wang in the Final, and was also a member of the Chinese trio that took Team gold.

King Kong

Chinese men's Doubles pairing Linghui Kong and Guoliang Liu teamed up to devastating effect at the Olympic Games at Atlanta in 1996. They lost only one game as they steamrollered their way to the gold medal. Liu also won the men's Singles at the same Games. Four years later, in Sydney, it was Kong's turn to win the men's Singles final after a tremendous struggle against Sweden's Jan Ove Waldner.

Comrade champion

Chinese star Nan Wang won two gold medals at the 2000 Olympic Games in Sydney. She won the women's Doubles and beat her doubles partner Ju Li in the Singles final. Her success brought with it some unexpected fringe benefits, such as being elected as a district representative to the Chinese Communist Party Congress. She retained her Doubles title with a new partner, Yining Zhang, at Athens 2004 and won further gold for China as part of the victorious squad in the Team event in Beijing. China's dominance of the Table Tennis competition at the 2004 Games was broken only when the Republic of Korea's Seung Min Ryu took gold in the men's Singles with a dramatic win over China's Hao Wang. The match went the full distance, and even then in victory the Korean conceded that his opponent had been the better player.

Taken for a ride

Chinese men's Doubles pairing Lin Lu and Tao Wang very nearly did not make it to their final at the 1992 Games in Barcelona. The bus that was supposed to take them from the Olympic Village to the arena failed to arrive, so they started out on foot. Eventually they were able to hail a taxi and reached the venue in the nick of time. Their match against the German pair Steffen Fetzner and Joerg Rosskopf went the full distance before the Chinese duo took gold.

← *China's Lin Lu (left) and Tao Wang (right) celebrate after they beat Germany's Steffen Fetzner and Jörg Rosskopf in the men's Doubles final at the 1992 Games in Barcelona.*

Sporting chance

China's Zhimin Jiao won bronze in the women's Singles and silver in the women's Doubles at the 1988 Games, but it was her romance with Korean men's Doubles bronze medallist Jae-Hyeong An that hit the headlines. The pair married in 1989, even though their countries had no diplomatic ties at the time, and had a son, Byeong-Hun An, who turned out to be a brilliant golfer and won the 2009 US Amateur Championship aged only 17.

Waldner breakthrough

Sweden's Jan Ove Waldner was the first non-Asian player to win an Olympic Games gold medal. After being knocked out in the quarter-final of the inaugural Table Tennis tournament at the 1988 Games, he was unstoppable four years later dropping only one game on the way to the final, where he beat Frenchman Jean-Philippe Gatien. He played in the first five Table Tennis tournaments at the Games, winning silver at Sydney 2000. His final Games appearance came at Athens 2004, aged 38.

London 2012

Clean sweep for China

Xiaoxia Li, in the women's events, matched the double-winning achievements of Jike Zhang in the men's competition. She beat compatriot Ning Ding in the women's Single final and they then formed, with Yue Guo, a formidable women's Team who took every match 3–0. China thus took all the four gold medals, just as they had at home at Beijing 2008 four years earlier. They have collected 24 of the 28 golds awarded since Table Tennis became an Olympic sport in 1988, and 19 of the last 20. Organisers estimated that more than 180,000 spectators had attended the tournament at ExCeL including software billionaire Bill Gates and Great Britain's Prince Philip, Duke of Edinburgh.

Bored of winning?

Germany's Timo Boll has been in the world's top 10 for a decade and hoped to stir up the dominant Chinese in the London 2012 Games Table Tennis tournament. In the event he was out of luck, but Europe's top men's player did enjoy the consolation of beating Jike Zhang, the men's Singles gold medal winner, in the Team semi-final – though Germany still lost 3–1. But the men's tournament did offer hints from Europe and Japan that the Chinese may not have it all their own way in future Olympic Games. Their dominance might even prove their undoing. 'I think even the Chinese are getting bored at China winning all the time,' said Boll as he and his German team celebrated bronze. One of the moments of the tournament was Nigerian Quadri Aruna's first-round victory over Spain's Carlos Machado. Aruna, who lost a shoe during the winning rally, was beaten in his next match.

← *China's Table Tennis squad won all four gold medals and silver, too, in the men's and women's Singles.*

Tennis

Tennis was one of the sports contested at the inaugural modern Games at Athens 1896 and featured at each of the first seven Games before being dropped after Paris 1924. After two appearances as a demonstration sport (in 1968 and 1984), it made a welcome return to the full-medal programme at the Seoul 1988 Games.

Greek classic

John Pius Boland, an Irishman studying at Christ's College, Oxford, was the first man to win a Tennis title at the Olympic Games. During the Easter holidays in 1896, he accompanied a Greek friend to Athens where the first Games of the modern era were about to take place. He was persuaded to take part in the Tennis competition, despite having had little experience of tournament play. Still, he won Singles gold and then partnered the German Fritz Traun to success in the Doubles.

On target in London

Charlotte 'Lottie' Dod may have been a five-times women's Singles champion at Wimbledon, but her only appearance at the Olympic Games came in the sport of Archery. She won a silver medal in the women's Individual competition at the 1908 Games in London.

⬆ *Legendary five-time Wimbledon singles winner Lottie Dod made a surprise appearance in Archery at the London 1908 Games and won silver.*

Winning for women

Great Britain provided the first female winner in Tennis at the Olympic Games. In fact Charlotte Cooper was the first woman to win any title at the Games. She beat Helene Prevost in straight sets to win Singles gold at Paris 1900. She also won gold in the Mixed Doubles, with R.F. 'Reggie' Doherty.

Tennis comeback

Exhibition and demonstration events in Tennis were held at the 1968 Olympic Games in Mexico City as the sport sought readmission to the official Games programme. But it was the demonstration event in 1984 that really paved the way for the sport's return. In Los Angeles the competition was an age-group affair (players had to be under 20): Sweden's Stefan Edberg won the men's Singles event, with West Germany's Steffi Graf winning the women's Singles.

Titanic achievement...

American Richard Norris Williams III could count himself fortunate to have taken part in the Olympic Games at all. He had been a passenger on the maiden voyage of the *Titanic* in 1912 and had swum away from the sinking ship before being rescued. He served in the military and won the Croix de Guerre in the First World War. A Wimbledon champion in the men's Doubles in 1920, he was selected for the USA team for the 1924 Games and partnered compatriot Hazel Wightman, a prolific player in the women's game, to gold in the Mixed Doubles.

➡ *Richard Norris Williams III was a Titanic survivor and a gold medallist at the Paris 1924 Games.*

Ins and outs in London

At the 1908 Games in London, the Tennis programme featured both indoor and outdoor tournaments. The indoor competitions were held at the Queen's Club in West Kensington, London. Arthur Wentworth Gore won an all-British Final against George Caridia in straight sets. Inspired by his success, he also won Wimbledon the following year at the grand old age of 41. A stalwart of the All England Club, he had competed there every year since 1888.

Golden gamble

Great Britain's Kitty McKane reached the last four in the women's Singles in 1920 but then, amazingly, withdrew from her semi-final so as to conserve her energy to partner Winnie McNair in the women's Doubles semi-final. The Britons were up against the legendary French player Suzanne Lenglen, partnered by her compatriot Elizabeth d'Ayen. The ploy paid off as the British women won in three sets and went on to win in the final to claim the gold medal.

↑ *Victory in the women's Tennis Final at Seoul 1988 saw Steffi Graf complete a memorable 'Golden Slam'.*

Graf's history lesson

1988 proved a golden year for Germany's Steffi Graf. When Tennis made its re-entry to the Games programme in Seoul, she became the first winner of the women's Singles title. She had already won the Australian, French, Wimbledon and US Open titles, the latter only a week before the Games began. Her straight sets win over Argentina's Gabriela Sabatini thus converted her 'Grand Slam' into what remains a unique 'Olympic Slam'.

Sky's the limit for Henin

Before the Athens 2004 Games, Belgium's WTA world No. 1 Justine Henin had been suffering from a virus, and when she arrived in Athens she had not played competitively in 11 weeks. At the Games, however, she was extended to three sets only once, by Russia's Alexandra Myskina, the French Open champion, in the semi-finals. In the final, Henin took only 78 minutes to beat France's Amélie Mauresmo in straight sets: she celebrated by trying out her new hobby – skydiving.

Agassi's heritage

Andre Agassi beat Spain's Sergi Bruguera in straight sets to win the gold medal at the 1996 Games in Atlanta, but he was not the first member of his family to take part in the Olympic Games. His father Mike Emanoul Agassi had boxed for Iran in the Bantam Weight division at the 1948 Games in London and also competed in the 1952 Games in Helsinki.

↖ *Andre Agassi beat Sergi Bruguera 6–2 6–3 6–1 to win men's Singles gold at Atlanta 1996.*

London 2012

Wonders of Wimbledon

Andy Murray walked away from Wimbledon in July burning with the pain of losing to Switzerland's Roger Federer in the All-England Championships final. Three weeks later he was back to turn the tables on Federer in the men's Singles final and take the bonus of Mixed Doubles silver. The Scot swept aside the world No. 1 in straight sets 6–2 6–1 6–4 before he and 21-year-old Laura Robson lost 2–6, 6–3, 10–8 to top seeds Max Mirnyi and Victoria Azarenka of Belarus.

Murray, the first Briton to win Olympic Tennis men's Singles gold since Josiah Ritchie at London 1908, described his victory as: 'The biggest win of my life. The support has been amazing, as at all the events. I had watched the athletics and the way Mo Farah won gave me a boost coming into my own final.'

The 25-year-old climbed up into the stands after his victory to celebrate with mother Judy, girlfriend Kim Sears, family, friends and aides.

Federer, gracious in defeat, said: 'For me, it's been a great month. I won Wimbledon, became world No.1 again, and I got silver. Don't feel too bad for me. Credit Andy for getting in the lead and then using the crowd to his advantage to come through. He did it unbelievably well.'

Earlier the USA's Serena and Venus Williams retained their women's Doubles with a 6–4, 6–4 win over the Czech Republic's Andrea Hlavackova and Lucie Hradecka. The sisters had also won Doubles gold at Sydney 2000 and Beijing 2008. With one Singles title each, they thus became the first Tennis players to win four golds each. Serena crushed Maria Sharapova 6–0, 6–1 in the women's Singles final.

⬇ *The Williams sisters, Serena (left) and Venus, added a third women's Doubles gold to their Olympic Games medal collection.*

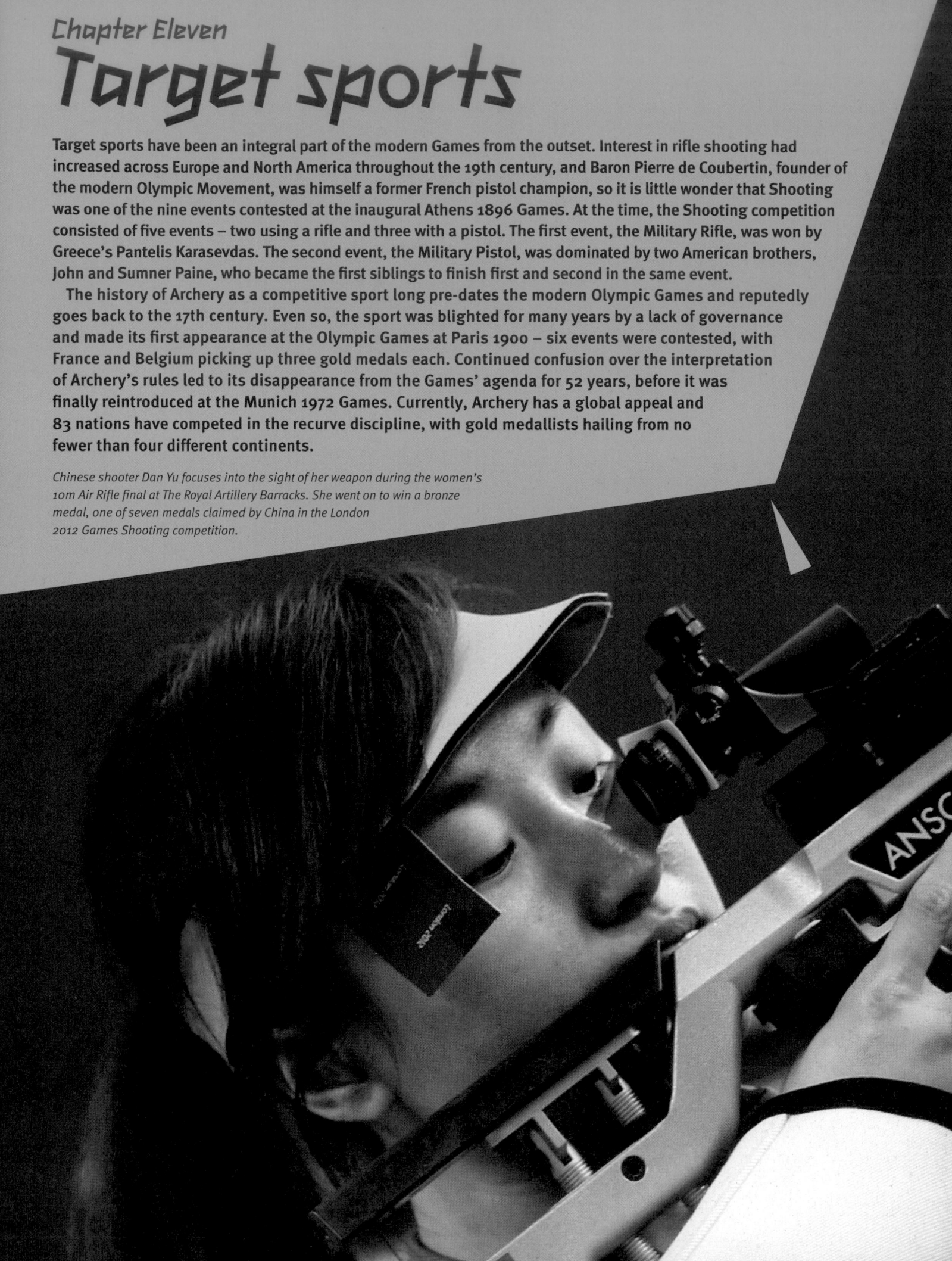

Chapter Eleven
Target sports

Target sports have been an integral part of the modern Games from the outset. Interest in rifle shooting had increased across Europe and North America throughout the 19th century, and Baron Pierre de Coubertin, founder of the modern Olympic Movement, was himself a former French pistol champion, so it is little wonder that Shooting was one of the nine events contested at the inaugural Athens 1896 Games. At the time, the Shooting competition consisted of five events – two using a rifle and three with a pistol. The first event, the Military Rifle, was won by Greece's Pantelis Karasevdas. The second event, the Military Pistol, was dominated by two American brothers, John and Sumner Paine, who became the first siblings to finish first and second in the same event.

The history of Archery as a competitive sport long pre-dates the modern Olympic Games and reputedly goes back to the 17th century. Even so, the sport was blighted for many years by a lack of governance and made its first appearance at the Olympic Games at Paris 1900 – six events were contested, with France and Belgium picking up three gold medals each. Continued confusion over the interpretation of Archery's rules led to its disappearance from the Games' agenda for 52 years, before it was finally reintroduced at the Munich 1972 Games. Currently, Archery has a global appeal and 83 nations have competed in the recurve discipline, with gold medallists hailing from no fewer than four different continents.

Chinese shooter Dan Yu focuses into the sight of her weapon during the women's 10m Air Rifle final at The Royal Artillery Barracks. She went on to win a bronze medal, one of seven medals claimed by China in the London 2012 Games Shooting competition.

Archery

As a military weapon, the bow and arrow dates back more than 1,000 years. King Harold of England was famously killed by an arrow fired by a Norman invader at the Battle of Hastings in 1066. As a sport, archery is believed to have begun as an Anglo-French event, so it was appropriate that Archery made its Olympic Games debut at Paris 1900.

Team after team

Archery as a team sport was added to the Games agenda at Seoul 1988 and has been dominated by South Korea's women's Archery team. From 1984 to 2008 they won 16 gold medals and retained their unbeatable tag with further gold in Beijing. At Sydney 2000, the country's archers, inspired by Seo Hyang-Soon, won three of the four events. The team put their success down to a healthy combination of preparation, scientific training – and the right DNA! World record holder Yoon Ok-hee claimed that Korean women were dexterous due to heightened sensitivity in their fingers.

Accidental outsider

There are countless examples of Olympians becoming movie stars. However, in Archery the reverse was the case when Hollywood actress Geena Davis took part in the qualifying for Sydney 2000. Davis competed in the semi-finals of the United States trials, but ultimately finished 24th and missed out. She said: 'This was a once-in-a-lifetime opportunity to be exposed to this amount of stress and level of competition. I just focus on my technique and not worry about the result.'

⬆ *Geena Davis, winner of the Best Supporting Actress Oscar in 1988, took part in the US trials for the Sydney 2000 Games but missed out on selection.*

⬆ *New Zealand's Neroli Fairhall made history at Los Angeles 1984 when she became the first paraplegic to appear in the Olympic Games.*

Fantastic Fairhall

The 1984 Games in Los Angeles saw one of the ultimate examples of inspirational endeavour. New Zealand athlete Neroli Fairhall had been paralysed from the waist down in a motorbike accident. Subsequently she took up archery and became the first wheelchair-bound athlete to compete at the Summer Games, finishing 35th overall. A national champion for many years, Fairhall won medals and held titles at the Paralympic Games, IPC-Archery World Championships and many international tournaments and was awarded the MBE.

Taking a time-out

Archery maintained a low-key presence at the 1904, 1908 and 1920 Olympic Games. However, there was no international consensus about the rules of the sport and differing interpretations were used by successive host countries, with the result that Archery was banished from the Games altogether. The emergence of the Fédération Internationale de Tir à l'Arc, in 1931, finally gave the sport much-needed governance and, more importantly, a standard set of rules. This paved the way for Archery's return to the Games at Munich 1972, four decades later, and only then as an Individual competition. It took a further 16 years before a Team competition was contested for the first time.

The most golden arrow

Archery's highest-profile moment came at the climax of the Opening Ceremony at the Barcelona 1992 Games. Billions of eyes around the world were captivated by the spectacular lighting of the Olympic Flame by an arrow fired from the bow of Spanish Paralympic archer Antonio Rebollo. He said later: 'There were no nerves: I was practically a robot, I focused on my positioning and reaching the target. Later people described to me how they saw it, what they felt, their emotions. That is what made me realise what such a moment actually meant.'

Always on target

In the pantheon of archers at the Games, Belgium's Hubert Van Innis arguably ranks highest of them all. He won six gold medals, despite competing at only two Games. At the 1900 Games in Paris, Van Innis struck gold twice, after which 20 years passed before his next appearance. At Antwerp 1920, he showed he had lost none of his control when he won another four gold medals. After his successes in 1920, Archery was banished from the Olympic Games during his lifetime, but in 1933, at the age of 67, he was still a team winner at the World Championships.

Golden years

Age has proved no barrier to women archers. At the 1908 Olympic Games in London, Britain's Sybil Fenton Newall (known as Queenie Newall) won the gold medal at the age of 53. Newall's score of 688 points gave her a 46-point victory over second-place finisher Lottie Dod. She remains the oldest woman ever to have won a gold medal at the Games.

⬇ *Fifty-three-year-old Queenie Newall showed the younger competitors how it was done when she took Archery gold at London 1908.*

London 2012

Fizzing with delight

The Republic of Korea maintained its monopoly of Olympic Archery by carrying off three out of four gold medals at London 2012. But pride of place went to the manner in which Jin Hyek Oh claimed the country's first men's Individual Competition gold as he defeated Japan's Takaharu Furukawa 7–1. The way had been cleared for Oh by the early-round defeat of Brady Ellison, the American favourite and world No.1. That was a twist of fate which rewarded Oh for his persistence in battling to earn a place in the Olympic squad ever since Sydney 2000. Oh also collected a Team Competition bronze but his achievements were outdone by girlfriend Bo Bae Ki, who won gold in both women's Individual Competition and women's Team Competition events.

⬆ *Jin Hyek Oh takes aim during the men's Individual Competition. He won gold in the Individual Competition and bronze in the Team Competition.*

Golden return

Korea beat China by one point to win the women's Team Competition, China's third straight loss to the Koreans in gold medal meetings. Bo Bae Ki, Sung Jin Lee and Hyeon Ju Choi scored 210 points from their 24 arrows – Ki scoring a nine with the last shot. Korean women archers have won 13 of the last 14 golds and going home without one was unthinkable. As Choi said: 'People think we should always win the women's Archery gold medal but coming here was so difficult. The hardest part was dealing with so many changes in the weather.'

World Record

Event	Name	Country	Record	Date
Men's Individual Competition	Dong Hyun Im	KOR	699	27 July
Men's Team Competition	Republic of Korea	KOR	2,087	27 July

Shooting

Shooting was contested at the first modern Games at Athens 1896 and, with the exception of St Louis 1904 and Amsterdam 1928, has been a feature at every Games since. Shooting today comprises nine events: 10m Air Rifle, 50m Rifle Prone, 50m Rifle 3 Positions, 10m Air Pistol, 25m Rapid Fire Pistol, 50m Pistol, Skeet, Trap and Double Trap.

Opening shots

Shooting was one of the nine events contested at the inaugural Olympic Games in Athens, in 1896. At those Games, five Sport Shooting events were contested. These took place at the newly constructed shooting range at Kallithea. They were organised and prepared by the Sub-Committee for Shooting. Some 61 shooters from seven nations competed in the five events: Military Rifle, Free Rifle, 25m Military Pistol, 25m Rapid Fire Pistol and Free Pistol. The host nation claimed three golds, with the United States bagging the other two.

Mixed results

Barcelona 1992 was a landmark Olympic Games for shooting equality as China's Zhang Shan took the gold medal in the mixed-gender Skeet competition, becoming the first woman to win a mixed event. Female shooters had been admitted to the Olympic Games only at Mexico City 1968 and it was not until 1984 that separate shooting events for women were introduced, in addition to mixed events. The International Shooting Union subsequently prohibited women from shooting against men.

↑ Zhang Shan created a slice of history at Barcelona 1992 when she claimed Skeet Shooting gold to become the first woman in history to win a mixed event.

Family business

When Sweden's Oscar Swahn won silver in the Running Deer Double Shot Team event, at the 1920 Olympic Games in Antwerp, he became the oldest person to win a medal at the Games. The 72-year-old had already won gold and bronze medals at the 1908 and 1912 Games, with his success at the latter, in Sweden, at the age of 64, making him the oldest gold medallist ever. His appearance in 1920 broke a further record: he became the oldest athlete ever to compete in the Summer Games. His gold medal-winning son Alfred, was by his side at every team event he competed in at Antwerp.

⬇ *(Left to right) Alf Swahn, Ake Lundberg, Oscar Swahn and Per Olof Arvidsson won Running Deer Double Shot silver for Sweden at the Antwerp 1920 Games.*

Pigeon relief

The Shooting contests at the 1900 Games in Paris were mired in controversy. Live pigeons were used as moving targets and it was reported that as many as 300 were shot dead. Clay pigeons were introduced in time for the following Games. The controversy did not stop there, however. Out of the 6,351 shooters listed, 96 per cent were from France. Also, values were compromised at the 1900 Games because prize money was awarded to virtually every winner in the Shooting events.

Shooting star

Carl Townsend Osburn holds the distinction of being the most successful competitor in Shooting at the Games in history. Until Michael Phelps's record-breaking performance in the swimming pool, Osburn was the all-time leading male medal winner for the United States in any sport at the Games, with a tally of 11. Osburn competed between 1912 and 1924 while serving in the US Navy, where he attained the rank of Commander. His shooting prowess saw him dominate the Shooting competition at the Antwerp 1920 Games, in which he claimed no fewer than six medals, four of which were gold. Such was his dominance, he would probably have added even more medals had the 1916 Games not been cancelled.

Teenage talent

Atlanta 1996 was the stage that produced the Olympic Games' youngest Shooting gold medallist: American Kimberly Rhode, who won the Double Trap event at the tender age of 17. She won a second gold medal at Athens 2004, but the elimination of Double Trap Shooting from the Games roster for women saw her focus on the Skeet. Having won the 2007 World Cup, during which she set a world record of 98 hits, Rhode won silver at Beijing 2008 and gold at London 2012.

➡ *Kimberly Rhode is the only United States athlete to have won an individual medal at five consecutive Olympic Games.*

London 2012

Wilson's ambition fulfilled

Peter Wilson's success in the men's Double Trap at The Royal Artillery Barracks in Woolwich was a reward not only for the Dorset-based shooter but for the vision and intent behind Great Britain's Olympic Ambition programme. The scheme had been created to offer possible future Olympians the chance to 'taste' the Olympic ambience. Wilson was duly inspired and after the Athens 2004 gold medallist Sheik Ahmed Al Maktoum agreed to coach him for free, results took off. Wilson topped the British rankings, won World Cup and European Championship team silver, set a double trap world record ... and Olympic gold.

⬆ *Peter Wilson's coach won gold at Athens 2004 and the pupil emulated the master at London 2012.*

Record for Rossi

Italian policewoman Jessica Rossi claimed a world record 99 out of 100 hits to win gold in the women's Trap – and the 20-year-old missed out on an unbeatable world mark only because she missed her 92nd shot. Slovakia's Zuzane Stefecekova took silver and France's Delphine Reau the bronze after a shoot-off. Britain's three-times Commonwealth champion Charlotte Kerwood, selected ahead of world No.4 Abbey Burton, was 16th. Another Shooting world record – also 99 clays out of 100 – was set by American Kimberly Rhode in the women's Skeet. This was her third Olympic Games gold and fifth medal in all. She is the only United States athlete to have won medals in an individual event at five successive Games.

World Record

Event	Name	Country	Record	Date
Women's Skeet (equalled)	Kimberly Rhode	USA	99	29 July
Men's 25m Rapid Fire Pistol	Alexei Klimov	RUS	592	3 August
Men's 25m Rapid Fire Pistol (finals, equalled)	Leuris Pupo	CUB	34	3 August
Men's 250m Rifle Prone (finals, equalled)	Sergei Martynov	BLR	705.5	3 August
Women's Trap (finals)	Jessica Rossi	ITA	99	4 August

Olympic Record

Event	Name	Country	Record	Date
Men's 10m Air Rifle (equalled)	Alin George Moldoveanu	ROM	599	30 July
Men's Skeet	Vincent Hancock	USA	148	31 July
Women's 25m Pistol	Kim Jangmi	KOR	591	1 August
Women's 50m Rifle 3 Positions (finals)	Jamie Lynn Gray	USA	691.9	4 August
Men's 50m Rifle 3 Positions (finals)	Niccolo Campriani	ITA	1278.5	6 August
Men's Trap (equalled)	Michael Diamond	AUS	125	6 August

Chapter Twelve
Water sports

Water sports – totally separate from Aquatics – have a long history at the Olympic Games. Rowing, for example, was included in the programme at Athens 1896 but the events had to be cancelled because of bad weather. The first Olympic Games water sports champions were thus hailed at Paris 1900.

Expansion saw Sailing entering the Games programme at Los Angeles 1932 and Canoeing at Berlin 1936. Women's Rowing first appeared at the Montreal 1976 Olympic Games, with the Lightweight events debuting at Atlanta 1996.

Down the years the balance and identity of the events in all three have evolved – with a RS:X (Windsurfer) competition being incorporated into the Sailing schedule at the Los Angeles 1984 Games.

The inclusion of Sailing at the Games meant extending the organisational challenge for Host Cities and conceding that the competition often had to be staged at venues that were often several hundred kilometers away from the Olympic Stadium. Thus the Sailing regatta at London 2012 took place on the south coast at Weymouth and Portland, some 110 miles (175km) away to the south-west of the capital.

All the water sports are themselves split into varied disciplines. For example, Rowing with a pair of oars is sculling, while Rowing with one oar is the sweep version. Canoeing employs a paddle with one blade, which is switched from side to side by the canoeist sitting in a half-kneeling position, while Kayak events use a paddle with blades at either end and alternating strokes.

Rowing courses at the Games varied in length before settling down to their current standard of 2000m (1.24 miles) at the Seoul 1988 Games. Rowing at the Paris 1900 Games was over a distance of 1750m (1.08 miles) , and the events were along the River Seine. The course at the London 1908 Games was 2414m (1.5 miles) long, on the River Thames at Henley. However, when Rowing returned to Great Britain (and to Henley) at London 1948, it was over a course 1883m (1.17 miles) in length.

Heather Stanning (left) and Helen Glover have a clear lead in the women's Pair final at Eton Dorney. They became Great Britain's first gold medallists in women's Rowing.

Canoe Slalom

Two types of boat are used in the sport: canoes, for one or two canoeists; and kayaks, for one, two or four kayakers. Slalom events were contested for the first time at the Munich 1972 Games and, after a 20-year break, at all of the five Games staged since Barcelona 1992.

East trumps west

For the Munich 1972 Games, the West German hosts spent DM17 million (US$4m) constructing an artificial river at Augsburg. A year before the Games, their East German counterparts studied the facilities and replicated them in Zwickau. And how it paid dividends: when the time came, the East Germans took gold in all four Slalom events.

Practice makes perfect

Some 24 years after the first Kayak Single event was held in Augsburg, during Munich 1972, a young man born in the city crossed the Atlantic to win gold in the event at the 1996 Olympic Games in Atlanta. Oliver Fix had first paddled on the course used at the 1972 Games when he was nine, becoming the youngest person to negotiate it. He visited the Atlanta canoeing site five times to familiarise himself with it and when he competed there in earnest he was victorious, with German rival Thomas Becker taking bronze.

Schmidt rises to the challenge

Germany's top-ranked Kayak Single competitor in the run-up to the 2000 Games was Thomas Becker, bronze medallist four years earlier and the 1997 world champion. But he was beaten in the selection races by Thomas Schmidt, who went on to defeat Britain's favourite Paul Ratcliffe – the winner of the pre-Olympic Regatta.

Elastic course

The first Olympic Slalom course, built for Munich 1972, was 600 metres long and included 30 gates. When the event was next held, at Barcelona 1992, it was 340m long and, at Atlanta 1996, 415m.

↑ Italy's Pierpaolo Ferrazzi struck men's K-1 gold at Barcelona 1992.

Second time lucky

Pierpaolo Ferrazzi of Italy managed only 17th place in the first run of the Kayak Singles competition at Barcelona 1992, but his second run, in which he incurred no penalties, earned him the gold with the fastest recorded time of 1:46.89.

Temporary River

The Canoe events at the Atlanta 1996 Games were staged on the Ocoee River in Tennessee – but there was a problem. The site of the course had been dry for almost 50 years and, although water had been redirected into the riverbed in 1994, it was diverted through a tunnel to a power plant to create electricity. In 1996, however, the water was released through one of the three dams into the 1-mile course for 77 days to allow for training, as well as a pre-Olympic event and the Games themselves.

➔ Michal Martikan won men's C-1 gold at Atlanta 1996 and silver in the same event at Sydney 2000.

Politics before sport

Czechoslovakia's Lukas Pollert won men's Canoe Singles gold at Barcelona 1992 when it was reintroduced to the Games after a 20-year absence. However, he said it had meant more to him to take part in the demonstrations that had led to the overthrow of Communism in his country three years earlier.

Double double

The 2000 Canoe Doubles title was won by twins – Pavol and Peter Hochschorner of Slovakia.

← *Twins Peter (back) and Pavol Hochshorner of Slovakia on their way to C-2 gold at the Sydney 2000 Games.*

Double golden

Slovakia's Elena Kaliska completed a rare Games double at Beijing 2008 as she successfully defended the women's Kayak Singles title she had won at Athens 2004.

So near, yet so far

Britain's Lynn Simpson, then the reigning women's Kayak Singles world champion, failed to live up to her billing as favourite at Atlanta 1996: she missed the 11th gate during her second run and finished in 23rd place.

Togo top man

Benjamin Boukpeti became the first athlete from Togo to win an Olympic Games medal when he won bronze in the men's Kayak Single event at Beijing 2008. Four years earlier in Athens, Boukpeti, who holds dual French-Togo citizenship, had become the first Togolese athlete to reach a Games semi-final. Boukpeti marked his bronze breakthrough by breaking his paddle over his kayak in celebration.

Celebrating in style

The Czech Republic's Stepanaka Hilgertova finished the Atlanta 1996 Games women's Kayak (K1) Slalom level on time, penalties and points with Dana Chaldek, who had also been born in the old Czechoslovakia, but was competing for the United States. Hilgertova won because her non-counting weaker run was better than Chaldek's, during which she had capsized, missed four gates and finished last. Four years later, at Sydney 2000, Hilgertova retained her title by a clear margin, finishing well clear of France's Brigitte Guibal after a faultless second run in her final that was three seconds faster than any rival. Asked if she had been motivated by the US$24,000 bonus she earned for winning, Hilgertova replied that she would have competed even if there had been no bonus, adding: 'First, I like winning, and second, as any woman, I like to be the centre of attention.'

London 2012

Family fortunes

Frenchman Tony Estanguet had a distinguished Olympic Games and maintained family honour. Having won men's Canoe Single gold in at Sydney 2000 and Athens 2004, he regained the title from his old Slovak rival Michal Martikan, another double Olympic gold medallist. In a superb final run the Frenchman finished ahead of Germany's Sideris Tasiadis. Martikan had to settle for bronze, his fifth Olympic medal after gold at Atlanta 1996 and Beijing 2008 as well as silver at Sydney 2000 and Athens 2004. Estanguet's father, Henri, won medals at the Whitewater Canoe World Championships in the 1970s while elder brother Patrice won bronze at Atlanta 1996.

Double top for Britain

One of the most remarkable achievements to take place at the Lee Valley White Water Centre was Great Britain's sweep of gold and silver in the men's Canoe Slalom Double (C2). Tim Baillie and Etienne Stott were ranked sixth in the world at the start of competition, for which they could enter only because the other Britons – David Florence and Richard Hounslow – had qualified as individuals. Remarkably Baillie and Stott set the standard and Florence and Hounslow came down the course last to take silver behind them and ahead of Peter and Pavol Hochschorner. The Slovak twins, invincible world champions for three years, had been chasing a fourth consecutive gold medal in the event.

↓ *Tim Baillie (left) and Etienne Stott led a Great Britain one-two in the men's Canoe Slalom Double (C2) at London 2012.*

Canoe Sprint

Sprint events in Canoeing and Kayaking were first contested at the 1936 Games in Berlin. Men compete over 200 metres and 1000m (in canoes and kayaks with one, two or four athletes), while women compete over 200m and 500m (in kayaks only with one or two athletes).

Electrifying speed

Cliff Meidl, who represented the USA in the Kayak Four event at the 1996 Games and in the Kayak Single at Sydney 2000, was so severely electrocuted at the age of 20 – while working for a construction company he received 30,000 volts, 200 times more than is normarly used for the electric chair – suffered three cardiac arrests and was unable to walk unaided for three years.

In and out

Sprinting events have been part of the Olympic Games since 1936 for men, and since 1948 for women. Kayak Single and Double races over 10,000 metres were held from 1936 to 1956, then discontinued.

Swedish flourish

The best medal haul at a single Games by one woman is the two golds and a silver amassed by Agneta Andersson of Sweden at the 1984 Games in Los Angeles. That feat was equalled at the 1988 Games in Seoul – by Germany's legendary canoeist Birgit Fischer-Schmidt, of course.

Birgit the best

Birgit Fischer-Schmidt is the most successful canoeist at the Games, having competed over a record 24-year period between 1980 and 2004, during which time she won a record eight golds and four silvers for East Germany and Germany. Her record of eight golds is shared with Hungarian fencer Aladar Gerevich, although she achieved that total in six Games – one fewer than Gerevich.

← *Birgit Fischer-Schmidt celebrates an eighth gold at Athens 2004.*

Little and large

Hungary's winners of the Canoe Double 500m gold at the 2000 Games in Sydney, Ferenc Novak and Imre Pulai, were known as 'The Monster and the Little Guy', as Pulai was 6ft 6in tall and weighed more than 15 stone, while Novak was 5ft 8in tall and weighed 12 stone. Because of strong winds on the day of the Final, Pulai played safe by taping his smaller partner's legs to the boat so he would not slip out.

Gert the great

The most successful male kayaker at the Games has been Sweden's Gert Fredriksson, who won six golds, one silver and one bronze from 1948 to 1960, all in the Kayak Single competition. Three golds in a single Games have been achieved by Vladimir Parfenovich, a 21-year-old PE instructor from Minsk, in the Soviet Union, in 1980, and Ian Ferguson of New Zealand four years later. Ferguson had retired after finishing seventh at the Moscow 1980 Games, but returned to the sport when the New Zealand Sports Federation offered kayakers increased financial support.

Kayaking in the blood

After winning a bronze medal in the men's Kayak Single (K1) 1000m at Sydney 2000, Tim Brabants delayed his medical studies to train for Athens 2004, where he finished fifth in the final. Having returned to medicine for a year, Brabants renewed his full-time sporting efforts in preparation for the Beijing 2008 Games. He won the Kayak Single (K1) 1000m gold and bronze in the Kayak Single (K1) 500m. Job done, he thought – and Brabants returned to medicine. A year later, however, he was back to full-time training once again, unable to resist the lure of London 2012. He made the final again, but finished in eighth.

← *Great Britain's Tim Brabants powers his way to Kayak Single 1000m gold at Beijing 2008.*

Triumph and tragedy

Matija Ljubek won gold and bronze medals for Yugoslavia at Montreal 1976 in the men's C-1 1000m and C-1 500m, and added two more medals in 1984 before becoming vice-president of the Croatian Olympic Committee. In 2000, however, Ljubek was shot dead while defending his mother from an estranged brother-in-law.

Comfortably numb

Clint Robinson, a 20-year-old from Queensland, worked so hard to outsprint Norway's two-time world champion Knut Holmann and earn gold in the K-1 1000m Final at the 1992 Games in Barcelona that his whole body went numb. He was also so dehydrated that it took him six hours to produce a urine sample for the standard doping test. His opponent Holmann went on to win the next two Kayak Single titles in a career that saw him take six medals in four appearances at the Games.

Silver to gold

Greg Barton, a mechanical engineer from Michigan, USA, won the K-1 1000m event at the Seoul 1988 Games, then lost it, then won it again – at least, that is how it seemed. Barton, who had been born with two club feet, was told immediately after his race by officials that he had narrowly beaten Grant Davies to win the gold medal. However, the scoreboard showed him as the silver medallist and the Australian started to celebrate. As Barton prepared for the Kayak Double Final, the jury of the International Canoe Federation studied the finish line photo and they duly announced that the American had won it after all – by 0.005 seconds, or less than a centimetre. So, in this bizarre manner, Barton became the first US kayaker to win gold at the Games.

Lifesaver's late flourish

Francis Amyot, who had once saved three Ottawa Rough Riders football players from drowning, took an early lead in the Canoe Single 1000m event at the Berlin 1936 Games, only to be overtaken by Czechoslovakia's Bohuslav Karlik after 750 metres. But the 31-year-old Canadian dug deep and burst to the front in the final 50m to win the event's first-ever Olympic Games title and become Canada's only gold medallist of the Games – despite having been refused financial support from the Canadian Olympic Committee.

London 2012

The 'Bolt of Eton Dorney'

Ed McKeever became another British competitor to win gold after leading from start to finish to triumph in the men's Kayak Single (K1) 200m at Eton Dorney. The 28-year-old from Bradford-on-Avon won in 36.346 seconds, a time slightly slower than that of his heats and semi-finals as he battled against a headwind to outpace Spain's Saul Craviotto Rivero and Canada's Mark de Jonge. Later McKeever said he had been so excited at the prospect of racing the final that he woke 'at 5am like a kid at Christmas wanting to open my presents'. Now that he had a medal he could feel more relaxed about his nickname as the 'Usain Bolt of the water'.

↗ Ed McKeever 'Bolted' to the gold medal in the men's Kayak Single (K1) 200m, the shortest and fastest event in the Canoe Sprint. He set a new Olympic Games record at the London 2012 Games.

Maori magic touch

Lisa Carrington stormed to victory in the women's Kayak Single (K1) 200m to earn New Zealand its first women's Olympic gold medal in the Canoe Sprint – with a little bit of special help from her father's Maori family. The 23-year-old tucked beneath her racing outfit a green stone necklace in the shape of a whale's tail which had been blessed for strength and protection. It also provided speed and determination and powered her to gold. Carrington was one of the smallest competitors in the event but she held a power to weight advantage over favourites such as Beijing 2008 Games gold medalist Inna Osypenko-Radomska from Ukraine and Hungary's Natasa Douchev-Janics. They took silver and bronze respectively.

World Record

Event	Name	Country	Record	Date
Women's Kayak Four (K4) 500m	Poland	POL	1:30.338	6 August

Olympic Record

Event	Name	Country	Record	Date
Men's Kayak Single (K1) 200m	Ed McKeever	GBR	35.087	11 August
Men's Kayak Double (K2) 200m	Russian Federation	RUS	33.507	11 August
Men's Canoe Single (K1) 200m	Ivan Shtyl'	RUS	40.346	10 August
Women's Kayak Single (K1) 200m	Lisa Carrington	NZL	40.528	10 August

Rowing

A scheduled event at the inaugural modern Games at Athens 1896 – only for the regatta to be cancelled due to bad weather – Rowing has been contested at every Games since Paris 1900 (by men) and since Montreal 1976 (by women). The current programme involves 14 events, all of which are contested over a 2000m long course.

Records eventually recognised

The Rowing events at recent Olympic Games have been held on still water, but weather conditions were considered too variable for official records to be set. However, as courses are now strictly regulated – they are a straight 2000 metres (1.24 miles) – records are recognised. The fastest average speed by a men's Eight is 22.51km/h (13.98mph), by the United States crew when they clocked 5:19.85 in a heat at Los Angeles 1984. Automatic timing was introduced at the Rome 1960 Games, and the narrowest winning margin in a men's event was when Great Britain's Coxless Four beat Canada by 0.08 seconds at Athens 2004.

⬆ *In the background, the Great Britain Coxless Four (from left: Steve Williams, James Cracknell, Ed Coode and Matthew Pinsent) celebrate gold at Athens 2004.*

Kelly gold

Just 30 minutes after the USA's John Kelly Senior had narrowly defeated Britain's Jack Beresford in the 1920 Single Sculls Final – after which both men were so exhausted they could not shake hands – he had recovered sufficiently to add another gold medal in the Double Sculls, in the company of Paul Costello. Kelly Senior, who won a record third gold with Costello four years later, had two children who also made their mark on the world. Son John Kelly Junior won a bronze medal at Melbourne 1956, and daughter Grace Kelly became a Hollywood film star before marrying Prince Rainier of Monaco.

Confusion in Paris

At the Paris 1900 Olympic Games, France's Coxed Fours crew from Roubaix won gold despite having finished one minute slower than the third fastest crew. The reason was the course was only big enough for four boats and officials held two separate finals. Crews were told that the four places in the final would go to winners of the three heats, along with the second-placed crew in heat three, which involved four of the ten entrants. But when the losers in heats two and three recorded faster times than the heat one winner, the officials announced an extra qualifying heat – only some of the crews could be contacted in time. Thus Roubaix, which had finished second in heat three, defeated two non-qualifiers to win gold in 7:11.00. The second final saw Germany's Ruder Club win in 5:59.00, while fellow Germans, Ruder Verein, finished third in 6:05.00.

Rowing for his life

Hugh 'Jumbo' Edwards, who won gold medals in the Coxless Pairs and Coxless Fours in the space of a single day at the 1932 Games in Los Angeles, used his prowess on the water to secure his personal safety 11 years later when, as an RAF squadron leader, he had to ditch his plane in the Atlantic Ocean and row four miles through a minefield.

⬆ *The Soviet Union's Coxless Pair team of Victor Ivanov (left) and Igor Buldakov (right) in action at the Henley Regatta in 1957.*

Throwing away the prize

Viktor Ivanov, an 18-year-old rower from the Soviet Union, was so thrilled at finishing second behind the United States in the Coxless Pairs at the 1956 Games in Melbourne that during the presentation ceremony he jumped up and down with joy – and dropped his silver medal into Lake Wendouree. Ivanov, who had partnered Igor Buldakov, dived into the water to search for it, but could not find it. After the Games, however, the International Olympic Committee took pity and gave him a replacement medal.

Oldest and youngest

The oldest Rowing gold medallist in Olympic Games history was Robert Zimonyi, who coxed the United States eight at the 1964 Games in Tokyo aged 46 years 180 days. The oldest oarsman to win gold was Guy Nickalls, who was in the victorious British eight at the 1908 Games in London aged 41 years 261 days. Fellow Brit Julius Beresford was 44 years 20 days old when won silver four years later. The youngest recorded gold medallist was Giliante D'Este, who was 18 years 141 days old when he rowed for Italy in the Coxed Fours at the 1928 Games in Amsterdam. The youngest medallist oarsman was Australia's Walter Howell, who was 16 years 346 days old when he was in the bronze medal-winning eight at Melbourne 1956. The youngest medal-winning cox was France's Noel Vandernotte, who won bronze in the Pairs and Fours at Berlin 1936 at the age of 12 years 232 days. The four included his father and uncle, Fernand and Marcel.

Redgrave the record

Immediately after he had won the Pairs gold in company with Matthew Pinsent at the 1996 Games in Atlanta, an exhausted Steve Redgrave, having just won his fourth successive gold medal at the Games, told a TV interviewer: 'If anyone sees me near a boat again, they have my permission to shoot me.' Four years later, Redgrave competed in the Four at Sydney 2000, collecting a record fifth consecutive gold medal and bringing his medal total to six. Redgrave, who later that year was voted BBC Sports Personality of the Century, achieved his record despite discovering three years beforehand that he was diabetic, and also required treatment for colitis shortly before the 2000 Games. His 1996 partner Pinsent, with whom he had won the Pair at Barcelona 1992, earned his third gold in the Four at Sydney 2000, and went on to add a fourth victory, also in the Four, at Athens 2004. Pinsent's fellow countryman Jack Beresford won one fewer gold medal, but two more silvers, as he became the first rower to win medals at five consecutive Games between 1920 and 1936. If the 1940 Games, scheduled for Tokyo, had not been prevented from taking place by the Second World War, who knows what the record would have been?

← *Sir Steve Redgrave poses with his five Olympic gold medals.*

No go rows

The line-up of Rowing events at the Games has changed over the years. In 1996, the Coxed Pairs and Coxed Fours, which had both been a part of the programme since 1900, were discontinued. Three other events made only one appearance at a Games: the Six-Man Naval Rowing Boats (won by Italy in 1906); the 17-Man Naval Rowing Boats (won by Greece in 1906); and the men's Coxed Four with Inriggers (won by Denmark in 1912). Quadruple Sculls were introduced to the Games in 1976, and Lightweight Double Sculls and Fours became part of the programme in 1996.

↑ *A butcher by trade and a long-standing member of the Vesta Rowing Club in Putney, London, Henry Blackstaffe won gold at London 1908.*

Experience pays off

At 40, the London 1908 Single Sculls gold-medal winner Henry Blackstaffe, who worked as a butcher, was twice the age of silver medallist Alexander McCulloch, but finished more than a length ahead of his fellow Briton.

Child's play

Benjamin Spock, a 6ft 4in student from Yale University, was in the USA eight that won gold at the 1924 Games in Paris. After graduating from medical school, Spock became a paediatrician and, in 1945, published a book – *The Common Sense Book of Baby and Child Care* – that sold more than 50 million copies in over 30 languages.

↓ *Benjamin Spock (sitting third from right) in action with the USA eight at the Paris 1924 Games.*

US women's Eight's once unofficial Games record

Women's Rowing was introduced at Montreal 1976, over a 1,000-metre (0.62 miles) course. From Seoul 1988, the course length was standardised to that of the men at 2,000m (1.24 miles). Also as with the men's competition, records are now recognised in Olympic Rowing. At Los Angeles 1984, the US women's Eight won a heat in a time of 5:56.55 – at an average speed of 20.19km/h (12.54mph). This once unofficial mark is now the official Olympic record.

Laumann the brave

Just 73 days before she was scheduled to race in the women's Single Sculls at the 1992 Games in Barcelona, Canada's Silken Laumann, the reigning world champion, was involved in a shocking accident while warming up for a race in Essen, Germany. The 27-year-old's shell was rammed by that of the German Coxless Pair, Peter Holtzenbein and Cohn von Ettingshausen, and a piece of wood smashed into her lower right leg, fracturing the bone, cutting her calf muscles and causing extensive nerve and tissue damage. After helping to save her, both the German rowers fainted at the sight. Laumann was told she would need six months to recover, but after five operations, and despite having to walk with a cane and having to avoid standing up for more than quarter of an hour at a time, she achieved her target of competing at the Barcelona Games. Incredibly, she took the bronze medal. Four years later she improved to silver, when she finished behind Belarus's Ekaterian Khodotovich.

Lipa – the greatest?

Romania's Elisabeta Lipa lays claim to being the most successful Olympic Games rower of all time, matching Steve Redgrave's record of five gold medals when she won at the Athens 2004 Games, 20 years after her first victory, at Los Angeles 1984. Two additional silvers and a bronze meant that Lipa finished her Olympic Games career with a total of eight medals – more than any other rower, and two more than Redgrave's tally. Lipa's compatriots dominated the individual medal table at Athens 2004. Doina Ignat, a member of the eight that won three straight golds, has amassed four golds and two other medals, while Georgeta Damian's victory in the Pair at the Beijing 2008 Games meant that she became the third rower in Olympic Games history to win five golds, having won the in Pair and Eight gold at the two previous Games. Viorica Susanu's total after the 2008 Games was four golds and a bronze, while Constanta Burcica has so far won three golds and a total of five medals in the Lightweight Double Sculls. Cox Elena Georgescu has also picked up five medals, three of them gold. Romania did not win a medal at London 2012, finishing fourth in the women's Eight final.

Romania's Elisabeta Lipa (second left) celebrates her fifth and final gold medal at Athens 2004.

Taxi trouble

After taking silver in the women's Pairs at her home Olympic Games in Sydney in 2000, Australia's Rachael Taylor celebrated too enthusiastically ... and ended up leaving her medal in a taxi cab. Her plight was publicised and a Sydney taxi driver returned the medal to her after finding it underneath his back seat.

↑ *Australia's Rachel Taylor (left) won women's Pairs gold at Sydney 2000 (with Kate Slatter) ... and left her medal in a taxi.*

Landmark achievement

In 1986, ten years after helping the USA eight to take bronze in the inaugural women's Olympic Games Rowing event in Montreal, Anita DeFrantz became the first black woman to be selected to serve on the International Olympic Committee. She was elected on to the IOC Executive Board in 1992.

Gift of life

Four weeks to the hour after winning silver behind Australia in the Coxless Pairs at the 1996 Games in Atlanta, United States rower Missy Schwen underwent an operation to donate her kidney to her brother, Michael.

London 2012

Grainger gold at last

A hugely popular success was that of Anna Watkins and Katherine Grainger in the Double Sculls. A wave of relief also greeted their success because Grainger – a multiple World Championship and World Cup winner – had been 'only' a silver medallist at Sydney 2000, Athens 2004 and Beijing 2008. In their preparation the duo tried as best they could to treat the event as 'just another competition'. Grainger said: 'It was really important that we made it as familiar as possible. We knew it was the final of the home Games with millions of people watching but if we had looked at all that too closely it would have been overwhelming.' Olympic victory left Grainger 'free' mentally to return to her PhD studies... in criminology.

First strike success

One of the most significant of all Great Britain's gold medals at London 2012 was the Pair victory at Eton Dorney of Helen Glover and Heather Stanning because this was the host nation's first gold in what proved to be a record modern haul of 29. British fans had to wait until five days after the Opening Ceremony to see Glover and Stanning lead from the first stroke. They were never challenged, achieving clear water by the 500m mark. This was also British women's first Olympic Rowing gold. Glover, educated at Millfield and briefly a member of the England satellite hockey squad, had taken up rowing only in 2008 through the Sporting Giants scheme. She and Stanning broke through at international level in 2010.

⬇ Helen Glover (left) and Heather Stanning celebrate their golden moment at Eton Dorney, and the first of 29 triumphs for Team GB at London 2012.

⬆ Katherine Grainger (left), after three silver medals, celebrates after partnering Anna Watkins to women's Double Sculls gold.

Team GB go one better

Great Britain commanded the regatta at London 2012. They headed the Rowing medals table with four gold, two silver and three bronze, the nine being one more than the team's previous record at the London 1908 Olympic Games and remarkable progress from the total two medals at Atlanta 1996.

Gregory steps up

Victory for Great Britain in the men's Four extended coach Jurgen Grobler's incredible record of having guided crews to gold at 11 successive Olympic Games since 1972. Parading gold fulfilled an ambition for Alex Gregory who had been a reserve at Beijing 2008. Steve Williams retired in 2010 and Gregory was brought in to winning effect at the World Championships the following year and then at London 2012 – Britain's fourth successive triumph.

New Zealand fliers

On the first day of the Rowing competition in the water at Eton Dorney, in the first heat of the men's Pair, New Zealand's Eric Murray and Hamish Bond shattered the world record with a time of 6:08.50. To no one's surprise, they later rowed to gold.

World Record

Event	Name	Country	Record	Date
Men's Pair	Eric Murray/Hamish Bond	NZL	6:08.50	28 July

Olympic Record

Event	Name	Country	Record	Date
Women's Pair	Helen Glover/Heather Stanning	GBR	6:57.29	28 July
Men's Double Sculls	Nathan Cohen/Joseph Sullivan	NZL	6:11.30	28 July
Men's Single Sculls	Tim Maeyens	BEL	6:42.52	28 July
Women's Double Sculls	Anna Watkins/Katherine Grainger	GBR	6:44.33	30 July
Men's Four	Australia	AUS	5:47.06	30 July

Sailing

Since the sport's Games debut at Paris 1900, results in Sailing have been determined on the basis of aggregate scores from a series of races, with the possibility of some results being discarded. The rules have altered over the years, as have the kinds of boats involved in competition. At London 2012, excluding the Windsurfer RS:X competition, there were five men's events and three for women.

Elvström – the great Dane

Denmark's Paul Elvström can claim to be the most successful yachtsman in Games history after becoming the first man to achieve four successive gold medals – from 1948 to 1960. His Games career did not finish there: he competed at Mexico City 1968 in the Star class (where he was fourth); the 1972 Soling class (17th), and the Tornado class in 1984 and 1988 (where he was fourth and 15th respectively).

⬇ *Denmark's Paul Elvström won the first of his four gold medals in the Firefly class at the London 1948 Games.*

Oldest and youngest

The USA's Everard Endt became the oldest gold medallist when he won the 6 Metre class in 1952 aged 59 years 112 days. The oldest winner in a single-handed race was Belgium's Leon Haybrechts, who won gold in 1924 aged 47 years 215 days. Franciscus Hin (Netherlands), who won the 12ft Dinghy event aged 14 years 163 days in 1920 with his brother Johannes is the youngest winner.

Scheidt's trap

In the 1996 Laser class, Britain's 19-year-old Ben Ainslie went into the final race in silver-medal position, trailing Brazil's Robert Scheidt by two points. As a result, there was much pre-race manoeuvring between the two as they jockeyed for position before the gun went. After four false starts, officials raised the black flag, meaning that anyone who crossed the start line early would be disqualified. As Scheidt headed for the line at the fifth attempt, he gambled that Ainslie would have to stick close to him to prevent him getting a decisive lead – and that if he crossed the line himself before the gun went, and got disqualified, the young Briton would suffer the same fate. Both crossed the line, both were disqualified – and Scheidt won gold.

⬆ *After being outsmarted by Brazil's Robert Scheidt, Great Britain's Ben Ainslie had to be content with a silver medal in the Laser class at Atlanta 1996. He would go on to win gold in 2000, 2004 and 2008.*

Ainslie's revenge

Four years after Ainslie fell into Scheidt's trap, the Sydney 2000 Laser class contest again came down to the last race, with Scheidt leading Ainslie by seven points. The only way Ainslie could win was by preventing the Brazilian from finishing 21st or better, so he harassed his opponent before the start, forcing him to commit an infraction that required a 720-degree penalty turn. Once they got underway, Ainslie blocked Scheidt's wind and repeatedly prevented him from passing, to the point where both trailed the rest of the fleet by 90 seconds. In his efforts to get clear, Scheidt collided with Ainslie's boat before moving up the field to 22nd place, but he could not get any higher and, despite filing two protests, both of which were rejected, as he was disqualified and the Briton was awarded gold. Ainslie then put on 40lb as he moved up to the Finn class, in which he won gold at Athens 2004, Beijing 2008 and London 2012.

Take the rest of the week off

Britain's pairing of Rodney Pattison and Christopher Davies won four of their first six races in the Flying Dutchman class at Munich 1972, which meant they were certain of the gold medal without having to race on the final day. In the same class at Mexico City 1968, Pattison had partnered Iain Macdonald-Smith, scoring the lowest number of penalty points – three – in Games history. After being, they felt, unjustifiably disqualified for interference after finishing first in the opening race, they won the next five on the trot, then played safe in the last race to finish second and ended up taking gold by a margin of more than 40 points.

Two for one

The only boat to earn two gold medals at a single Games was *Scotia*, crewed by Britain's Lorne Currie and John Gretton, which won the 0.5-1 Ton and Open classes at the Paris 1900 Games. The USA yacht *Llanoria* won the 6 Metre class at London 1948 and Helsinki 1952, skippered on both occasions by Herman Whiton.

Brotherly crews

Sailing has often been a family affair. At Antwerp 1920, four Norwegian brothers won gold in the 12 Metre (1907 rating) class: Henrik, Jan, Ole and Kristian Ostervold. Eight years earlier, Amédée, Gaston and Jacques Thube (France), won the 6 Metre class. Sweden's Ulf, Jorgen and Peter Sundelin (5.5 Metre class) equalled the feat at Mexico City 1968. The only gold medal-winning twins were Sumner and Edgar White (United States, 5.5 Metre class) at the Helsinki 1952 Games.

Sailing dynasties

The Antwerp 1920 Games saw the first victory by a father and son pairing when Belgium's Emile and Florimond Cornellie won the 6 Metre (1907 rating) class. Sailing's most prominent dynasty is Norway's Lunde clan. Eugen started it all off at Paris 1924, winning gold in the 6 Metre class; his son Peder and daughter-in-law Vibeke won silver in the 5.5 Metre class at Helsinki 1952, with Vibeke's brother also aboard; and grandson Peder junior won gold at Rome 1960 in the Flying Dutchman class. That made it three generations of Lundes as Olympic Games medallists. The London 1948 Star class event saw gold go to USA sailors Paul Smart and his son Hilary, with silver being won by another father and son team, Cuba's Carlos De Cardenas Culmell and Carlos De Cardenas Junior.

Zeros to heroes

At Seoul 1988, Britain's Michael McIntyre and Bryn Vaile were in fourth place in the Star class going into the final race. To earn gold they needed to win it, with the US leaders, Mark Reynolds and Hal Haenel, placing no higher than sixth and Brazilians Torben Grael and Nelson Falcao no better than fifth. It was a tall order, but Fate was with the British pair. While the Brazilians finished eighth and the Americans failed to finish after their mast broke, McIntyre and Vaile duly won the race by 11 seconds. McIntyre, from Salisbury, said afterwards: 'In my wildest dreams I thought we could win – but not in any other state of mind.' It was a great victory for the Britons in what was Scotsman McIntyre's second appearance at the Olympic Games and Vaile's one and only. McIntyre had finished seventh at Los Angeles 1984 in the Finn class.

↑ *Great Britain's Michael McIntyre (back) and Bryn Vaile (front) won the final race to take Star class gold at the Seoul 1988 Games.*

Power of eight

The first woman to win a medal in Sailing at the Olympic Games was Britain's Frances Rivett-Carnac at the London 1908 Games. She was part of the gold medal-winning crew of four sailing in the 7-Metre class. The next time a woman won a gold medal at the Games was at Antwerp 1920, when another Briton, Dorothy Wright, was also part of the victorious 7-Metre class crew. Another eight years would pass before the next female medallist, France's Virginie Hériot, at the Amsterdam 1928 Games. The eight-year cycle for women winning medals continued when Sweden's Dagmar Salen of Sweden was part of the bronze-medal crew of five in the 6-Metre class at the Berlin 1936 Games. After the Second World War interrupted the Olympic Games, there were no women medallists until the Helsinki 1952 – again a gap of two Games. This time two women went home with medals: Norway's Vibeker Lunde won the silver medal as part of the crew of three in the 5.5-Metre class and the United States' Emelyn Whiton was one of six crew members who took the gold medal in the 6-Metre class.

Countess with the mostest

The first woman to compete in the Olympic Games was a sailor. When women's events were introduced at the 1900 Games – not in major sports – Hélène, Countess de Pourtalès, of Switzerland, became the first woman to make her mark as she crewed for her father, Count Hermann de Pourtalès, in the 1–2 Tonnes Sailing event. And they won, making the Countess, at 31, the oldest female gold medallist of the 1900 Games, and her father the oldest gold medallist of the Games at 53 years 55 days. However, as the 1900 races were handicapped, most observers do not consider them to have been part of the Olympic Games proper.

➜ *Hélène, Countess of Pourtalès, is credited with being the Games' first female starter. She won gold.*

Oldest and youngest

The oldest female gold medallist was Virginie Hériot (France), who won in the 8-Metre class at the 1928 Games aged 38 years 16 days. The oldest female medallist was Pease Glaser (United States), who took silver in the 470 class at Sydney 2000, aged 38 years 314 days. The youngest female gold medallist was Kristine Roug (Denmark), who won the Europe class at Atlanta 1996 aged 21 years 141 days. The youngest female medallist was Natalia Via Dufresne Perena (Spain), who took silver in the Europe class at Barcelona 1992.

Golden coach

Guided by their coach, Viktor Kobalenko, the Ukraine pairing of Ruslana Taran and Olena Panholchik, 470 class bronze medallists at the 1996 Games, won three consecutive world and European titles. But when their coach moved to Australia their form began to falter – and that of the Australian pair, Jenny Armstrong and Belinda Stowell, started to improve under his guidance. The Ukraine pair won another bronze at Sydney 2000, while the gold went to Armstrong and Stowell – who had originally come from New Zealand and Zimbabwe respectively.

On the up

In the Sailing competitions at both Athens 2004 and Beijing 2008, women represented 35 per cent of the competing athletes (139 out of 400). That represented a 32 per cent increase in women's participation since the 2000 Games in Sydney (95 out of 402).

Sensini supreme

A total of 90 medals have been won by women sailors at the Olympic Games, but Italy's Alessandra Sensini is the only woman sailor to have won four medals – one gold (in 2000), one silver (in 2008) and two bronzes (in 1996 and 2004).

Yngling, Yngling, gone…

Sarah Ayton was a member of the British crew that won the Yngling class – an event for a three-person keel boat – when it was introduced to the Olympic Games in 2004. Her partners in Athens were skipper Shirley Robertson and Sarah Webb. Four years later at Beijing 2008, Ayton was skipper of a British crew that won Yngling gold again, this time partnered by Webb and newcomer Pippa Wilson. Having won the world title as well, the British trio were looking forward to completing a hat-trick in their home Games in 2012 but, in 2009, the International Federation dropped Yngling from the Games programme.

⬆ *From left to right: Shirley Robertson, Sarah Webb and Sarah Ayton celebrate their Yngling victory at Athens 2004.*

From four to the fore

Shirley Robertson missed out on a medal in the Europe class by just two points at Atlanta 1996. Four years later, in Sydney, she was in with a shout for gold with just two races remaining, needing to finish fourth or better in either. When she could only manage 16th place in the first of them, the pressure was on to finish ahead of Holland's Margriet Matthijsse, winner of the penultimate race. The Dutchwoman won the last race too, but Robertson finished in third place to secure gold. At the next Games, at Athens in 2004, the Scotswoman skippered Britain to gold in the newly established Yngling class.

London 2012

Ainslie flies the flag

Ben Ainslie, as befitted his status as the most-decorated Olympic sailor of all time, carried Great Britain's flag at the Closing Ceremony of London 2012. Ainslie's fourth gold medal, won in the Sailing men's Finn, added to the silver he won at Atlanta 1996 and made him the first British Olympian to win medals in an individual event at five consecutive Games. The 35-year-old described his Finn class victory over Denmark's Jonas Høgh-Christensen after a week of Olympic sailing off Dorset's coast as 'the most nerve-racking race of my life.'

Taste of silver

The one set of British Olympic competitors who missed out on the immediacy of crowd support were the sailors. To make amends they were granted open-top bus parade through Weymouth and Portland where the Sailing events were staged. The team won a gold and four silvers, and Luke Patience, who won silver with Stuart Bithell in the men's 470 class, said: 'The public have been amazing, it's something we don't get to experience as much because we are out on the water.' Patience and Bithell, who teamed up in 2009, taste the seawater, out of superstition, before setting sail. But they did not taste ultimate success after losing narrowly to Australia's Mathew Belcher and Malcolm Page.

⬆ Ben Ainslie won gold at London 2012 in the men's Finn to become Great Britain's most decorated Olympic sailor of all time.

All over with Olivia

Spain won Match Racing gold in the women's Elliott 6m class after Australia lost their skipper Olivia Price overboard during a tacking manoeuvre in winds of up to 27 knots off Weymouth and Portland. The 20-year-old went over during the third of five head-to-head races. That cost the Australians crucial minutes as Nina Curtis and Lucinda Whitty hauled Price back on board. Spain, the 2011 European champions with a crew of Tamara Echegoyen Dominguez, Sofia Toro Prieto Puga and Angela Pumariega Menendez, went on to win the deciding fifth race by a clear 100 metres for a 3-2 overall success. This was Spain's second Sailing gold at the London 2012 Games.

Kiwi power

New Zealand's Jo Aleh and Olivia Powrie fulfilled a pledge to go one better than their men by winning the women's 470 class. Aleh and Powrie left Britain's Hannah Mills and Saskia Clark behind after they had started the final medal race joint first. Mills and Clark chose the left side in the first upwind beat while the Kiwis struck out on their own course after a slow start and stayed in front to the end. Aleh said: 'We had taken a look at the course before the race and we were pretty happy the right would be fine. We needed to strike out on our own'. Earlier in the week Aleh had said she and Powrie would surpass the silver medal achieved by fellow Kiwis Peter Burling and Blair Tuke in the men's 49er.

⬇ Jo Aleh (helm) and Olivia Powrie of New Zealand won the gold medal in the women's 470 class at London 2012. In the sea off Weymouth and Portland, Dorset, they outmanoeuvred Great Britain's Hannah Mills and Saskia Clark in the final medal race.

Windsurfer RS:X

Windsurfer RS:X is a class that combines the elements of sailing and surfing and is often referred to as sailboarding, as it takes place on a board with a sail on it. In competitions at the Olympic Games, all competitors use identical equipment.

Herminator-style

Christoph Sieber, Austria's unexpected winner of the event at the 2000 Games in Sydney, credited his success to the winter weight-training training he had undertaken in the snow with the Austrian skiing legend Hermann Maier.

↑ *Christoph Sieber held off Charles Espinola (Argentina, silver) and Aaron McIntosh (New Zealand, bronze) to take Windsurfing gold at Sydney 2000.*

Rubbish luck

Michael Gebhardt (USA) took Windsurfer class silver at Barcelona 1992 and might have won gold had it not been for a stray rubbish bag. There had been complaints before the competition got underway that the course at the Parc de Mar venue was not fit for purpose because of the amount of refuse floating in it. On the last lap of his seventh race, a bag became caught on the end of Gebhardt's board. By the time he had disentangled himself from it, the American had been passed by six rivals.

Breezing in

The Windsurfer class for men was first contested at the Los Angeles 1984 and the women's event became part of the Games programme eight years later at Barcelona 1992. Different styles of board have been used at different Games. For the inaugural event at Long Beach in Los Angeles, a Windglider was used – a board 12 feet 9 inches long and 25½in wide that carried a sail of 70sq ft. At Seoul 1988 and Barcelona 1992, the Lechner Division II board was chosen – a 12ft long, round-bottomed sailboard with a 78.6sq ft sail. In 1996, 2000 and 2004, the Mistral board was used, a 13ft 11in long board made of fibreglass with a sail of 7.4sq m. Beijing 2008 saw the introduction of the Neil Pryde RS:X board.

Safer at sea

At the 1988 Games in Seoul, heavy winds gusting up to 25 knots on the fifth day of racing created waves almost two metres in height, and only 19 of the 43 men starters finished. Conditions favoured heavier windsurfers, but the gold went to New Zealand's Bruce Kendall, who weighed just over 10 stone. Kendall, aged 24, had encountered more difficulties on dry land, having grazed his hand badly after falling off his skateboard while listening to rock music on his Walkman. New Zealand team officials banned him from further skateboarding until after the Games were over.

Going Dutch

The first Windsurfer class gold medallist at the Olympic Games was Holland's Stephan van den Berg, who held off the competition from home contender Randall Scott Steele off Long Beach, California, in 1984. Van den Berg was favourite to win, having been world champion for the three previous years. This was Holland's first Sailing gold since Berlin 1936, when Daniel Kagchelland had won the Finn class at Kiel. Eight years later, Van den Berg competed at the 1992 Games in Barcelona, finishing seventh.

Back to the drawing board

The originator of the first sailboard is generally believed to have been an American named Newman Darby who, as a 20-year-old in 1948, had the idea of mounting a hand-held sail on to a small catamaran. Darby, however, did not patent his idea. The first patent on a windsurfing boat was taken out by two Californians, Jim Drake and Hoyle Schweitzer, who named their design the Windsurfer. Fittingly, the Windsurfer class event was contested for the first time at the 1984 Olympic Games in Los Angeles.

Sister power

Four years after her brother Bruce, had won gold for New Zealand in the Windsurfer competition at the Seoul 1988 Games, Barbara Kendall did likewise at Barcelona 1992 to become the first female Olympic champion in her event. It was a remarkable performance by Kendall because, in early 1992, just seven months before the start of the Games, she had been thrown from a power boat, suffering a severed tendon in her arm and a broken scaphoid bone in her wrist. China's Xiaodong Zhang finished runner-up to Kendall to become the first Asian athlete to win an Olympic Games Sailing medal. Kendall became the first New Zealand woman to compete at five Games, winning silver at Atlanta 1996 and bronze third at Sydney 2000, before finishing fifth at Athens 2004 and sixth at Beijing 2008. She retired in 2010.

Close encounter

Endra Ha-Tiff, of the Seychelles, almost did not make it to the start line at the 2000 Games in Sydney, having narrowly escaped with her life after a close encounter with a ferry while training in Sydney Harbour. Luckily it left her with nothing worse than a scraped knee.

Home Heroine

Jian Yin (who had finished second at the previous Games in Athens) provided China with a home champion at Beijing 2008 as she held off the challenge of the 2000 champion Alessandra Sensini of Italy, and won four of the event's ten races (including the first three) to take gold in the Windsurfer class. Bryony Shaw finished third to win Britain's first Windsurfer class medal at the Games and celebrated the feat by breaking down in tears.

⬇ *Having picked up a silver medal in the Windsurfer class at Athens 2004, China's Jian Yin thrilled the home crowd when she took gold at Beijing 2008.*

London 2012

⬆ *Dorian Van Rijsselberghe (right) was the last Windsurfer gold medallist.*

Gold and farewell

Dutchman Dorian Van Rijsselberghe wrote a final page in Olympic history as last winner of gold in the Windsurfer RS:X category. Kiteboarding will replace windsurfing at Rio 2016 – and Van Rijsselberghe has already said he intends to follow the switch. The 2011 world champion scored six firsts in the 10 qualifying races and was well clear by halfway. Trailing in his wake were London 2012 silver and bronze medallists Britain's Nick Dempsey and Przemyslaw Miarczynski of Poland, as well as the second and third at Beijing 2008, Julien Bontemps of France and Shahar Zubari of Israel.

Wife's winning sacrifice

Nick Dempsey had barely collected his men's RS:X silver medal before acknowledging the sacrifice made by his wife Sarah Ayton so he could chase his own dream. Ayton, a double gold medallist in the Yngling class in Athens 2004 and Beijing 2008, retired at the start of 2011 to care for their son, so Dempsey could concentrate on improving from his fourth place at Beijing 2008 and bronze at Athens 2004. Dempsey said: 'I owe this all to Sarah. When she retired from sailing a little part of it was so that I did not have to compromise. She would have won a gold medal at these Games.'

Chapter Thirteen
Weightlifting

Weightlifting is one of the cornerstone sports at the Games, reflected in the third part of the Olympic Motto – 'Citius, altius, fortius' (faster, higher, stronger). The sport has been part of the Games programme since Athens 1896 and has produced some of the most colourful moments in the event's history.

The fascination of Weightlifting lies not just in the demonstration of physical prowess but also in the tactics, which are intriguing but easy to understand. Every competitor has three attempts at two movements: the snatch and the clean & kerk – a third, the press, was discarded after the Munich 1972 Games.

In the snatch the bar is lifted overhead in one movement; in the clean & jerk it is pulled into the top of the chest, usually with the competitor squatting beneath the weight to receive it, and then jerked overhead, invariably with one leg going forward and the other back for support.

The best performances on the two lifts are then aggregated, with the competitor who has recorded the highest total adjudged the winner.

Key to the sport's tactics is the fact that once a weight has been selected, the competitor cannot go down. If the athlete fails in an attempt, he must either retake the lift using the same weight again or increase it. If two competitors have the same total, the man or woman with the lighter bodyweight wins.

There are eight bodyweight divisions for men and seven for women. Women's Weightlifting was first contested at Sydney 2000 and has been dominated by China.

Ilya Ilyin of Kazakhstan set a new Weightlifting world record in the men's 94kg clean & jerk by lifting 233kg. His lift total of 418kg was another world record as Ilyin successfully defended his Olympic title from Beijing 2008.

London 2012

Weightlifting

The first two men's Weightlifting competitions at Athens 1896 featured no weight limits. They were introduced for the first time at Antwerp 1920, have been modified several times over the years and, since 2000, feature eight categories from 56kg to Over 105kg. Women's Weightlifting made its debut at the Sydney 2000 Games and features seven weight categories from 48kg to Over 75kg.

The strongest man

Charles Rigoulot was one of France's most famous figures during the 1920s, not because he won the light-heavyweight title at the 1924 Games but because of his career afterwards. In 1925, he was challenged by a professional French strongman, Ernest Cadine, a gold medallist at Antwerp 1920, for the title of 'The World's Strongest Man'. Rigoulot won. Subsequently he became a professional wrestler, continued to train with weights, raced cars for Peugeot and was imprisoned in a concentration camp during the Second World War for hitting a German officer.

⬆ *Charles Rigoulet became a huge celebrity in the 1920s.*

Family support

Khadr El Touni was a decisive winner of the 1936 middleweight title, setting a world record with a lift of 387.5 kilograms. At London 1948, he signed himself out of a London hospital, to which he had been admitted, to take part in the competition and could only finish fourth. His last major victory came when he won the world title in 1950. He died six years later after electrocuting himself attempting to do a domestic repair.

Winning gambles

Born in Israel and the son of a Brooklyn rabbi, Issy Berger won featherweight gold at Melbourne 1956 and then the world title in Stockholm in 1958. He was renowned for placing wagers on lifts and was nicknamed 'Betcha' Berger. One weight he twice failed to lift, despite impressive performances in the gym, was the 152.5 kilograms he needed to retain his title at the Rome 1960 Games, leaving the Soviet Union's Yevgeny Minayev, the only man in the competition to complete all nine attempts, as the champion.

Beating the system

In 1932, France's Louis Hostin, runner-up in 1928, took the light-heavyweight title in Los Angeles, finishing 5 kilograms ahead of Denmark's Svend Olsen. Hostin continued to improve and was the clear favourite for Berlin 1936. There he led his main rival, Germany's Eugen Deutsch, by 5kg on the press, and on the snatch he raised 117.5kg, with Deutsch failing to raise 110kg three times. The Germans then protested that one of Deutsch's attempts had been valid and the Jury of Appeal, under considerable pressure, allowed one effort to be ratified. The British Olympic Association's official report noted: 'This was keenly resented by many present.' However, Hostin held on for his second successive victory.

Bowling them over in Bond...

Harold Sakata was one of the few weightlifters to achieve international fame, but not because of his exploits in the sport. He finished second in the light-heavyweights at the 1948 Games, became a professional wrestler and went on to become the Canadian tag team champion. However, his greatest role was still to come: he played the role of Oddjob in the Bond film *Goldfinger*.

⬅ *Harold Sakata in action at the London 1948 Olympic Games.*

Bars to prison bars

The USA's John Davis reigned supreme among weightlifters for 15 years. He won his first world title at light heavyweight in 1938, aged 17. After the war, he won two gold medals at the Games and five world super heavyweight titles, even though, at only 100 kilograms, he was much lighter than many of his opponents. In 1950, Davis lifted the famous Apollon railway axle, which had defied many people over the years, although he needed four attempts to do so because his small hands were not suited to grasping the thick bar.

Fast food route to gold

The bespectacled American Norbert Schemansky was the first weightlifter to win four medals at the Games, as he moved between the mid-heavyweight and heavyweight divisions from London 1948 to Tokyo 1964, when he finished third at the age of 40. His career, in which he took three world titles, was interrupted by serious back injuries. 'Skee' was not helped by a diet that owed little to healthy nutrients. When once asked of what it consisted, he replied: 'Hamburgers. Pizza. Beer.'

Conquering not just asthma

Born in Sacramento of Japanese extraction, Tamio 'Tommy' Kono was an asthmatic child, but, having been introduced to Weightlifting in a relocation camp during the Second World War, he became perhaps the greatest competitor the sport has ever known. Between 1952 and 1959, he won two Olympic and six world titles, in the lightweight and light heavyweight categories.

↑ Celebration time for Soraya Jimenez Mendivil at the Sydney 2000 Games.

The sweet smell of success

When women's Weightlifting was introduced to the Games programme at Sydney 2000, the organisers enterprisingly gave red carnations to all the female competitors and spectators. Few deserved it more than Soraya Jimenez Mendivil. The 23-year-old Mexican produced the performance of a lifetime – she managed to jerk an impressive 127.5 kilograms (15kg more than her best performance at the previous year's World Championships) – to take the 58kg gold medal from North Korea's Ri Song-Hui, who failed her second jerk attempt. When asked afterwards whether females should compete in Weightlifting, Mendivil replied decisively: 'This is a sport for women. All sports are for women.'

Martin the master

Louis Martin, who was born in Kingston, Jamaica, but who went on to represent Great Britain, was his adopted country's greatest-ever weightlifter, winning four world titles and mid-Heavyweight silver and bronze medals at the Olympic Games, at Rome 1960 and Tokyo 1964 respectively. His last chance for gold came in Mexico City in 1968, but it was not to be. Trailing going into the clean & jerk, he went for 192.5kg in a bid to get the bronze medal. Three times he got up with the bar. Three times he jerked it overhead. Three times he failed.

↗ Louis Martin won bronze at Rome 1960 and silver at Tokyo 1964 in the -90kg category.

Cold War weights

When the Soviet Union competed for the first time at the Olympic Games in 1952, the Cold War was at its peak. This gave a special edge to the rivalry between the United States and the Soviets, and nowhere was this keener than in the Weightlifting competition. The light heavyweight class in 1952 was perhaps the most controversial in the history of the sport, with Trofim Lomakin and Arkady Vorobyev trying to take away the title from the American Stan Stanczyk. There were constant protests from both sides and two judges resigned after their decisions were reversed. Lomakin eventually won, with Stanczyk second, but Vorobyev just failed with his last clean & jerk when he tried a world record lift of 170 kilograms. He got the bar to arms' length, but the sudden roar from the crowd applauding his feat seemed to unsettle him and he dropped the weight.

If at first...

After being the first person to train at the US Olympic Center in Colorado in three different sports, Tara Nott-Cunningham finally competed at the Games in Weightlifting. The 1.54-metre tall Texan was originally a gymnast, but had failed to qualify for the Games. Then she tried volleyball, basketball and finally football, in which she played internationally, but was not picked by the United States for Atlanta 1996. She took up weightlifting for fitness and became Pan American champion in 1999. In Sydney, she finished second in the 48kg category – becoming the first American to win a Weightlifting medal since 1960 – and was subsequently elevated to the gold medal position.

Lei Cao powers to gold

China dominated the women's Weightlifting competition at the Beijing 2008 Games winning four of the seven gold medals on offer, and the star of the show was Lei Cao. A former junior world champion and the reigning senior world champion (having taken the title in both 2006 and 2007), the 24-year-old dominated the 75kg category, setting new Olympic Games records in both the snatch and clean & jerk disciplines (with lifts of 128kg and 154kg respectively). Her total score of 282kg was also a new Games record. She may have failed with her final world record attempt (159kg in the clean & jerk), but it mattered not: she had lifted a combined 16kg more than her closest competitor (Kazakhstan's Alla Vazhenina) to win gold.

⬆ *Cao Lei dominated the 75kg category at Beijing 2008.*

Worthy contender

The impressive performance of Yanqing Chen at Beijing 2008 (left) was emulated by Chinese team-mate Chunhong Liu, who won her second 69kg crown at the Games. Russia's Oxana Slivenko, the world record-holder in snatch, had been expected to challenge Liu, but the Chinese competitor set new Games and world records –
not bothering with her final clean & jerk to win the title by 31 kilograms, with a total of 286kg. The official magazine of the International Weightlifting Federation suggested she was a worthy contender to be considered the best woman lifter of all time.

Strongest and longest

Confusion reigned briefly at Beijing 2008, when a seemingly unknown Thai weightlifter won the 53kg class – the bantamweights. Jaroenrattanatarakoo Prapawadee also had the distinction of having the longest name of all the competitors in the Games. However, after she had raised a total of 221 kilograms to claim gold, the truth emerged. The winner revealed that, following a run of bad luck, including not being picked for the previous Games, she had consulted a fortune-teller and was told she would be successful at the 2008 Games if she changed her name from Kuntatean Junpim, by which she had been known earlier when she won senior and junior world titles.

More weight

The supreme super heavyweight at Beijing 2008 was South Korea's Jang Mi-Ran, who added an Olympic Games gold medal to her six world crowns. She had begun weightlifting aged 16, and in 2008 won the gold medal by 49 kilograms, setting new world records with both her snatch lift and her overall total.

Now you see her...

Beijing 2008 witnessed one of the outstanding Weightlifting feats in history, when China's Yanqing Chen retained her Olympic Games title to become the first woman in history to win two gold medals in the Games. This was the climax of an international career that had begun 11 years earlier, in 1997, when she won the world middleweight title. Despite winning the lightweight crown two years later, she was not picked for the 2000 Games in Sydney, but came back at Athens 2004 to win her first Olympic Games gold medal. However, after the Asian Games in Doha she had another period away, taking a BSc in psychology, before returning successfully once again.

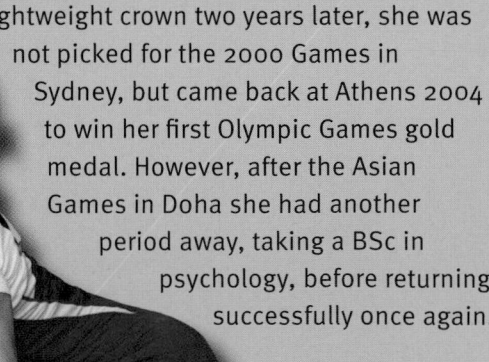

⬅ *China's Yanqing Chen won the 58kg Weightlifting category at Beijing 2008 to become the first woman in history to defend her title at the Games.*

London 2012

Salimi The Strong

Iran's Behdad Salimikordasiabi seized the unofficial crown as strongest man at London 2012 when the 'man mountain' won gold in the Over 105kg category. The 22-year-old 'Salimi' – already world champion – took victory with a winning total of 455kg and two lifts to spare. His winning total comprised a 208kg lift in the snatch round and a 247kg clean & jerk. That put him 6kg ahead of training partner and fellow countryman Sajjad Anoushiravani. Together they paraded an Iranian flag for delighted fans. His only failure was in missing a 264kg clean & jerk which would have taken the world record from former Olympic champion Hossein Rezazadeh who, as Iran's Weightlifting president, was cheering him at ExCeL. The party atmosphere spread far beyond east London. Salimi said: 'In Iran I know they're all partying in the street already.'

Pole's slight difference

Adrian Zielinksi celebrated Poland's first Weightlighting gold medal for 40 years thanks to the fine margin of 130 grams in terms of body weight. Zielinski and Russian Federation teenager Apti Aukhadov tied on a total weight of 385kg in the 85kg category but Zielinski had the advantage in build. Zielinki, world champion two years earlier, said: 'This is the fulfilment of all my dreams. I wasn't sure I would get a medal then, in the last lift, I felt a new strength and decided to go for it.' This was Poland's first Weightlifting gold since Zygmunt Smalcerz won the men's 56kg title at Munich 1972. China's defending Olympic champion Yong Lu led after the snatch, lifting 178kg, but he failed to register a weight in the clean & jerk.

Off the gold standard

China topped the Weightlifting medals table with five golds but that was a slip from eight at Beijing 2008. Lulu Zhou won the country's fifth and final gold medal in the 75kg category with a world record 333kg but still described the team's overall performance as: 'Mission unaccomplished'. Her total extended the aggregate world record 328kg she had set at the world championships in Paris the previous November. A Chinese selection choice which misfired was that of Zhou Jun in the 53kg category though, she was not alone in upsetting predictions. Other medal tips who came up short with her included Dominica's Yuderqui Contreras and Turkey's Aylin Desdelen.

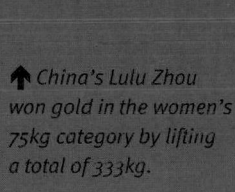

↑ *China's Lulu Zhou won gold in the women's 75kg category by lifting a total of 333kg.*

World Record

Event	Name	Country	Record	Date
Women's 53kg	Zulfiya Chinshanlo	KZH	131kg (clean & jerk)	29 July
Men's 62kg	Un Guk Kim	PRK	327kg (total)	30 July
Men's 77kg	Xiaojun Lu	CHN	175kg (snatch)	1 August
Men's 77kg	Xiaojun Lu	CHN	379kg (total)	1 August
Men's 94kg	Ilya Ilyin	KAZ	233kg (clean & jerk)	4 August
Men's 94kg	Ilya Ilyin	KAZ	418kg (total)	4 August
Women's Over 75kg	Tatiana Kashirina	RUS	151kg (snatch)	5 August
Women's Over 75kg	Lulu Zhou	CHN	333kg (total)	5 August

Olympic Record

Event	Name	Country	Record	Date
Men's 56kg	Yun Chol Om	PRK	168kg (clean & jerk)	29 July
Women's 53kg	Zulfiya Chinshanlo	KAZ	226kg (total)	29 July
Men's 62kg	Un Guk Kim	PRK	153kg (snatch)	30 July
Men's 62kg	Oscar Albeiro Figueroa Mosquero	COL	177kg (clean & jerk)	30 July
Women's 58kg	Xueying Li	CHN	108kg (snatch)	30 July
Women's 58kg	Xueying Li	CHN	246kg (total)	30 July
Women's 63kg	Maiya Maneza	KAZ	245kg (total)	31 July
Women's 75kg	Natalya Zabolotnaya	RUS	131kg (snatch)	3 August
Women's 75kg	Svetlana Podobedova	KAZ	161kg (clean & jerk)	3 August
Women's 75kg	Natalya Zabolotnaya	RUS	291kg (total)	3 August
Women's Over 75kg	Lulu Zhou	CHN	187kg (clean & jerk)	5 August

Picture credits

The publishers would like to thank the following sources for their kind permission to reproduce the pictures in this book. The page numbers for each of the photographs are listed below, giving the page on which they appear in the book and any location indicator (C-centre, T-top, B-bottom, L-left, R-right).

Action Images: 80B, 109BL, 114; /Carlos Barria/Reuters: 108BL; /Kin Cheung/Reuters: 194BL; /Nir Elias/Reuters: 86T; /Mike Finn-Kelcey/ Reuters: 171BL; /Caren Firouz/Reuters: 123T; /Zainal Abd Halim/ Reuters: 174L; /Jim Hollander/Reuters: 127T; /Kim Kyung-Hoon/ Reuters: 159BL, 160; /Kai Pfaffenbach/Reuters: 76L; /Oleg Popov/ Reuters: 206B; /Jason Reed/Reuters: 82BL; /Reuters: 162TR, 170BL, 175BL, 200; /Sporting Pictures: 150T; /Topham: 62TR, 140TR; /Rick Wilking/Reuters: 48B

Corbis: /Colorsport: 137BL; /Underwood & Underwood: 138L, 139L, 178B

Getty Images: 14R, 15T, 37B, 54T, 56T, 70B, 98BL, 116R, 140L, 142; /AFP: 33L, 46, 52R, 130R, 140BR, 158TR; /Odd Andersen/AFP: 102BR, 110-111; /Nicolas Asfouri/AFP: 20; /Frank Barratt: 18L; /Natalie Behring/ Bloomberg: 139R; /Al Bello: 31TR, 35TR, 38L, 39TR; /Hamish Blair: 105R; /Clive Brunskill: 5TR, 85TR, 91L, 112R, 132L, 172-173, 179BR; /Simon Bruty: 197; /Martin Bureau/AFP: 5C; /Matt Campbell/AFP: 182BL; / David Cannon: 101T, 118T; /Matt Cardy: 23TR; /Central Press: 12B, 23TL, 61T, 64T, 68B, 88T, 205TR; /Rich Clarkson/Time & Life Pictures: 29T, 106B; /Fabrice Coffrini/AFP: 113TR; /Chris Cole: 177TL; /Yuri Cortez/AFP: 189BR; /Ralf Crane/Time & Life Pictures: 70T; /Creutzmann/AFP: 130L; / Mark Dadswell: 99T; /Adrian Dennis/AFP: 93BR; /Tony Duffy: 33T, 34T, 36L, 38R, 50BL, 52L, 56BL, 72L, 73T, 84L; /Emmanuel Dunand/AFP: 102BL, 135BL; /Johannes Eisele/AFP: 6; /Elsa: 107BR; /Don Emmert/ AFP: 33B; /David Eulitt/MCT: 163; /Eric Feferberg/AFP: 139TR; /Franck Fife/AFP: 69TR; /David Finch: 159TR; /Julian Finney: 51L; /Focus on Sport: 32B; /Stu Forster: 4, 63BR, 67TR, 67BL, 75L, 77TR, 77BL, 89TR; / Fox Photos: 22B; /Romeo Gacad/AFP: 88B; /Gamma-Keystone: 31BL, 204L; /Michel Gangne/AFP: 176; /Lluis Gene/AFP: 137T; /Paul Gilham: 69BL, 166-167, 171TR, 183R; /George Gobet/AFP: 165TR; /Jeff Gross: 103R; /Paul Hackett: 87R; /Alexander Hassenstein: 15R, 59BL, 71TR, 75BR, 79TR, 81L, 91TR, 93TL, 95TR, 95BL; /Alexander Hassenstein/ Bongarts: 78T, 100BR, 185TR; /Scott Heavey: 146-147, 153TR, 153L; / Julian Herbert: 125T; /Mike Hewitt: 47T, 53TR, 55BR, 89BL, 115BR, 186-187, 202-203; /Harry How: 49TR, 51TR, 55L, 191; /Hulton Archive: 10B, 40T, 42C, 90T; /IOC Olympic Museum: 158L, 164L; /Jed Jacobsohn: 190B; /Alexander Joe/AFP: 107L; /Hannah Johnston: 141BL, 161BL; / Mark Kauffman/Time & Life Pictures: 16TR; /Keystone: 16L, 30L, 74TR, 150B, 152BL; /Toshifumi Kitamura/AFP: 74BL, 157BL; /Heinz Kluetmeier/ Sports Illustrated: 28L; /Christof Koepsel: 21; /Patrick Kovarik/AFP: 103TL; /LOCOG: 25TR; /Robert Laberge: 192L; /Nick Laham: 87TL; /Lake County Museum: 168L; /Pascal Le Segretain: 47BR; /David Leah/ Mexsport: 40B; /Streeter Lecka: 13, 49BL, 61BL; /Bryn Lennon: 59TR; /

Kevin Levine: 24BR; /Feng Li: 177BL; /Alex Livesey: 120-121, 123BR, 125B, 127BR; /Marco Longari/AFP: 161TR; /John MacDougall/AFP: 105BL; /Bob Martin: 132T; /Ronald Martinez: 19R, 128-129, 135TR; /Clive Mason: 199TR, 199BL, 201TR; /Darren McNamara: 98T; /Aris Messinis/ AFP: 22T; /Damien Meyer/AFP: 118BL; /Jeff J Mitchell/AFP: 11T; /Gray Mortimore: 50T; /Marwan Naamani/AFP: 180-181, 185R; /New York Daily News Archive: 36B, 145T; /Kazuhiro Nogi/AFP: 133BL, 137BR, 144C; / Pascal Pavani/AFP: 80T; /Doug Pensinger: 108R; /Ryan Pierse: 96-97, 141TR; /Alberto Pizzoli/AFP: Front endpaper, 157TR; /Popperfoto: 28B, 36R, 48T, 60TR, 126, 155BR, 162BL, 169, 196TR; /Mike Powell: 72T, 82T, 118BR, 119TL, 143B, ,T; /Steve Powell: 76T; /Adam Pretty: 112BL; /Gary M Prior: 193BL; /Mark Ralston/AFP: 99B; /Michael Regan: 83TR, 101BR, 175BR; /Rolls Press/Popperfoto: 66B, 138B; /Quinn Rooney: 195BL; / Clive Rose: 17B, 26-27, 29R, 39BL, 41BR, 43BR; /Martin Rose/Bongarts: 42B; /STF/AFP: 151B; /Sankei Archive: 134BR; /Oli Scarff: 23BR; /Ezra Shaw: 57L, 73BR, 79BL; /Cameron Spencer: 19BL, 35BL, 53BL, 145BR, 165BL; /Jamie Squire: 5BR, 19T, 81BR, 109TR, 143R, 170R, 207, Back endpaper; /Michael Steele: 57BR, 60BL, 65TR, 71L, 78B, 83BL, 85L, 205L; /Billy Stickland: 86B; /John Stillwell: 8-9; /Henri Szwarc/ Bongarts: 143T; /Bob Thomas: 34B, 116BL, 136B, 149L, 179TL, 182TR; / Bob Thomas/Popperfoto: 10T, 100T, 178L; /Topical Press Agency: 104L, 183BL, 193R; /Phil Walter: 113BL, 117R, 119R, 195TR; /Ian Walton: 44-45; /William West/AFP: 18R; /Nick Wilson: 24L, 194R

Press Association Images: 32R, 63T, 68R; /AP: 12T, 58T, 64B, 84T, 92C, 94L, 131R, 132B, 148L, 155L, 164TR, 192R; /Bernat Armangue/AP: 201BL; /Matthew Ashton: 115T; /A. Bibard/Panoramic: 124; /Bildbyran: 184BL; / Zhang Chen/Landov: 174BL; /Paul Chiasson/The Canadian Press: 206TL; /DPA: 32T, 37T, 43T, 62L, 94TR, 134TR, 148B; /David Davies: 198L; /Wang Dingchang/Landov: 41L; /Matt Dunham/AP: 25B, 134BL; / Empics Sport: 104R, 156, 184R, 193BR; /John Giles: 117T; /David Guttenfelder/AP: 190L; /Ma Hailin/Landov: 11B; /Petr David Josek/AP: 103BL; /Peter Kneffel/DPA: 24TR; /Lehtikuva: 168B; /Tony Marshall: 98BR, 189TL; /Don Morley: 136L, 151T; /Phil O'Brien: 188L; /David J Phillip/AP: 65L; /S&G and Barratts: 14L, 17TR, 54B, 149T, 154, 196L, 204B; /Amy Sancetta/AP: 144BL; /Schimer Sportfoto/DPA: 66T; / Topham Picturepoint: 58L, 122, 131T, 131B; /Aubrey Washington: 100BL, 188BR; /Wu Wei/Landov: 152BR; /Valeria Witters: 90B, 174TR, 179BL; / Liu Yu/Landov: 30B

Private Collection: 133T, 198TR

Topfoto.co.uk: /RIA Novosti: 92B, 106T

Every effort has been made to acknowledge correctly and contact the source and/or copyright holder of each picture and Carlton Books Limited apologises for any unintentional errors or omissions that will be corrected in future editions of this book.